ROMANS UNLOCKED
POWER TO DELIVER

RENÉ A. LOPEZ

FOREWORD BY
ELLIOTT E. JOHNSON

21ST CENTURY
PRESS
PUBLISHING WITH PURPOSE
WWW.21STCENTURYPRESS.COM

WHAT LEADERS ARE SAYING

For those interested in a fresh look at the Book of Romans, let me recommend René Lopez' commentary to you. It is well outlined and documented, giving all of the basics in a clear and understandable way, which is most helpful, but the thing I like best about it is that Lopez gives fresh, and sometimes challenging, insights and ideas on almost every page. Few of us need another commentary on Romans in our library, but a stimulating one is hard to find. It is also, and I like this, not one of those long drawn out tomes that no one ever any longer finds the time to read. It is concise, as well as fresh.

Gary G. Cohen, Th.D., Litt.D.
One of the translators of the NKJV
Professor of Biblical Studies, Trinity International University

Finally! In this important volume, we now have in print a systematic work on the entire text of the book of Romans that follows Paul's thought in his categories, as opposed to imposing previous categories from Systematic Theology upon Paul's thought! René Lopez, a first rate scholar with a pastor's heart has written a commentary that is not only accurate exegetically, it also maintains an exquisite balance between analysis and synthesis which allows the reader to understand Romans at both a micro and a macro level. While René interacts with the major scholarly literature on Romans throughout this volume, his commentary flows nicely and is a joy to read. This volume has instantly become the first reference work

I will go to whenever I interact with the text of Romans. I highly recommend it to others both scholars and laymen.

Brad McCoy, Ph.D.
Pastor of Tanglewood Bible Fellowship
Adjunct Professor Cameron University
Adjunct Professor: Messiah Evangelical Seminary
Visiting Professor: Jordan Evangelical Theological Seminary

Because the Church sees the enormous importance of Romans, many commentators have taken in hand to exposit it. An example-perhaps the best commentary, period—C. E. B. Cranfield gave us. In light of the plethora of material available, one might ask "Why another commentary on this New Testament book?" Authors approach a book carrying with them theological perspectives. Thus, whether one comes from an Arminian, Orthodox, Reformed, or Roman, frame of reference, his theology tends to color how he handles scripture. What has been missing is a commentary from a free grace perspective that seeks to build theology from the text up, permitting God's grace to remain truly free grace. René Lopez has given us a commentary that does an admirable job of filling this gap in our literature. His treatment, for example, of Romans 4 provides a refreshing and uncompromising exposition of how God granted Abraham eternal salvation-dealings that were strictly based on free grace, involving no works before, during, or after Abraham's initial faith in the Messiah. Lopez's work is a must have for those wanting a balanced commentary that adheres to context without undue influence from a theological system.

George E. Meisinger, D.Min.
President
Chafer Theological Seminary

The writing of books is endless and wearisome to the soul. This is evermore true with the abundant literature on the book of Romans. But hold everything. Here is a book that creatively blends precision, passion and practicality as the theme and theology of Romans is exposited. This commentary is not merely the gathering of exegetical data or theological dogma. It is a systematic and synthetic exposition. A rare combination these days it includes technical analysis as well as pastoral insight to guide the reader to an understanding of the Apostle Paul's greatest epistle. René Lopez has introduced and validated some viewpoints that have been overlooked by recent commentary literature that will challenge the reader to make some theological decisions. Pastors and laymen alike will glean valuable insights from this work for both sermon preparation and personal spiritual life study. This is a book that every serious student of the bible needs to have in their library.

Fred Chay, Ph.D.
President of GraceLine Inc
Assistant Professor of Theology &
Director of Doctoral Studies
Phoenix Seminary

Breaking from the interpretive status quo that views Romans as a treatise on justification, René Lopez has introduced us to Paul's Epistle to the Christians in Rome as a treatise on the sanctified life, for believers both new and mature, including the warning that those who are exempted from God's final wrath may taste His present wrath if they fail to live obediently by faith. He shows us that a free-grace understanding of the gospel does not lead to antinomianism as some of its opponents accuse, but includes a clear description of the believer's responsibility to obey, and accountability before, our righteous God who is both just and justifier of those who come to Him by faith alone in Christ alone.

Gary W. Derickson, Ph.D.
Professor of Biblical Studies, Western Baptist College
Associate Professor of Biblical Studies, Oregon Theological
Seminary

I have come to expect any commentary on Romans to disappoint with interpretations that contradict or compromise the gospel of grace. This is the first commentary I have seen that is consistent in its theme and its treatment of the gospel and the Christian life. Careful exegesis combines with convincing synthesis to leave the student of Romans appreciating both the simplicity and the complexity of the epistle's message. René Lopez has made a unique and useful contribution that must be in the library of everyone who wants to better understand this foundational book of God.

Charlie C. Bing, Ph.D.
Pastor/Executive Director of Grace Life Ministries

One of the more misunderstood books in the Bible is the Book of Romans. René Lopez does an excellent job of explaining the power of the gospel for the Christian life. If you are interested in growing as a Christian, this book is for you.

Robert N. Wilkin, Ph.D.
Executive Director
Grace Evangelical Society

If you are not familiar with the writings of René Lopez in the Journal of the Grace Evangelical Society or Chafer Theological Seminary Journal, this commentary on Romans is a good place to start. This new work is biblically and exegetically sound. His argument that the main thrust of the book is that "only those justified by faith can be delivered to experience and express Gospel-life to others" is right on.

Stephen R. Lewis, Ph.D.
President
Rocky Mountain Bible College & Seminary

If you like to dig deep and want a good commentary on Romans from a dispensational, free grace perspective, this work by René Lopez is for you. He deals with critical passages with precision, but he doesn't wear you out with options. He has a nice balance between synthesis and analysis. Well done.

David R. Anderson, Ph.D.
President
Grace School of Theology
Senior Pastor of Faith Community Church

The author of this study of Paul's letter to the Romans, based on the original text, perceives Paul's theme through the epistle to be "the gospel" (Rom 1:16-17). However that theme relates not just to justification (Rom 1:18-5:21) but also to sanctification (6:1-8:27), glorification (8:28-39), Israel's future (9:1-11:36), and applies to the life of the believer as well (12:1-16:27). Thus the gospel answers the sinner's need and the believer's need in his struggle with his sin nature as well and promises eventual glorification in the final redeemed state in His presence along with a future for Israel. The grace of God provides a total answer to the sin question.

A serious layman will profit greatly by studying the Epistle to the Romans under the author's guidance of this volume. It is highly recommended as the basis for an in depth study.

J. Dwight Pentecost, Th.D.
Distinguished Professor Emeritus in Bible Exposition
Dallas Theological Seminary

With careful exegesis and faith attention to the doctrines of grace, René Lopez has produced a much needed and wonderfully written commentary on this key book of the New Testament. All students of this book will be encouraged, have points of interpretation clarified, and be challenged to live a life consistent with the mercies of God. I heartily recommend this new work.

Joseph C. Dillow, Ph.D.
President
Biblical Education by Extension

A commentary with a special niché, this book is technical enough to meet the needs of the Bible Institute student who has little or no knowledge of Koine Greek, or the pastor who has been away from seminary and has not stayed fluent in his Greek. Lopez challenges those who have forgotten their Greek vocabulary while providing a commentary that helps the student of the Bible see the importance of language training. This well written and well-documented work will fill the void between those simple commentaries generally written for the laity and the highly technical works of renowned Bible scholars. This work belongs on the desk of every Bible study leader.

Robert C. Beatty, D.Min.
Director of the Master of Arts and Religion
Trinity International University

This concise commentary on the book of Romans will prove to be a helpful tool for pastors and any serious student of Scripture. Lopez has included useful grammatical notes and offers proper consideration for the context of the portion of Scripture under discussion.

Ed Glasscock, Th.D.
Assoc. Professor of Greek and New Testament
and acting Director for Post-Graduate Studies
Central Baptist Theological Seminary

ROMANS UNLOCKED

Published by 21st Century Press
Springfield, Missouri U.S.A.
Printed in U.S.A.

21st Century Press is an evangelical Christian publisher dedicated to serving the
local church with purpose books. We believe God's vision for 21st Century Press
is to provide church leaders with biblical, user-friendly materials that will help
them evangelize, disciple and minister to children, youth and families.

It is our prayer that this book will help you discover biblical truth for your own
life and help you meet the needs of others. May God richly bless you.

21st Century Press
2131 W. Republic Rd.
PMB 41
Springfield, MO 65807
800-658-0284

Library of Congress Cataloging-in-Publication Data
Lopez, René A., 1963-
Romans unlocked: power to deliver / René A. Lopez
Includes bibliographical references.
ISBN 0-9766243-0-3

Cover: Lee Fredrickson
Book Design: Terry White
Visit our web-site at: 21stcenturypress.com

2131 W. Republic Rd., PMB 41.
Springfield, MO 65807
lee@21stcenturypress.com

DEDICATION

This book is dedicated to my grandmother (Sofia), mother (Daisy) and my wife (Marialis). Thanks for loving me unconditionally and for always supporting me.

ACKNOWLEDGEMENT

Writing a commentary involves more people than the name appearing on the cover. Numerous people have worked hard behind the scenes to make this volume possible. Many thanks to all the reviewers who gave me suggestions and took the time to make this tome as sharp as it could be. But this author, especially, owes a great deal to three individuals. Jon Tretsven was involved in editing and in compiling the author, Scripture and subject list that allows researchers easy access to the information. While juggling various projects as usual, Mike Makidon sacrificed much of his time to typeset and to also be involved in the editing process. Finally without the incomparable editing of Cathy Beach the commentary would have never reached its final polished form. A great deal of gratitude and indebtedness goes to my mentor and friend Zane C. Hodges whose views of "wrath" and "salvation" in this commentary were originally derived from and allowed Romans to become unlocked for me. Finally, without my loving and overly sacrificial wife, Marialis, this commentary would have remained a dream. Thanks for your exhaustive patience. You are God's greatest gift to me besides the gift of eternal life.

TABLE OF CONTENTS

ABBREVIATIONS

ASV	American Standard Version
BBC	*Believer's Bible Commentary*
BAGD	*A Greek-English Lexicon of the New Testament and Other Early Christian Literature*, by W. Bauer, W. F. Arndt, F. W. Gingrich, and F. W. Danker, 2d ed. (Chicago: University of Chicago Press, 1979)
BDAG	*A Greek-English Lexicon of the New Testament and Other Early Christian Literature*, by W. Bauer, F. W. Danker, W. F. Arndt, and F. W. Gingrich, 3d ed. (Chicago: University of Chicago Press, 2000)
BDF	*A Greek-English Grammar of the New Testament and Other Early Christian Literature*, by F. Blass, A. Debrunner, and R. W. Funk (Chicago: University of Chicago Press, 1961)
BDB	*A Hebrew and English Lexicon of the Old Testament with an Appendix Containing the Biblical Aramaic* (1906; reprinted Peabody, MA: Hendrickson, 1979)
BKC	*Bible Knowledge Commentary*
CLE	*The Complete Life Encyclopedia*, by Frank Minirth, Paul Meier, and Stephen Arterburn (Nashville, TN: Thomas Nelson Publishers, 1995)
DSS	Dead Sea Scrolls (Qumran documents)
EBC	*The Expositors Bible Commentary*, edited by F. E. Gaebelein et al., 12 vols. (Grand Rapids: Eerdmans, 1976)
EDT	*Evangelical Dictionary of Theology*, edited by Walter A. Elwell (Grand Rapids: Baker, 1984)
E.g.	*exempli gratia*, for example
Et al.	*et alia*, and others
Fn	footnote
Gk	Greek

Ibid.	*ibidem*, in the same place		
I.e.	*id est*, that is		
ISBE	*The International Standard Bible Encyclopedia*, edited by G. W. Bromiley et al., 4 vols. (Grand Rapids: Eerdmans, 1979–88)		
KJV	King James Version		
Lit.	Literally		
LSJM	*A Greek-English Lexicon*, by H. G. Liddell, R. Scott, H. S. Jones, and R. McKenzie, 9th ed., with a new supplement added (1940)		
LXX	Septuagint (Greek Translation of the Hebrew Scriptures)		
MM	*The Vocabulary of the Greek Testament: Illustrated from the Papyri and Other Non-literary Sources*, by J. H. Moulton and G. Milligan (1930; reprinted Grand Rapids: Eerdmans, 1997)		
MS(S)	manuscript(s)		
NASB	New American Standard Bible		
NET	New English Translation		
NIV	New International Version		
NKJV	New King James Version		
NT	New Testament		
NTS	New Testament Survey		
OT	Old Testament		
RSV	Revised Standard Version		
SNT	*A Survey of the New Testament*, by Robert H. Gundry, 3 ed. (Grand Rapids: Zondervan, 1994)		
Str-B	*Kommentar zum Neuen Testament aus Talmud und Midrash*, by H. L. Strack and P. Billerback, 6 vols. (München: Beck, 1922-61)		
TDNT	*Theological Dictionary of the New Testament*, edited by G. Kittel and G. Friedrich; translated and edited by G. W. Bromiley, 10 vols. (Grand Rapids: Eerdmans, 1964–76)		
YNG	Young's Literal Translation of the Bible		

Hebrew Bible		1 Kgs	1 Kings
Gen	Genesis	2 Kgs	2 Kings
Exod	Exodus	1 Chr	1 Chronicles
Lev	Leviticus	2 Chr	2 Chronicles
Deut	Deuteronomy	Ezra	Ezra
Josh	Joshua	Neh	Nehemiah
Judg	Judges	Esth	Esther
Ruth	Ruth	Job	Job
1 Sam	1 Samuel	Ps (*pl.* Pss)	Psalms
2 Sam	2 Samuel	Prov	Proverbs

Eccl (or Qol)	Ecclesiastes
Song	Song of Songs
Isa	Isaiah
Jer	Jeremiah
Ezek	Ezekiel
Dan	Daniel
Hos	Hosea
Joel	Joel
Amos	Amos
Obad	Obadiah
Jon	Jonah
Mic	Micah
Nah	Nahum
Hab	Habakkuk
Zeph	Zephaniah
Hag	Haggai
Zech	Zechariah
Mal	Malachi

Other Jewish and Writings
Apocryphal/Deuterocanonical Books

Tob	Tobit
Jdt	Judith
Add Esth	Additions Esther
Wis	Wisdom
Sir	Sirach
(Ecclesiasticus)	
Bar	Baruch
Let Jer Jeremiah	Letter of
Azar/Song Thr	Prayer of Azariah and the Song of the Three Jews
Sus	Susanna
Bel	Bel and the Dragon
1 Macc	1 Maccabees
2 Macc	2 Maccabees
1 Esd	1 Esdras
Pr Man	Prayer of Manasseh
Add Ps	Psalm 151
3 Macc	1 Maccabees
2 Esd	2 Esdras
4 Macc	1 Maccabees

For further Jewish writings see the *Pseudepigrapha* 2 vol. Also, for more Jewish writings see the Rabbinic Tractates (Babylonian Talmud, Palestinian or Jerusalem Talmud, Mishnah and Tosefta) and Josephus and Philo.

New Testament

Matt	Matthew
Mark	Mark
Luke	Luke
John	John
Acts	Acts
Rom	Romans
1 Cor	1 Corinthians
2 Cor	2 Corinthians
Gal	Galatians
Eph	Ephesians
Phil	Philippians
1 Thess	1 Thessalonians
2 Thess	2 Thessalonians
1 Tim	1 Timothy
2 Tim	2 Timothy
Titus	Titus
Philem	Philemon
Heb	Hebrews
Jas	James
1 Pet	1 Peter
2 Pet	2 Peter
1 John	1 John
2 John	2 John
3 John	3 John
Jude	Jude
Rev	Revelation

FOREWORD

Consider Unlocking Romans

Romans, among biblical books, is weighty theology. Its scope and depth of message makes it a book in which a guide is needed to navigate a reader through it.

Commentaries today are written with such diverse agendas that one may find it difficult to recognize the path that a commentary seeks to cut for the reader. René Lopez has written to follow Paul's thought and from a carefully considered theological conviction. That perspective is that God's grace infuses His work of justification so that His offer comes with no strings attached. Careful attention is given that nothing is added to nor taken away from the free offer of the gospel. Yet this message is not easy believism because the demands that sanctification place upon the believer reflects the holy God who alone provides deliverance.

Further, the commentary is written with the conviction that Paul's epistle is a unified and coherent letter. No interpretation can claim to be valid which does not trace a message as developed through the whole letter. Then the component parts were written to express and support this developing message and establish the argument.

Romans Unlocked is written from a clear theological insight of faith and with the conviction that a letter must be read as a whole.

The author is familiar with the interpretive literature surrounding Romans, as well as the broader discussion of Paul and second Temple Judaism. Where the literature relates to the message of Romans, Lopez validates his interpretation in light of the current scholarly discussion. As part of his academic awareness, Lopez carefully utilizes the original language to provide a more careful hearing of what Paul says.

All believers need to spend time in the theology of Romans, and this commentary will enrich the reader's experience as he follows the thought of Paul.

Elliott E. Johnson, Th.D.
Distinguished Professor of Bible Exposition
Dallas Theological Seminary

I

INTRODUCTION

Authorship

Typical of Pauline letters, he identifies himself by name at the beginning of the epistle, "Paul, a bondservant of Jesus Christ" (Rom 1:1). Both external and internal evidence indicates that Paul wrote Romans.

External evidence indicates that the post-apostolic writers (like Clement, Ignatius, Polycarp, Irenaeus, Justin Martyr, Hippolytus, etc...) accepted Pauline authorship without reservations. Furthermore, every list of New Testament books of the early church attributes Romans to Paul. Even ancient heretics acknowledged Pauline authorship (Witmer, "Romans," in *BKC*, 435).

Internal evidence indicates Pauline authorship since he greets Priscilla and Aquila (Rom 16:3), whom he knew from Corinth (Acts 18:2-3). Paul also mentions a collection for "the poor among the saints who are in Jerusalem" (Rom 15:25-27), which if compared with Acts 19:21; 20:1-5; 21:15, 17-19, 1 Corinthians 16:1-5, and 2 Corinthians 8:1-12; 9:1-5, establish identical subject matter. Paul's tribal ancestry from Benjamin, attested in Philippians 3:5, appears in Romans 11:1. Further disclosure of Paul's plan to visit Rome in Acts 19:21 is confirmed in Romans 1:10-13 and 15:22-32. As noticed by some, once Pauline authorship is accepted elsewhere, like Galatians and the Corinthian epistles, no substantial difficulty arises in attributing Pauline authorship to

Romans since similar content appears in these letters (Harrison, "Romans," in *EBC*, 3-4).

Paul probably dictated the letter to his secretary, Tertius (Rom 16:22). Thus, no significant reasons are given that ascribes authorship to another.

Date of Composition

Paul penned Romans after writing the two Corinthian letters (A.D. 55-56) from Macedonia before going to Achaia (Greece). Hence he continuously mentions the collection being made for the saints in Jerusalem (1 Cor 16:1-4; 2 Cor 8–9). After completing the charitable collection, Paul must have written Romans before parting to Jerusalem (cf. Rom 15:25). He intended to arrive at Jerusalem on the day of Pentecost (Acts 20:16). Since he spent Passover and the Feast of Unleavened Bread in Philippi, it seems probable that he wrote Romans in the later part of winter or early spring of A.D. 56-57. With relative certainty, one can date the epistle around A.D. 56-57, while Nero reigned.

Historical Background

Place of Composition. Paul wrote the epistle at the end of his third missionary journey, while staying at Corinth for three months (Acts 20:3), as he finalized the love-gift-collection for the poor in Jerusalem (Rom 15:26-28). The mention of Phoebe (the letter bearer) coming from Cenchrea (an eastern port of Corinth, cf. 16:1-2) and the believer Gaius from Corinth who hosted Paul (cf. v 23; 1 Cor 1:14) present strong evidence it was written from Corinth.

Recipients of Romans. The letter's recipients are "saints" (Rom 1:7) whose "faith" is recognized throughout the region (1:8, 15). They are believers, and their ethnic backgrounds were Jew and Gentile. For example, Priscilla and Aquila were Jews (Acts 18:2), as others (Rom 16:7-11). Rome had a small colony of Jews (see Acts

28:11-24). Major Jewish sections (chapters 2–4; 9–11; 16), along with heavy Old Testament use and imagery, clearly show that Hebrew-Christians are part of the letter's recipients. However, the Roman church, being in a Gentile city, was also composed primarily of Gentile-Christians. Paul identifies himself as "an Apostle to the Gentiles," who addresses Gentiles in the letter (1:13; 11:13; 15:16). He calls the Gentile mission field his "ministry" (11:13). Therefore, both groups are the recipients of this letter.

Destination of Romans. These Jew and Gentile Christians composed one of probably many house churches in Rome that met in Priscilla and Aquila's house (Rom 16:3-5). Unlike today's megachurches, the early church met in houses composed of small groups of believers. Hence, Paul does not speak of the "whole church" coming "together in one place" (as in 1 Cor 14:23), but greets the "saints," who he later names individually (Rom 16:5-15). However, since Rome was hostile to Christians, perhaps they met in different houses to divert attention.

A Biographical Sketch of Paul. Saul was born and raised in Tarsus, the main city of Cilicia (Acts 22:3). This was one of the greatest learning centers in Greek culture and of the Eastern world. Saul's parents resided in Cilicia. They were Jewish with Roman citizenship, a position Saul inherited (Acts 22:25-29). Like all Jewish males, Saul learned a manual trade to survive in the hard world of the Middle East (cf. Kiddushin 4:14 in the *Mishnah*). He specialized in tent making (Acts 18:3). Since Saul's father was a wealthy Pharisee, he was able to give him the best formal training (Acts 23:6) under the best teacher of the Law, Gamaliel (Acts 5:34; 22:3). Saul must have graduated in the top of his class, for he was one of the most zealous Jewish leaders in regards to their traditions and laws (Gal 1:14). He is found in Acts consenting and holding the coats of all the people who stoned the first Christian martyr, Stephen (Acts 7:58). After Stephen's death, Saul departed to persecute and bring all

Christians to justice by either killing or imprisoning them (cf. Acts 9:1; 22:4; 26:9-11; Gal 1:13). On his journey to Damascus to persecute Christians (Acts 22:5; 26:12), Saul encountered the Lord Jesus Christ who redirected his whole life to promote Christianity. After becoming a believer (Acts 9; 22:6-15; 26:13-16), Saul became one of the greatest promoters of Christianity by becoming the Apostle to the Gentiles (Acts 9:1-16; 26:17-18; Rom 11:13; Gal 1:11-16; 1 Tim 1:12-16). Not long after his conversion, Saul, a Hebrew name, began to be referred to by his Roman name of Paul (Acts 13:9). It seems logical to begin calling him Paul since he was commissioned to be the Apostle to the Gentiles (Rom 11:13; Gal 1:16). However, before being commissioned, Paul spent three years in Arabia, Damascus and the Judean area (A.D. 33-36; cf. Acts 19:29; Gal 1:17-21). After spending fifteen days in Jerusalem trying to see Peter, Paul was only able to see the Apostle James, the Lord's brother (Gal 1:18-19). Then Paul returned to Tarsus, where he ministered there for about nine or ten years (A.D. 36-45; cf. Acts 9:30). After this time, Barnabas went to Tarsus. While there, he encouraged Paul to go with him to minister at Antioch of Syria, where the church was growing at an enormous rate (A.D. 45-48; cf. Acts 11:25-30; 12:25). Initially, Paul began teaching Christianity in his hometown of Tarsus, but Antioch became the home base for his three missionary journeys. This is where believers "were first called Christians" (Acts 11:26). During the first and second missionary journeys, Paul possibly wrote Galatians and attended the Jerusalem council of Acts 15. Paul's third missionary journey ended when he arrived at Jerusalem (see chart below for a synthesis of Paul's ministry).

While going to Jerusalem, Paul received a prophetic warning that he would be imprisoned there (Acts 21:11-13). As prophesied, he was arrested in Jerusalem when a riot broke out due to his teaching. Paul was then transferred to Caesarea, where he remained imprisoned for over two years (A.D. 57-59; Acts 21:17–26:32; cf. 24.27). Because Paul appealed to Caesar, he was taken to Rome through a rough voyage, where he spent another two years under house arrest (A.D. 60-62; Acts 27:1–28:30). During this time Paul wrote Ephesians, Colossians, Philippians and Philemon, (known as the prison epistles). Though no scriptural evidence appears on the

A Synthesis of Paul's Missionary Journeys
The Apostle to the Gentiles (Rom 11:13)

Journeys	Scripture	Time	Visited	Books & Places
First	Acts 13:1–14:28	A.D. 47–48	Seleucia, Cyprus (Salamis, Paphos) Perga, Antioch in Psidia, Iconium, Lystra, Derbe	None None
Second	Acts 15:36–18:22	A.D. 49–52	Syrian-Antioch (Cilicia, Derbe) Lystra, Phrygia, Galatia, Mysia Troas, Samothracia Neapolis, Philippi, Thessabnica, Berea Athens, Corinth Ephesus, Corinth Caesarea, Jerusalem	1 Thess (A.D. 50) Corinth 2 Thess (A.D. 51) Corinth Gal (A.D. 49) Syr.-Antioch Jerusalem Council Acts 15
Third	Acts 18:23–21:17	A.D. 52–57	Galatia, Phrygia Ephesus, Macedonia Corinth, Philippi Troas, Assos, Mitylene Chios, Samos, Trogyllium, Miletus, Coos, Rhodes, Patara Tyre, Ptolemais, Caesarea, Jerusalem	1 Cor (A.D. 54) Ephesus 2 Cor (A.D. 55) Macedonia Romans Corinth
1st Prison Term	Acts 21:27–26:32	A.D. 57-59	Caesarea	**Books** Luke wrote his gospel
	Acts 21:18–28:31	A.D. 60-62	Rome—Prison Epistles	Ephesians, Philippians Colossians, Philemon
4th Mission Journey not Recorded in Acts	1 Tim 1:3 & Titus 1:3	A.D. 62-66	Crete, Ephesus, Macedonia	1 Timothy (A.D. 62-66) Titus (A.D. 62-66)
2nd Prison Term	None	A.D. 64-67	Rome—Martyrdom	2 Timothy (A.D. 67)

subject, after Paul's release he resumed ministering in Crete, Ephesus and Macedonia (A.D. 62-66; cf. 1 Tim 1:3; Titus 1:5). At this time, Paul wrote 1 Timothy and Titus. Not long after Nero began persecuting Christians he was imprisoned again (A.D. 66-67). During Paul's last imprisonment, he pens 2 Timothy, where he expresses the expectation of imminent death (2 Tim 4:6). Early church tradition records that Paul was beheaded in A.D. 67 in the city of Rome and buried underneath the city, in one of its many catacombs (cf. Gromacki, *NTS*, 177-79).

Purpose

There are several purposes for writing Romans with one central purpose. First, after returning from Jerusalem, one of Paul's main objectives was to visit Rome (Acts 19:21; Rom 15:24, 28-29), as well as Spain, with the financial help taken at Rome. Since Paul had the Roman church in his prayers and desired to build their faith (1:9-12), but was unable up to this point (1:13), one of his purposes for writing this epistle was to inform them of his future visit and to have them pray for its fulfillment (15:30-32).

A second purpose for writing this letter was to ease the tension between Jews and Gentiles created by Judaizers. Similar content shared between Romans and Galatians argue for such a purpose (see Rom 14:1–15:13; Galatians).

Finally, there is a link between the founding of the Roman church and Paul's ultimate purpose for writing the epistle. No one knows who founded the Roman church. Paul does not greet Peter, since he was not there yet. This is further established by Paul's pioneering statement and lack of apostolic founding mentioned in Romans 15:20. Maybe Priscilla and Aquila founded it, since they were in Italy as early as A.D. 49, when Christians began to be expelled from Rome (Acts 18:2, see *Claudius* 5.25 §4, p 53). However, a better option suggests that the Pentecost believers from

Rome (in Acts 2:10) founded the church, since they probably took the Christian message back to Rome as early as A.D. 33. Hence, since the founders were new converts, perhaps the church needed sound apostolic doctrine. Thus, out of this need, one can safely deduce that Paul's central purpose for writing the epistle is to present a detailed account of the entire Christian gospel from cover to cover (e.g., see 1:1, 9, 15-16; 2:16; 10:15-16; 11:28; 15:16, 19-20; 16:25). This gospel has a broad scope that encompasses justification, sanctification, glorification and a future for Israel (10:15-16; 11:26-28).

Clarifying the Theme

Frequently, many have suggested that the message or theme of Romans is "the righteousness of God," "salvation," or simply "the gospel." While these options have something to commend them, they fail to account for the book's entire content, since these terms are interpreted to have a "forensic" (legal) meaning, which section ends in 4:25.

It is widely recognized that Romans 1:16-17 constitute the theme verses of the epistle. However, what goes unrecognized are the various terms that Paul distinguishes. For example, "salvation" and "justification" are distinguished in Romans 5:9-10 and in 10:9-10 (see commentary). Furthermore, God's present "wrath" in 1:18 is later interpreted to always mean eternal-judgment. Yet, wrath should be understood as God's displeasure and display manifested against sin in time and not in eternity, whether one is unjustified or a justified-sinning-believer (cf. Lopez, *Wrath of God*, 45–66). Failure to make such distinctions will distort the theme of the book: The gospel produces power to be justified and to be delivered from God's wrath brought by sin. This enables the believer to experience life, as well as expect God's promises to Israel to be fulfilled in the future.

Unique Characteristics

Though Paul wrote thirteen epistles in total, Romans is his magnum opus. Various unique characteristics make this letter stand out:

1) Paul's most comprehensive letter that covers largely, if not all, theological points of the New Testament is found in the book of Romans. It is a systematic treatise in itself.

2) Romans is the most theological out of all of Paul's epistles.

3) Romans is the longest of Paul's letters containing 7,114 (Gundry, *SNT*, 341) words. Compared to an average size letter in New Testament times of 1,300 words and Paul's shortest letter, Philemon, of 335 words, Romans is a long letter (see Gromacki, *NTS*, 183 whose number of words in Romans 7101 varies slightly).

4) Romans is the most formal of all of Paul's letters.

5) Of all of Paul's Old Testament quotations in his letters, more than half of them are in Romans.

6) Others have opined over the incredible value of this letter as follows:

Thiessen notes what **Shaw** says, "'Great intellects, like those of **Augustine** and **Luther** and **Calvin**, have discussed it only to discover depths beyond their depths.'"

Luther said, "It is the chief book of the New Testament."

Godet said, "O St. Paul, had thy one work been to compose an Epistle to the Romans, that alone should have rendered thee dear to every sound reason." He added: "It is a Cathedral of Christian education."

Griffith W. Thomas said, "It is a theological education in itself."

B. H. Carroll said, "It is the most fundamental, vital, logical, profound, and systematic discussion of the whole plan of salvation in all the literature of the world."

Romans' Message

The gospel produces power to be justified and delivered from God's wrath brought by sin that enables believers to experience life that will benefit them and others. Furthermore, the term *gospel* also includes the unconditional promises to Israel that will be fulfilled in the future (10:15-16; 11:26-32). Thus the gospel encapsulates the message found in the entire book of Romans (i.e., justification, sanctification, glorification and a future for Israel).

 OUTLINE OF ROMANS

I. Introductory Issues (1:1-17)
   A. The Author and Subject: The Bondservant Apostle Paul and Gospel (1:1)
   B. The Subject Matter: The Gospel (1:2-7)
   C. The Recipients and Trip to Rome: The Roman Christians (1:8-15)
   D. The Theme: The Gospel's Power to Justify and Deliver the Justified to Experience Life (1:16-17)
II. The Body of the Epistle Unfolds the Gospel: Only Those Justified by Faith Can Be Delivered to Experience Life, Expect a Future for Israel and Express Gospel-Life to Others (1:18–15:13)
   A. Unrighteous Humanity Suffers God's Wrath (1:18–3:20)
      1. The Gentile world suffers God's wrath (1:18-32)
      2. The moralist (Jew) under God's principles of judgment suffers wrath (2:1-16)
      3. The Jew unable to keep the Law suffers God's wrath (2:17–3:8)
      4. The world stands under God's wrath condemned (3:9-20)
         a. No exception: Jew and Gentiles stand condemned (3:9-18)
         b. No exception: Justification does not come by the Law (3:19-20)
   B. The Propitiation for Sinners Seen in the Gospel Comes by Way of Sacrifice: Righteousness Comes by Faith Alone in Jesus Christ Alone (3:21–4:25)
      1. God's righteousness comes by faith alone in Christ alone (3:21-31)
      2. God's righteousness by faith alone originated in the Old Testament as illustrated in Abraham (4:1-25)

C. The Power of the Gospel Delivers: Only the Righteous Can Experience Life and Expect Ultimate Deliverance (5:1–8:39)

   1. Justification endows one with sanctifying-power to be delivered from God's wrath to experience life (5:1-11)
   2. Grace-righteousness reigns in life over sin's reign of death (5:12-21)
   3. Justified believers should live resurrection lives (6:1-23)
   4. Justified believers have changed dominions: from the Law to the Spirit (7:1-6)
   5. The Law's inability to sanctify believers (7:7-25)
   6. The Spirit's ability to sanctify believers (8:1-17)
   7. Justification guarantees glorification but suffering enhances a greater kind of glorification (8:18-39)

D. The Promise of the Gospel Stands: God is Vindicated through His Sovereign Choice, in Rejecting Israel, by Extending Mercy to All and by His Wisdom (9:1–11:36)

   1. God's sovereign choice vindicates Him (9:1-29)
   2. Israel's rejection vindicates Him (9:30–10:21)
   3. God's mercy extended to all vindicates Him (11:1-32)
      a. Gentiles experience present salvation (11:1-25)
      b. Jews experience permanent future salvation (11:26-32)
   4. God's wisdom vindicates Him (11:33-36)

E. The Practical Outworking of the Gospel is to Serve: Only the Justified Can Express Gospel-Life in Service to Others (12:1–15:13)

   1. Service of the church (12:1-21)
      a. Expect to sacrifice in light of God's mercy (12:1-2)
      b. Exercise spiritual gifts to serve the church (12:3-8)
      c. Extend sincere love, kindness and mercy to all (12:9-21)
   2. Service to the state (13:1-7)
      a. Honoring the state honors God (13:1-2)
      b. Dishonoring the state dishonors God (13:3-7)
   3. Serve by loving others in light of the future (13:8-14)
      a. Serve by loving others (13:8-10)
      b. Serve in light of the future day (13:11-14)
   4. Serve by being sensitive to others (14:1–15:13)
      a. Practice love by not judging on nonessential issues (14:1-12)

1
SALUTATION AND THE SIN PROBLEM

A. The Author and Subject: The Bondservant Apostle Paul and Gospel (1:1-1)

1:1. Paul introduces the letter by identifying his position as a willing **bondservant** (*doulos*, lit. means "slave," BDAG, 260) **of Jesus Christ** and **called** *to be* **an apostle.** "Bondservant" identifies his relationship as a "slave" owned by Jesus Christ, showing his total commitment to his Master's cause. The formal title of "apostle" gives his position of authority to establish God's doctrine in Rome. This title in a strict sense belonged only to a select group of men, who as Paul had seen the risen Lord (Acts 1:22; 1 Cor 9:1). Paul was also **separated** (*aphōrismenos*) directly by God (as the passive voice of the Gk verb suggests) for His purpose (cf. Acts 9:15; Gal 1:1, 15).

Paul's mission statement is summarized in one pithy phrase: *separated* **to the gospel of God** (cf. 15:16; 1 Cor 9:16; 2 Cor 11:7; Gal 1:6-9, 11; 1 Thess 2:2, 8-9). The term *gospel* (*euaggelion*), also known as "good news," occurs twelve times in Romans (1:1, 9, 15-16; 2:16; 10:15-16; 11:28; 15:16, 19-20; 16:25). Paul uses the term *gospel* four times in a symmetrical form to introduce his topic from 1:1-16 and another four times to conclude his topic from 15:16–16:25. Thus, the gospel encapsulates the message found in the entire book of Romans (i.e., justification, sanctification, glorification and a future for Israel). Usually unrecognized, the term *gospel* also includes the unconditional promises to Israel that will be fulfilled in the future (10:15-16; 11:26-32).

B. The Subject Matter: The Gospel (1:2-7)

1:2. Lest anyone think Paul's gospel comes through innovative means, he recalls it was **promised** by God **through the prophets** located **in the Holy Scriptures**. In typical Pauline fashion, he validates his gospel message through the Old Testament Scriptures (e.g., 4:3; 9:17; 10:11; 11:12; 15:4; 16:26; 1 Cor 15:3; Acts 17:2; 24:14-15; 26:22-23; 28:23).

1:3-4. Thus, Paul defines the content of the gospel as God's **Son Jesus Christ our Lord**, who equally shares humanity and deity. A further link to God's Old Testament promise (Gen 12:3; Jer 33:14-15) shows His royal lineage coming from **the seed of David** as the promised ruler (2 Sam 7:16; Ps 89:3, 19; Is 11:1, 10; Jer 23:5; Ezek 34:23; 37:24), also confirmed in the New Testament (Matt 1:1-16; Luke 1:27, 32, 69; 2:4; 2 Tim 2:8; Rev 5:5; 22:18).

The phrases **according to the flesh** (*kata sarka*) and **according to the Spirit of holiness** (*kata pneuma hagiōsynēs*) do not refer to Jesus' unique nature, but to His relationships in two spheres. Since the phrase "His Son" (1:3) already conveys deity and "seed of David" conveys human existence and lineage of the highest order, to add the phrase *according to the flesh* is redundant and unnecessary, unless it indicates human frailty. On the other hand, the phrase *according to the Spirit by the resurrection from the dead* implies endowment of resurrection-power through the Spirit, as apposed to the frailty of the flesh. Translators are incorrect in rendering the participle **declared** (from *horizō*), since the eight times it appears in the New Testament it carries the sense "to appoint or determine." Thus, Paul does not mean Jesus was *declared* Son of God through the resurrection, but "appointed Son-of-God-in-power by the resurrection" (NET). Jesus was born in frail humanity (with reference to *the flesh*, v 3) and limited Himself by taking on human nature (Phil 2:7), but at the resurrection the Spirit raised Him in power (John 17:5). This shows Jesus' newly appointed function and ability in the new sphere as the God-man. Hence, only after Jesus' resurrection, He told the disciples in Matthew 28:18: "All authority has been given to Me in heaven and on earth." Later in chapter 6, Paul develops how people at regeneration (similar but not exactly like Jesus) also enter into a new sphere and acquire resurrection power. This endows believers with a new disposition to obey God.

1:5. Through Him (i.e., Jesus), therefore, Paul could say he **received** his call and enablement of *grace and apostleship*. Perhaps he uses **we** not as a reference to other Christians as recipients of grace, or to associate apostles, but as an editorial plural of himself (cf. 3:8-9; 1 Cor 9:11; 2 Cor 1:12) as having *received* **grace and apostleship** (*charin kai apostolēn*). One may understand his call as "the gift of apostleship" granted unmeritoriously in order to further Christ's purpose **for** (*eis*, i.e., "to bring about") **obedience to the faith among all nations for His name.**

The phrase "for obedience to the faith" (*eis hypakoēn pisteōs*) occurs here and in 16:26. This expression is understood in various ways: (1) *obedience to* [the] *faith*, i.e., as the body of doctrine of the Christian faith, (2) *believing obedience*, i.e., obedience motivated by a life of faith, (3) *obedience that consists in faith*, i.e., obeying the call to believe in Jesus, or (4) *obedience consisting and produced by faith*, i.e., obedience to believe consists of faith and to follow is produced by faith (cf. Cranfield, *Romans*, 1:66).

The first three options have things to commend them, but not without problems. Jesus' purpose is for all nations to obey Him—not just to simply trust Him—as the Great Commission suggests in Matthew 28:19-20. Romans 1:5 and 16:26 may be the Pauline version of the great commission, thus ruling out view three because of its narrow scope. Furthermore, in the Greek text, *faith* lacks the definite article "the." Perhaps Paul did not intend for it to be understood as *the body of apostolic truth* since it was customary for him to add the article in front of *faith* when he meant this (cf. 12:6; 14:1; 1 Cor 16:3; 2 Cor 13:5; 1 Tim 3:9; 4:1, 6; 5:8; 6:10, 12; 2 Tim 4:7; Titus 1:13). Consequently, before urging the nations to allow a faith-life to motivate their obedience to apostolic doctrine, they must first obey the call to believe, thus ruling out views one and two. The last option fits best for the following reasons: This phrase must be understood in light of the subject currently under discussion, i.e., the gospel in Romans encompasses justification, sanctification and glorification. Thus, *for obedience to the faith* means: *Obedience to believe consists of faith and obedience to follow is produced by faith.* This phrase encompasses all of these elements of the gospel as found in the book of Romans (cf. 10:16). For example, God calls all nations to believe in Christ (3:29; 4:17-18; 9:24; 10:19; 11:11-13). To obey this call requires faith. All nations are also called by God to obey Christ (6–8; 12–15:19; 16:19, 26). To generate obedience faith is also necessary (cf. Gal 2:20; 5:1–6:10; 10:5-8). Paul uses the phrase *for obedience to the faith* in a symmetrical form in 1:5 and 16:26 that forms an *inclusio* (i.e., a similar word, phrase or clause that begins and ends a literary unit that serves as a framing device to unite a paragraph, section or book treating the same theme), thus encapsulating everything found in Romans "so that all nations believe and obey him" (the NIV rendering of 16:26; cf. 15:18). Hence, fundamental to the meaning of Romans, both conditions are necessary to escape God's present wrath (1:16-18): For the unregenerate to believe and the believer to obey (Lopez, *Wrath of God*, 45–66).

1:6-7. Paul's Roman readers were **among** those Gentiles who exhibit "obedience to the faith," **called of Jesus Christ** (i.e., belonging to Jesus Christ). This call (*klētoi*), similar to Paul's calling (1:1), is an effectual **call *to be* saints** or literally *called saints* (since *to be* is not in the Gk) initiated by God. The term *saints* means "set-apart." The New Testament calls believers *saints* (BDAG, 11) because by their position they are set-apart to God (8:27; 12:13; 15:25; 1 Cor 6:1; 2 Cor 1:1; Eph 2:19; Col 1:4; 1 Tim 5:10) as here, but elsewhere it also refers experientially to believers being made *increasingly holy* (set-apart) (2 Tim 2:21).

Finally, Paul concludes his salutation from vv 1-7 by combining the common greeting of the day: **Grace** (*charis*, of the Gk culture) and **peace** (*eirēnē*, Hebrew *šālôm* of the Jewish culture) comes **from God our Father and the Lord Jesus Christ**, which strongly implies the Son's equality to the Father. Thus, his salutation contains in germ form everything he will develop later throughout the letter.

C. The Recipients and Trip to Rome: The Roman Christians (1:8-15)

1:8. Usually Paul began his letters by thanking **God** for his audience (1 Cor 1:4; Eph 1:16; Phil 1:3; Col 1:3; 1 Thess 1:2; 2 Thess 1:3; 2 Tim 1:3; Phlm 4) **through Jesus Christ** and encourages them by mentioning how their **faith is spoken of throughout the whole world**, a hyperbole (i.e., an exaggerated term for the purpose of emphasis or heighten effect that conveys more than what is literally meant) that perhaps means it echoed throughout the Roman Empire (cf. Luke 2:1). Hence, this leaves no doubt that his audience were believers (1:7).

1:9-10. As believers, Paul felt concern for their spiritual welfare and assured them **that without ceasing** he mentioned them **always in** his **prayers**. As part of his prayers, he was also **making request, if by some means, now at last** God in His sovereignty allows (understood best by the passive participle, *euodōthēsomai*="the way may be opened" in the NIV, instead of **I may find a way** in the NKJV) his trip to materialize. Perhaps he waited for more than two years before this prayer was answered (cf. v 13; Acts 24:27), thus encouraging perseverance in prayer.

1:11. The reason (*gar*) Paul wanted to see the Roman Christians may be understood in approximately three parallel purpose statements: To **impart to you some spiritual gift** (v 11), "to be encouraged mutually by one another's faith" (v 12) and to "have some fruit among you" (v 13, cf. Moo, *Romans*, 59, for a slightly different view). The literal Greek phrase *spiritual gift* (*charisma pneumatikon*) does not refer to the type of "gifts" imparted to the church, since when speaking of such it always appears in the plural (12:6; 1 Cor 12:1; 14:1). Elsewhere, when a special ministerial *gift* appears, in the singular form, the combination of *spiritual* and *gift* does not occur (1 Tim 4:14; 2 Tim 1:6). Thus the mutual encouragement, referred by "faith" in v 12, further supports that spiritual benefits, not the Church's gifts, are in view. Hence, *spiritual gift* refers to imparting the *spiritual benefit* that Paul wishes to share with his readers throughout the book. As a result, they will be **established** (i.e., their faith will be *strengthened*; cf.16:25).

1:12. In return, Paul and the Roman believers will be mutually *established* (lit. Gk. to be made *firm, strengthened* or *supported*) and **encouraged** by each other's faith (vv 11-12). Paul will share his God-given-spiritual-insights resulting in their spiritual-enrichment. In turn, they will share in Paul's ministry by accepting him (15:20-24) and by giving to further the cause of faith. This is a valid trade off as taught in 15:26-27 and elsewhere (1 Cor 9:11).

1:13. Again Paul reaffirms (cf. vv 10-11) his desire to see his readers, but now more emphatically than before, because he states one of his main purposes for coming: **that I might have some fruit among you also, just as among the Gentiles.** Having *fruit* *among* the Roman believers does not refer primarily to winning converts for two reasons: First, the preceding verses refer to the spiritual-blessings that he will impart to believers at his coming. Second, in Romans, *fruit* refers to the benefits of holiness and the results of the Christian experience (cf. 6:21-22; 7:4; 15:28), as well as the *fruit* Paul had elsewhere "among the Gentiles" (Gal 5:22; Eph 5:9; Phil 1:11, 21-25; 4:17). Perhaps Paul's use of *fruit* refers broadly to the spiritual results of his ministry in Rome that includes making converts, but they are not the primary focus since he wrote to believers (1:7-8, 15).

1:14-15. Thus Paul expresses his reason for wanting fruit among the Gentiles, because he is **a debtor both to Greeks and to barbarians, both to wise and to unwise.** His readers to which he felt obligated (since he was appointed "Apostle to the Gentiles") were the people in Rome; but the people in Rome are divided in two camps: linguistically and culturally (which assumes intellectuality). By using the term *Greeks* (*Hellēsin*) Paul did not necessarily mean Greek by race, but those who were highly educated (wise) that shared Greco-Roman culture. Conversely, the rest of the Gentiles who belong to another uneducated (unwise) culture, who spoke an uncommon language, were known as "barbarians" (*barbarois*). The term *barbarois* was onomatopoeic and it was formed phonetically by repeating "bar, bar, bar." This sound denoted a rough sounding foreign language that to the cultured Greco-Roman world sounded like gibberish, which many considered *unwise* and unintelligent.

Being a *debtor both .. to wise and unwise* was a common way of speaking by Romans and other cultures that were among Paul's readers, to whom he says: *I* **am ready to preach the gospel to you who are in Rome** (cf. v 1). Specially important in understanding this verse and the book of Romans as a whole is how the word *gospel* is used in 1:15. Looking at the immediate context, the plural *you* (*hymin*) appears ten times, each referring to the Roman believers (1:6, 7, 8, 9, 10, 11, 12, 13 [twice]). But how can Paul preach the gospel to "saints" (1:7) whose "faith is spoken throughout the world" (v 8)? This implies the *gospel* in Romans includes a much broader concept than merely justification (cf. v 1). In addition the *gospel* also furnishes power through Christ's resurrection for the believer to live victoriously now by the Spirit and be delivered from God's wrath brought by sin in the believer's life.

D. The Theme: The Gospel's Power to Justify and to Deliver the Justified to Experience Life (1:16-17)

1:16. Thus the theme verses of the epistle connect the *gospel* aimed at believers, in v 15, by the explanatory **"For"** (*gar*), which Paul is **not ashamed** to call **the gospel** (cf. vv 1, 15) **of Christ.** Why mention shame? Perhaps Paul had unbelieving Greeks (1:5, 14) in mind who think preaching a crucified Savior is foolish (1 Cor 1:23). Furthermore, with persecution in Rome, these believers were subject to fear and ridicule. If Christians are ashamed they will not confess (cf. Mark 8:38; Luke 9:26; 2 Tim 1:8). If they will not confess there is no deliverance, according to Romans 10:9-10 (to clarify 10:9-10 see commentary). This topic becomes relevant in Romans since 10:11 links "shame" that could hinder public confession of calling on the Lord (10:9-14) with deliverance that believers can experience.

After all, Paul need not be ashamed of this gospel; **for** (*gar*) as he explains, **it** furnishes **the power of God to salvation**. Here Paul does not clarify the meaning of salvation (*sōtēria*). One does not hear of "salvation" again until 5:9, which is defined as salvation from wrath to one already justified. Hence one does not find the term *sōtēria* or *sōzō* mentioned in the justification section

(3:21–4:25), but only in places where it is clearly distinguished from justification (see 5:9 and 10:9-14). Thus, one is hard pressed in Romans to define *salvation* as justification (as commonly done in Eph 2:8-9). Hence the connection of v 16 with v 18 becomes vitally important since *salvation* and *wrath* are linked at the inception and theme of Romans. Paul defines this *salvation* from the beginning as *deliverance from God's present wrath brought by sins.* Therefore, in Romans, it serves the interpreter best to understand and translate *salvation* as *deliverance*, which focuses more on freeing the believer from sin's grip.

A closer look at v 18, 2:5, 8 and 3:5 show God's wrath to be a present, not eternal, judgment whereby He turns the sinners over to the bondage of sin (1:18–3:20). Therefore Paul is saying that to be delivered (*sōtēria*) from this wrath one must have a life of victory over sin (cf. 1:16-18; 5:9-10; 10:9-14; 13:4-5), not just simply be justified. Nevertheless, justification is the first sequential step of deliverance, first by faith in Christ (3:21–4:25) and then by following Christ (5:1–8:39).

Hence the gospel furnishes the "power" (*dynamis*) which is able to deliver (*sōtēria*) **everyone who believes** (i.e., faith becomes the only condition necessary to appropriate the power that is able to deliver; cf. 3:22; 4:11; 10:4,11). Therefore, *salvation* does not merely result upon believing in Christ but has as its goal *to deliver* (*eis sōtēria*) experientially all believers from the effects of sins. Thus believers, subsequent to justification, have power through the Spirit provided by Christ's triumphant resurrection to be delivered from sin's power (cf. 1:4; 6–8).

In Romans, *dynamis* and its derivatives appear thirteen times carrying the usual meaning *of an ability produced by God* (1:16, 20; 15:13-14, 19; 16:25) or *a lack of ability stemming from one's nature* (8:7-8, 38-39). Perhaps, Paul thinks of God's personal power to deliver or judge His people (Exod 9:16; Ps 77:14-15; Jer 16:21) found in the Old Testament (cf. Moo, *Romans,* 66). This *power* is now available to all believers, **for the Jew first and also for the Greek.** Even if this *power* is equally given to all, Paul continues his customary pattern throughout his ministry to visit the *Jew first* (2:9-10; Acts 13:14-15, 42; 14:1; 17:1, 10, 17; 18:4, 7, 19, 26, 19:8; 22:19; 26:11).

1:17. Paul clarifies v 16 by using the explanatory **For** (*gar*) that further explains a major component of "the gospel" by the phrase **in it the righteousness of God is revealed.** The words *in it* (*en autō,* neuter singular) refer to the "gospel" (*euaggelion,* neuter singular) in 1:16.

Hence, the gospel reveals *the righteousness of God.* This expression appears eight times in the New Testament, once in 2 Corinthians 5:21, and seven times in Romans (3:5, 21-22 [twice], 25, 26; 10:3 [twice]). One may understand the expression *righteousness of God* in a broad sense as referring both to His judicial acceptance, granted "to all and on all who believe" (3:22), and His delivering activity, given in resurrection-power (6:1-14) through the Spirit that enables the believer to live righteously (8:1-17). Perhaps Paul may be thinking of God's righteousness, connected in numerous Old Testament deliverance texts, whereby God *delivers* His people on the basis of His *righteousness* (Pss 40:10-13; 71:1-3, 16, 19, 24; 98:2; 119:123; Isa 46:13; 51:5-6, 8; cf. Lopez, *OT Salvation–From What?* 49-64). Unlike the Old Testament era, now God, the Holy Spirit, comes to indwell all believers at the moment of justification (8:9; John 3:1-8) to empower them in order to overcome the experience of sin (Rom 8:1-13). Once believers appropriate God's power, they will immediately experience deliverance from His wrath brought by sins. Thus, the *righteousness of God* should not only be understood as a legal declaration, upon faith alone in Christ alone, but as also bestowing all believers with resurrection-power through the Spirit's indwelling that aids them to live righteously (6–8; 12:1–15:13, see BDAG, 249) and escape God's present wrath (1:18; 5:9-10; 10:9-14; 13:4-5).

Therefore, one may take **from faith to faith** to mean, "*on the basis* of faith *directed* by faith" to describe not only the forensic aspect of "the righteousness of God," but the life that stems from that righteousness on the basis of faith (cf. 6:12-13; 10:5-8). That is, God justifies the ungodly *on the basis* of faith from beginning, and continues to aid the believer in sanctification *directed* by faith, to the end (cf. 10:5-21). Hence faith becomes the sole means for justification and the life-blood for sanctification.

Yet, it is not coincidental for Paul to inseparably link "faith" (*pisteōs*) to "justification" (*dikaios*) in the quote taken from Habakkuk 2:4: **The just shall live by faith.** Perhaps a better translation makes the inseparable link between *dikaios* and *pisteōs* immediately apparent: "*The one who is righteous by faith shall live.*" This has better support contextually since *pistis* appears three times and twice it is linked to "righteous" in v 17. Thus a particular emphasis is given to both words to mean that only those *justified by faith* shall live (*zaō*). Of course, Paul gives faith an important role in the Christian life (e.g., Gal 2:20). This concept lies at the root of Romans 6–8 and directly in 10:5-21. However, in Romans, Paul does not usually link the term "faith" to the theme of sanctification-deliverance leading to "life," except when addressing the Jews in 10:5-21, for specific reasons shown there.

The letter's structure provides evidence by connecting *pistis* with *dikaios* and not with *zaō* (Nygren, *Romans*, 81-92). A purely statistical observation develops this. The noun *pistis* and verb *pisteuō* appear twenty-seven times in chapters 3–4. Those chapters show that God's righteousness comes through faith. Then both verb and noun dramatically disappear, only occurring three times from chapters 5–8. Two of the three occurrence, found in 5:1-2 (where a transition is taking place), appear with its customary meaning pointing back to the justification section in chapters 3–4.

Conversely, the noun *zōē* and verb *zaō* appear twenty-five times from chapters 5–8 where Christians can experience the "resurrection-life" known as sanctification. But both verb and noun are virtually non-existent, appearing only three times (1:17; 2:7; 4:17). It logically follows from this evidence that Paul connects "righteousness" to *faith* and *not* to *live*, which link allows the following translation of Habakkuk 2:4: "The one who is *righteous by faith* shall live."

Thus, Paul means to emphasize "life" since his definition of the gospel is not limited to justification. To Paul those who on the basis of faith are declared righteous shall live (i.e., have the capacity to experience life), since intrinsic to the gospel lays the power to deliver from wrath everyone who appropriate it: first to unbelievers by possessing God's righteousness through faith alone in Christ alone (3:21–4:25) and second to believers by living the resurrection-life of Christ (5–8; 12:1–15:13) that is able to deliver everyone from God's present wrath.

A. Unrighteous Humanity Suffers God's Wrath (1:18–3:20).

Before revealing the righteousness of God provided on the basis of faith, Paul first establishes why unrighteous humanity needs it. Everyone stands condemned under sin and unable to conquer the power of sin to live. Humanity needs God's righteousness provided by grace. Thus, in four sections, Paul shows how everyone stands condemned and experience God's wrath because of sin.

1. The Gentile world suffers God's wrath (1:18-32)

1:18. Not wanting to leave anyone darkened (*skotizō*, see v 21), Paul begins this major section, which subject matter extends to 3:20, by reasoning why humanity finds itself in such a state of degradation: **For the wrath of God is revealed ...** because of **all ungodliness and unrighteousness of men.** The particle *for* (*gar*), beginning in v 18 carries a causal sense and refers back to the clause "God's righteousness is revealed" (present tense) in 1:17. Therefore, since God's righteousness is presently being revealed (same verb and tense as in 1:18), this wrath must be understood as presently occurring. Hence God's present wrath is evidenced in vv 24, 26, and 28, as He lifts His protection and allows sin to run its course.

The original Greek word for *wrath* (*orgē*) means "anger" and "strong displeasure" (BDAG, 720). When speaking of wrath in the New Testament, God is usually at the center, and it always appears to refer to God's *strong displeasure against sinful actions* expressed in time (as here) or at the future tribulation period (Rom 2:5, 8; 1 Thess 1:10; 5:9). Whether God's wrath should ever be understood as eternal judgment (cf. 2:12) is highly questionable (see for detail discussion Lopez, *Wrath of God*, 45-66), since biblically human sin always manifests itself in time by **ungodliness** (*asebeia*) **and unrighteousness** (*adikia*).

Both *asebeia* and *adikia* ought to be understood as a "violation by words and deeds." Perhaps *asebeia* refers vertically to human violation of the first four commandments directed at God, since the context refers to idolatry (1:19-23), and *adikia* refers horizontally to violations of human rights by disregarding the last six commandments (1:24-32, cf. Shrenk, *TDNT*, 1:155-56, see v 29 where it begins the list of vices).

Paul does not attribute humanity's present condition to passive ignorance. Instead, humanity has actively chosen to **suppress the truth in unrighteous**. To "suppress" (*katechontōn*) literally means "*to hold*." Here it means to *stifle* (in a sense to *deny*) through *unrighteous* behavior, *the truth*, presented by creation giving evidence of God's existence.

1:19-20. This "truth," showing God's existence through creation in v 18, cannot be denied **because** (*dioti*, is a "marker used to indicate why something just stated can reasonably be considered valid, BDAG, 251) **what may be known of God is manifest.** First, God made it crystal clear **in** (*en*) **them** before He visibly showed it **to them.** While the phrase *to them* captures the external evidence explained (with "**For**," *gar*) in v 20 that God makes plain of Himself through natural revelation (i.e., creation), the phrase *in them* refers to the knowledge about God that all humans possess inherently. That is, humans are not intrinsically atheist, agnostic or devoid of moral knowledge (2:14-15). Discoveries of all civilizations show the opposite, for all of them give evidence to having a god-conscience by their cultic-worship-systems and rule of law.

Thus, God "may be known," as v 19 indicates, through **the creation of the world** since **His invisible *attributes* are clearly seen, being understood by the things that are made.** What may be known are **His eternal power and Godhead** (*theiotēs*, means divinity). The phrase *His eternal power,* linked to *theiotēs*, refers to God's creative activity that is properly associated with One having a divine nature (BDAG, 446). However, since "God is Spirit" (John 4:24), He reveals Himself to the physical eye and mind through creation. Even depraved mankind is **without excuse** because he possesses the physical and mental capacity to recognize God's existence. Therefore, they are held responsible.

1:21. Paul explains the last clause, why humanity is "without excuse" in vv 21-23, by using the same conjunction "**because**" (*dioti*) as he did in v 19 (cf. *dioti* there for definition) to explain the last clause of v 18 (i.e., although humanity "suppress the truth" they "are without excuse"). Mankind has no excuse because **they knew** (*gnontes*) **God.** The aorist participle *gnontes* expresses mankind's experience that precedes their failure to recognize Him and act accordingly. Hence one may render it as "having known God." Nevertheless, **they did not glorify** *Him* **as God,** having been created for this very reason, **nor were** they **thankful. But** they **became futile in their thoughts, and their foolish hearts were darkened.** Both verbs *became futile* (*emataiōthēsan*) and *darkened* (*eskotisthē*) are aorist passive, which phrase began with the strongest contrastive conjunction in the Greek *but* (*all'*). Paul uses the passive verbs to imply how God's wrath allows sin to sink the sinner deeper, causing a spiritual stupor. Thus, what causes this *futility* and *darkness*—that only God can remove—is *sin* that takes over and controls humanity if allowed to run its course (Gen 4:7; Acts 16:14; 2 Cor 4:1-4; Col 1:13).

1:22. Sin usually causes intellectual illusion (cf. v 21) and moral folly as Old Testament wisdom literature shows. **Professing to be wise** becomes the claim of deceived people (1 Cor 3:18), leading to moral bankruptcy (Ps 36:3), as **they became fools.** The term *emōranthēsan* (*became fools* or stupid) appears in the aorist passive that could be rendered "made themselves fools" (Murray, *Romans,* 1:42) due to sin's influence on the person (v 21). Foolishness leads to idolatry as v 23 shows, as also the LXX translation of Jeremiah 10:14 indicates since the same aorist passive verb *emōranthē* (senseless) appears linked to idolatry (cf. Isa 19:11).

1:23. As a result of sin, man **changed the glory of the incorruptible God.** Mankind refuses to acknowledge God because automatically they become accountable for their behavior. Consequently, today, sinful man created a natural process called evolution that explains how all things originate apart from God, so that they do not have to be accountable to anyone. It was no different in the Old Testament as men created their own origins of species method through a plethora of myths and animal worship system (Exod 32; Ps 106:20; Jer 2:11). Instead of behaving like God in whose image man was created (Gen 1:26-27), man reversed it by behaving according to the god created in his image. Paul may be thinking about the biblical narrative after Adam's fall, by his use of **birds, four-footed animals and creeping things** (reptiles), that along with *glory, image* and *made like* all appear in Genesis 1:20-26. According to Paul in 1 Corinthians 10:20, when anyone sacrifices to idols they do it unto demons. Today, as then, idolatry becomes anything that takes the place of God's preeminence in one's life (e.g., money, family, sports, etc…).

1:24. Therefore (*dio*) indicates emphatically the result of God's response to the degrading effects of sin described in vv 22-23. Because mankind stubbornly persists in the sin of idolatry, the descent into which they fall becomes evident from vv 24-32. Thus Paul says: **God also gave them up**. The verb *gave up* (*paredōken*, found in vv 24, 26, 28) becomes highly important to understanding God's wrath and *how* it functions. Since this section highlights God's response, the verb *paredōken* specifically describes how God's wrath is presently being revealed (v 18). He basically hands people over **to uncleanness, in the lusts of their hearts, to dishonor their bodies among themselves.** The verb *paredōken* implies how God lifts His hand of protection to turn people over to another entity (a common NT use, cf. 4:25; 8:32; Matt 17:22), sin's powerful control.

1:25. Thus, instead of humans displaying God's image and glory (to achieve the purpose of being created), they display sin's control as shown by its fruits of corruption mentioned in the list of vices (vv 24, 29-32). Paul continues describing in detail those **who exchanged the truth of God for the lie.** The literal phrases *the truth* and *the lie* suggest Paul has a specific idea in mind. Verse 25 repeats the general sense of v 23. Comparing both verses show: *the truth* parallels "the glory of the incorruptible God" manifested in creation and *the lie* parallels "an image," which they traded for God. As a result, humanity **worshipped and served the creature rather than the Creator,** whom Paul described as **blessed forever** (a Jewish benediction), with a strong affirmation, **Amen** (cf. 9:5; 11:36; 15:33; 16:24), that means "let it be." Only when humanity learns to love the Blessed more than the blessings of material things, can they be free from idolatry.

1:26-27. For this reason (*dia touto*) connects Paul's indictment to what follows with v 25, in the same manner "therefore" (*dio*) joined v 24 to vv 22-23. At this point, the link of sinful behavior found in v 26 to idolatry must be obvious. Paul says the reason **God gave them up** (cf. v 24) **to vile passions** stems from choosing to control their destiny by worshipping the creature. This implies that God (in Gentiles eyes) becomes superfluous. Hence, God gives them up by lifting His grace and allowing their wish.

An absence of God's general grace allows human sin to go unchecked that results in a greater perversion of sin. Paul explains those sins of "vile passions" (lit., "passions that disgrace," BDAG, 748): **For** (*gar*) **even their women exchanged the natural use for what is against nature.** Paul thinks of lesbianism, something rarely mentioned in ancient literature. Here Paul diverges from the common pattern of the day.

Likewise … men … burned for one another, men with men committing what is shameful. He may have gotten a picture of homosexuality from Corinth, where he wrote this letter. One of Rome's most notorious sins was homosexuality. Hence Paul spills more ink on this sin than any other on the list of vices.

The terms used by Paul, "female" (*thēlys*) and "male" (*arsēn*), are adjectives and are *not* the common words used for "women" (*gynē*) and men (*anēr*). However, they are appropriately used here since they stress sexual distinctions, which is a common use elsewhere (Gen 1:27 [LXX]; Matt 19:4; Mark 10:6; Gal 3:28).

Unwisely some homosexuals suggest these verses refer to a heterosexual engaged in homosexual relations. Then it is sinful, but not for homosexuals since it happens to be their natural preference. Some have gone on to argue for a homosexual *gene.* Three answers may be given: (1) Nowhere does the Scripture condone acting on feelings or natural tendencies, whether indulging in homosexuality or heterosexual fornication (1 Cor 6:13). (2) Furthermore, since human nature was distorted by sin, intrinsic desires are not the best guides. (3) Whether or not a homosexual gene exists is irrelevant, because homosexuality in the Scripture refers always to an action, not a feeling. Hence Scripture condemns the action and not the feeling. As a result, the Bible forbids homosexual acts (cf. Gen 19:4-25; Lev 18:22; 20:13).

Paul knew **the penalty of their error** came in different forms. Today AIDS, brought by sexual sins, is an example of one of the most common penalties.

1:28. Another step downward comes because men **did not like to retain God in *their* knowledge.** There is a word play here in the original Greek. Man did not want to "retain" (*dokimazō*) God, which can be understood as "useless." As a result, **God gave them over to a debased mind** (cf. vv 24, 26). Because man thought that having a God-conscience is useless, God handed them over to a "debased" (*adokimon*) mind, which may be understood as "worthless." Thus, since human thought did not desire God and regarded Him as useless, He turned them over to "worthlessness," **to do those things**

which are not fitting. The same Greek term *kathēko,* used for *fitting,* was a commonplace word used in Stoic philosophy that expressed behavior contrary to the moral norms imposed by nature. Men will, therefore, sink deeper by doing immoral acts since God turned them over to sin that ultimately mars their God-conscience even more.

1:29-31. By dismissing God, their minds were **being filled** (*peplērōmenous,* perfect passive tense) **with** pure malice. In English *being filled* implies *filled full* of **all** kinds of sins, which occurs as a result of God giving them over (vv 24, 26, 28). What follows is a list of vices commonly used of unbelievers in Greek literature of this period and well attested in the Bible (13:13; 1 Cor 5:10-11; 6:9-10; 2 Cor 12:20; Gal 5:19-21; Eph 4:19, 31; 5:3-5; Col 3:5; 1 Tim 1:9-10, etc...). Grouping these vices has been a matter of dispute among commentators. However, two things are certain: There seems to be three divisions (5-5-12), and within them, all of these things are terrible: (1) **unrighteousness** (injustice, *adikia,* cf. v 18), (2) **sexual immorality** (all forms of illicit sex, the term absent in some early ms, but does appear in the majority of mss; it is also easy to delete because of the similarities of the Greek words *porneia* with the following word for *wickedness, ponēria*), (3) **wickedness** (evil in general), (4) **covetousness** (greed), and (5) **maliciousness** (hatred with intent to harm). The noun **full of** (*mestous*) governs the following specific vices stemming from the general term *adikia* above: (1) **envy** (jealousy), (2) **murder** (unlawful killing; Rom 13:3-5), (3) **strife** (quarrel), (4) **deceit** (liar), and (5) **evil-mindedness** (bitter or mean). The last twelve are expressed in more specific terms, while the last four terms within the twelve in v 31 begin with the Greek letter *alpha* ("a" in English), a common way to negate a word (e.g. like the English word *a*theist).

1:32. Paul concludes by echoing the verb *know* of v 19 and v

21 thus reiterating a similar concept by accusing mankind as a whole of **knowing** (*epignontes*) **the righteous judgment of God.** Therefore, **those who practice such things** know they **are deserving of death ...** and **approve of those who practice them.** The *righteous judgment* (*dikaiōma*) refers to the righteous requirement of the Law as used elsewhere in 2:26; 5:16, 18; 8:4, but here it refers to man's innate-legal-mechanism called the conscience, which knows the appropriate retribution for immorality (2:14-15). Nevertheless, they disregard it and instead promote it.

Just because something is legally correct does not mean it is morally right. Regardless, many try to rationalize their sins, but they know better because God at creation placed a moral mechanism within man called the conscience. Hence, even if pornography, abortion, etc... are within the legal bounds of man's law, the conscience bears witness to God's moral Law convicting them otherwise.

GOD'S STANDARD 2 OF JUDGMENT

2. The moralist (Jew) under God's principles of judgment suffers wrath (2:1-16)

After having dealt with man's unrighteousness (*adikian* in 1:18) and their refusal to respond to general revelation from 1:18-32, Paul turns to the moralist Jew to reprove their self-righteousness. Though he does not reveal their identity until v 17. Because Jews possessed special revelation showing how to act before God (2:1-29), they considered themselves an exception to sinful humanity. Hence, Jews upheld their moral behavior to be above others but misunderstood God's principle of judgment that equally applied to all. Paul will correct this misunderstanding: judgment comes (1) according to truth (vv 2-4), (2) according to deeds (vv 5-11) *and* (3) according to revelation (vv 12-16).

2:1. Therefore, Paul transitions from the first group (1:18-32), who are "without excuse" (1:20), to the second group (2:1-16), who are also **inexcusable** (2:1). This is important to note; just as the first group experiences God's wrath, contextually the wrath in 2:5, 8 should also be seen as a present reality. *Therefore* (*dio* in 2:1) acts as a connector linking both groups. However, one should not understand *therefore* to relate primarily to the sins of the Gentiles described in 1:21-32, but to God's wrath in 1:18 (Lopez, *Wrath of God*, 57-58). It follows then that **man, whoever you are who judge**, is found wanting, **for you who judge practice the same**

51

things (i.e., the moralist performs the sins of the previous group, 1:18-32). Important to note here and throughout Romans is Paul's style of communication ancients referred to as *diatribe*. That is when objections in the form of a question are placed in an imaginary critic's mouth in order to be answered or rebutted (2:1, 17, 21-23; 3:1, 5-6, 9, 31; 4:1, 9; 6:1; 7:7, 13; 9:19-21; 11:17-24; 14:4, see S. K. Stowers, *Diatribe in Romans*, 85-118).

Those in 1:32 "approve of those who practice" sin because perhaps it makes them feel good to have others around like them. Likewise, but in a perverse way, those in 2:1 set a false standard of judgment by using sinful humanity to make themselves appear better, but *practice* the same things.

2:2. Now Paul explains the first principle found in God's courtroom: judgment comes according to truth. Jews together with Paul can say **we know** (*oidamen*) **the judgment of God is according to truth**. The expression *oidamen* usually appears in places where both parties agree intuitively with the statements that immediately follow (cf. 3:19; 7:14; 8:22, 28; 1 Cor 8:1, 4; 2 Cor 5:1, et al.). Hence, this group has no excuse, for God's *judgment* is *according* to absolute *truth* (i.e., factual, *not* hypothetical, circumstantial, or incomplete data). He judges justly, unlike men who in their false standard judge others and at the same time they **practice such things**. Moralists need reminding of certain truths. For example, breaking one commandment makes one guilty of breaking them all (Jas 2:10). Even a lustful thought, apart from the act, becomes tantamount to committing adultery (Matt 5:28). Merely resolving not to sin is not enough, for omitting to do right is just as bad (Jas 4:17).

2:3-4. Moralists ignore the fact exhibited according to God's truth that they are not completely flawless. In Jewish literature Wisdom 15:1–16:2 suggests that there were Jews who thought

God would somehow over look their sins because they were not idol worshippers (as the first group) and possess the Law, thus implying God is partial to them. One of God's major attributes is His justice that is based on absolute truth. He is called four times "the God of truth" (Deut 32:4; Ps 31:5; Isa 65:16 [2x]), as Jesus is the personification of "Truth" (John 14:6) that came "to bear witness to the truth" (18:37). When it comes to God's courtroom, the principles by which He judges are always based on unbiased truth.

The irony then may be found in their capacity to **judge those practicing such things,** which does not exonerate them from escaping **the judgment of God.** Because the Jews knew better, it increased their guilt. Man should not confuse or **despise the riches** (*ploutou*, indicates exceedingly "abundance") **of His goodness** (*chrēstotētos*, "a benevolent activity" also used in 11:22; Eph 2:7; Titus 3:4)**, forbearance, and longsuffering** (cf. 3:25; Acts 14:16; 17:30) and assume that everyday sin goes unpunished or that it means nothing will ever happen (cf. 2 Pet 3:4-8). Instead, because God is exceedingly good, this **goodness of God leads** to **repentance** (*metanoian*, appears only once in Romans) before the second advent of "the day of the Lord" (Rom 2:5) that Peter also mentioned in 2 Peter 3:8-15. *Metanoia* means change of direction that obviously includes a change of mind (BDAG, 640). As in 2 Peter 3:6-9, God desires men to turn (*metanoia*) from sin to Him in order not to perish physically, thereby escaping wrath. While justification by faith alone in Christ alone (Rom 3:21–4:25) places one in a position of possessing the power to escape God's wrath, apart from repentance, His wrath cannot be avoided (cf. 1:18). Jonah's preaching of repentance to the Ninevites exhibits this last point (Jonah 3:1-10; Matt 12:41). Nothing in Jonah's book shows how to resolve the eternal destiny issue of the Ninevites, other than reading more into the word "repent" than the context allows.

Perhaps Jonah told the Ninevites about God's plan of justification, but that is mere speculation. Thus, all that the text merely shows (in Jonah and here) is God's desire for all to do a 180° turn to Him (2 Pet 3:9) in order to escape His wrath.

2:5. But, Paul contrasts what should lead Jews to repent, as mentioned in the previous verse, to what is actually occurring to them: **in accordance with** the **hardness** of their **impenitent heart** they **are treasuring up for** themselves **wrath in the day of wrath and revelation of the righteous judgment of God.** The first use of term the *wrath* (*orgēs*) grammatically refers back to *treasuring up,* which points to the present wrath of 1:18. Several reasons argue for this view: (1)

Dio in 2:1 acts as a connector linking both groups. Thus, since the first group experiences God's present wrath due to their practices, the second group who alike practices those sins must logically experience the same result. Otherwise, God's judgments are unfair. (2) This group can only store-up for the future something that is presently available. (3) The broad context presents the present problem of sin and wrath in 1:18–3:20 for unbelievers that God will begin to remedy with a present solution in 3:21–4:25 by becoming believers.

Paul begins to develop the second principle of God's judgment *according to deeds* (vv 5-11). Therefore, in verses 5-8, Paul juxtaposes those who obey and receive "eternal life" (which Law-claimers would have to do perfectly [not just hear, 2:13]), to those who do not obey and receive "indignation and wrath." One should not assume "the day of wrath and revelation of the righteous judgment of God" refers to the Great White Throne Judgment of Revelation 20. The term "the righteous judgment of God" in Romans 2:5 appears only once in the entire New Testament. However, a variant occurs in 2 Thessalonians 1:5: "righteous judgment of God." Upon a closer examination of the context of 2 Thessalonians 1:4-9, one discovers other terms like "tribulations," "revealed," "flaming fire" (=judgment, cf. Rev 1:14; 2:18), "everlasting," "obey," and "glory", which are all found in Romans 2:5-8. Of course, 2 Thessalonians 1:4-9 refers to Revelation 19:11-16, which is part of "that day," "the day of wrath," and "the day of the Lord." In 2:5, Paul refers to "the day of wrath" (*en hēmera orgēs*), also known as "the day of the Lord," which occurs in the seven-year tribulation period when God will judge the world. Numerous passages point to this coming day (Isa 2:12; 13:6, 9; 24:21; Jer 24:21; Joel 2–3; Ezek 7:7; Zeph 1:7, 14-15, 18; 2:3; Mal 3:2; 4:1; possibly Rom 9:22; 1 Thess 1:10; 5:9). It will culminate at the tribulation. For Paul, Christ's imminent return provides a way out of the day of wrath (1 Thess 4:13–5:11) for the regenerate. In turn, for the unregenerate, the rapture means that the "day of wrath" (cf. 1 Thess 5:1-3) has merely begun. God's wrath in Romans 2:5, 8 is addressed to the moralist who thinks he can earn eternal life through the Law, which is impossible (3:20).

2:6. Now, Paul clarifies "the day of wrath and revelation of the righteous judgment of God" by the relative pronoun **who** (*hos*) that refers back to God as the One rendering this judgment. Having just cautioned the moralists of their self-righteousness as this day draws near, Paul develops it in more detail (vv 6-11). Therefore, on that day of tribulation God *will render to each one according to his deeds* (cf. Ps 62:12; Prov 24:12; Matt 16:27). Thus, if the moralist claims his *deeds* (*ergon*, lit. "works") as a means of justification, doom awaits because they are guilty of the same thing they accuse others of doing (vv 1-3).

2:7-8. However, Paul does not state the obvious. He presents hypothetically (as if the moralist could obey flawlessly) the principles on which God judges and rewards deeds: **eternal life to those who by patient continuance in doing good seek for glory,**

honor, and immortality. This statement may be understood in various ways: (1) Deeds cannot justify or earn one eternal life before God (3:20; 4:2), but they may be viewed as evidence of a changed life, which is an element that many find to be pervasive in Romans (e.g., see Moo, Cranfield, Witmer, Murray, Harrison). (2) Since the subject of this verse is judgment, not justification, believers may be in view. That is, believers who continue in good works will receive rewards in the future since works are never the basis for receiving eternal life but for judging believers at the judgment seat of Christ (1 Cor 3:15; 2 Cor 5:10-11). Hence when eternal life appears as a present possession and is based on faith (John 3:16; 6:47, et al.) it refers to a gift, but when it appears as future possession based on works (Gal 6:8; 1 Tim 6:17-19; Titus 1:2) it refers to rewards. (3) If anyone obeyed perfectly, by patiently persisting in doing good, then eternal life could be earned. Hence, eternal life is a future possession, because as long as the person lives he may not persevere perfectly. Unfortunately, Paul states later no one can accomplish such a feat: "There is none righteous, no, not one…none who seeks after God" (3:10-11). This view fits best because the immediate context (2:5-8) addresses the moralists who claim God's favor on the basis of works, thus God lays the principle on approaching Him by works. One can see grammatically the connection from v 5 to v 8 as each verse modifies the previous. Finally, the overall context 1:18–3:20 refers to unbelievers, *not* to the evidence of a changed life or of rewards for believers.

Paul lays down the principle verdict of failure by a strong contrasting particle, **but.** Verse 7 "to those" (*tois men*) and v 8 *but* **to those** (*tois de*) introduce markers (*men ..de*) identifying a set of items in contrast to one another. Thus, *to those* **who are self-seeking and do not obey the truth, but obey unrighteousness—indignation and wrath** awaits them.

The meaning of *truth* should be understood contextually by how its been used (2:1-4). This is not the truth of the gospel, but the absolute truth as revealed in God's Law that are the principles of His judgment (cf. 2:2, 13), for those who claim deeds as the basis of justification before Him. Hence *obey the truth* is juxtaposed to the phrase *but obey unrighteousness*, which *adikia* has been used by Paul so far to denote godless behavior (1:18, 29).

The phrase *indignation and wrath* (*orgē kai thymos*) is used three times by John in Revelation 14:10; 16:19; 19:15 to refer to God's judgment in the tribulation. Verse 8 further strengthens the idea that Paul is referring to the tribulation period (mentioned in v 5) by his use of *indignation and wrath*. Although the LXX uses the combination of *orgē kai thymos* in a general sense for God's anger (Deut 29:22; Ps 68:25; Isa 10:5), it also uses this same combination to refer to the day of the LORD (Isa 13:9; 30:30; Jer 7:20; 21:5). Therefore, for the unbeliever to continue on that course will only cause him to experience and accumulate wrath that will culminate in the ultimate day of wrath known as the tribulation (cf. 2:5).

2:9. Paul further qualifies this day of "indignation and wrath" as characterized by **tribulation and anguish** (parallel to v 8) that will come **on every soul of man who does evil**. The phrase *soul of man* (*psychēn anthrōpou*) merely means "everyone," similar to "each one" in v 6. The term *psychē* is an idiom reflecting merely the Hebrew term *nepeš* meaning "human being" (cf. the LXX in Gen 12:5; 17:14, 19:20; Num 31:40; Deut 10:22). As already mentioned, wrath comes upon the unrighteous because they practice evil, and more so on **the Jew first** (cf 1:16) since his privilege was greater by receiving special revelation. Jews will also be prominent in the tribulation period since God will again turn to them (cf. Rom 11:26-32) as a prophetic fulfillment of the week (=7 years) missing in the 70-week prophecy in Daniel 9:24-27. Of course, **the Greek** (=Gentile) will also experience wrath at this time of tribulation (Revelation 7).

2:10. Again Paul contrasts the previous verse with **but**. The literal Greek may be translated *but even* (*de kai*), but omitting "even" eliminates redundancy and awkward English. This verse should be seen parallel to v 7 as further describing those who persevere in **glory, honor, and peace to everyone who works what is good** (cf. v 7), **to the Jew first and also to the Greek** (cf. 1:16).

2:11. Ending this section which unit of thought begun in v 6 (note the chiastic structure), Paul explains the reason why God is a fair judge: **For there is no partiality with God.** The basis for God's judgment, spoken by Paul until now, is absolutely impartial. Fear should come upon the self-righteous (vv 1-5) because they will approach God on the basis of their works. If this is the case, as Paul will shortly say, condemnation awaits. However, there is another type of righteousness for those who stand before God can claim: righteousness by faith. Even in dispensing this "righteousness" God was impartial. That is, God could not declare a sinner righteous apart from someone meeting the Judge's righteous standards as previously mentioned (cf. 3:25-26), or else God would be lawless in allowing sin to go unpunished. Since the principles of God's judgment stand on the basis of works, Christ's perfect life becomes the only acceptable human works before God. Hence Christ died on behalf of sinners and provided for them the righteous standard demanded by God. The difference, however, for the believer, unlike the moralist, when he stands before God, is that Christ's imputed righteousness appears on his account (cf. 3:21-22, 25-26; 4:3). Thus God is impartial indeed!

2:12. After having summarized the previous section in v 11, Paul shifts his focus to the related issue of judgment based on the

Law. While self-righteous man accumulates wrath-judgment according to deeds, the culmination, when God repays directly, refers to the tribulation period in vv 5-11. Similarly, God's final-judgment on the self-righteous, who claim the Law, will also be based on deeds. Wrath and eternal-punishment, however, are not synonymous concepts. God's wrath occurs temporally until the final ruling of eternal punishment. For example, a victim's relative was once asked, before the execution of the man who killed her brother, whether she was still wrathful about the horrendous crime. She responded, "I am not angered or wrathful anymore because justice has been served." Thus, God's wrath subsides in eternity because eternal justice has been served. Sin that is not dealt with incurs God's wrath, but sin that is dealt with subsides His wrath. All sin will have been dealt with in eternity; either by grace or law (see Stählin, *TDNT*, 5:434, for a distinction between "wrath" and "eternal punishment").

Although wrath rewards men according to deeds in time, so final-judgment rewards men according to deeds in eternity. Devoid of God's righteousness (cf. 3:21–4:25), the latter concept relates to man's final justification before God on the basis of Law (*nomos*). Considerable debate exists on Paul's meaning of the term *law* here. There are four nuances found in Romans: (1) Generic, "a law" (4:15; 7:1[?]), (2) figurative, law as *principle* (2:14; 3:27; 7:21, 23, 25; 8:2), (3) a reference to the entire Old Testament (3:2, 19, 31), or (4) in the majority of cases that *nomos* appears, with or without the article, it refers to the Mosaic Law (Torah) (2:12-15, 17-18, 20, 23, 25-27; 3:19-21, 27, 28; 4:13-15, 16; 5:13, 20; 6:14-15; 7:2-9, 12, 14, 16, 22, 23, 25, 25; 8:3-4; 9:31; 10:4; 13:8-9) (see J. A. Fitzmyer, *Romans*, 131-32). Paul seems to refer to the Mosaic Law here. Thus, in vv 12-16, Paul takes a further step in developing the concept of God's impartiality; in the final analysis He deals with men according to the revelation they possessed. Yet, favoritism will not be shown to those deprived of the Law: **For as many as have sinned without law will also perish without law**, no more than those who possess it but do not keep it: **and as many as have sinned in the law will be judged by the law.** Those devoid of special revelation (1:18-32) will be held just as guilty as those having it (2:1–3:8). Perhaps the difference will be on the degree of punishment to those that possessed more light, since they knew better and did nothing about it. Then *the law* will be a witness against them.

2:13. Hence, Paul now makes it explicitly clear: **for not the hearers of the law *are* just in the sight of God, but the doers of the law will be justified.** Justification here is the legal term discussed in the theme 1:16-17 by the Greek term *dikaios* (cf. 3:24). No one will be exonerated or declared righteous merely by hearing *the law*, but by doing it perfectly, something impossible to accomplish (3:19-20). Jews must have felt special and perhaps justified before God, because they heard the Law read in synagogues in addition to having possession of it (cf. see commentary in 2:3-4; 4:13). Hence Paul attacks such deception.

2:14-16. By using the explanatory **for** (*gar*) Paul explains how **Gentiles,** as an example of those **who do not have the law, by nature do the things in the law.** This further implicates those that have *the law* but do not absolutely keep it. Conversely, Gentiles do **not** have **the law** and **are a law to themselves.**

Clearly in v 12, Paul said Gentiles would equally perish without *the law.* Consequently, this makes Paul's case of accusing the Jews, through the example of the Gentiles, even stronger since those *not* having the details of *the law* (who equally perish without it) comply with its essence. Paul's point is that unbelieving Gentiles normally obey their parents and do not rob or murder (Moo,

Romans, 150). They obey the righteous principles that are fundamentally the essence of *the law* (see R. E. White, "Biblical Ethics," in *EDT,* 376). Intuitively Gentiles **show the work of the law written in their hearts** by *nature.* They practice the basic moral principles of *the law* by loving, which fulfills the principles of *the law* (13:8-10). Thus, even before Israel had the Law inscribed on tables of stone, traits of the Law (hence the word "work" used by Paul refers to something other than the complete Law) were also found inscribed in Gentile hearts. Some see Paul alluding to Jeremiah 31:31-34. If so, Gentile Christians are in view in Jeremiah's passage. Yet, this is unlikely for three reasons: (1) Jeremiah refers to the actual Law, not *the work of the law,* being written in their hearts. (2) As a result of *the law* being *written in their hearts* a full knowledge of God will occur, not partial. (3) Jeremiah's prophetic context refers to Israel. The context here speaks clearly of unbelieving Gentiles. Moreover, since unredeemed man's heart is a tainted parchment that can be easily corrupted (Jer 17:9), God's Law objectifies trespasses by inscribing what man tries to suppress (1:18, 23).

God being aware of man's corrupt state gives him another supplemental mechanism to help him along. This mechanism analogous to a computer chip called the **conscience also** bears **witness** to the validity of God's Law within man. The *conscience* records all moral and immoral thoughts and innately knows and communicates to man the distinction between right and wrong (cf. Minirth, Meier, and Arterburn, "Mind," in *CLE,* 414). Hence Paul says **between themselves *their* thoughts accusing or else excusing *them*.** Yet, what a person wrongly experiences in certain cultures may help program his conscience or sear it (1 Tim 4:2). Conscience may not be the best reliable guide. Regardless, everyone knows, from primitive tribes to modern man, common moral principles.

All cultures know that lying, cheating, murder, and even denying the existence of God (cf. 1:18-20) is wrong. Therefore, even if in some cultures certain immoral practices are accepted (e.g., cannibalism), it cannot occur without searing some aspect of the conscience, and even then a total reprogramming never occurs. Or else Paul could not say that on judgment day peoples' thoughts will accuse or excuse them.

Thus **in the day** of final-judgment, **when God will judge the secrets of men by Jesus Christ**, "the law written in their heart" and the "conscience" (e.g., analogous to a computer hard drive) will divulge all of its information. Both of these elements within man will act as witnesses against them (perhaps like Deut 17:6; Matt 18:16) **according to** Paul's (i.e., **my**) **gospel**. That is, Paul's gospel includes the absolute certainty of final-judgment on sin (1 Cor 4:5). Though God judges (cf. Rev 20:11-15), this judgment comes through the divine Agent, Jesus Christ (John 5:22, 27, Acts 17:31).

3. The Jew unable to keep the Law suffers God's wrath (2:17–3:8)

2:17-20. Previously, Paul had in mind the self-righteous sinner in 2:1-4, who was warned of the coming wrath in vv 5-11 and of final-judgment in vv 12-16. But now he explicitly identifies the self-righteous group by name, **called a Jew.** His national ethnicity (chosen of God, Deut 7:6; 14:2), possession of **the law** and relationship of **boast**[ing] **in God** are all sources of pride and confidence.

Their self-righteousness and confidence may further be viewed in its totality, from vv 17-20, by the six main verbs and three participles in the Greek describing their privilege and pride: (1) *called a Jew* (chosen and a member of the covenant people); (2) *rest on the law* (enough to approach God); (3) *boast in God* (pride in God); (4) **to know** *His* **will** (to possess special revelation); (5) to **approve** (moral discernment) modified by two participles **excellent** (cf. Phil 1:10) things as **instructed out of the law**; and (6) **confident** (or persuaded) of being **the guide to the blind**, and **a light to those .in darkness** because "you have" (participle, NIV) the **knowledge and truth in the law.** The *light* to guide one's path was connected with *the law* (Pss 119:105, 130; Wis 18:4). Ironically, God's Servant, Christ (Isa 42:6-7; 49:6, identified in some sense with Israel) as well as Paul (cf. Acts 26:18) guided and lit others paths (for passages showing that Christ and Paul served as lights see Matt 4:16; 5:15-16; Luke 1:79; John1:4-9; Acts 13:47; Acts 26:23) where Israel failed (Matt 15:14) and were both rejected by Israel.

2:21-24. Hence, from vv 21-23, Paul asks five rhetorical questions in a diatribe form (cf. 2:1) to indict Israel with hypocrisy: (1) **You, therefore, who teach another, do you not teach yourself?** (Ps 50:16-21; Matt 23:3); (2) **You who preach that a man should not steal, do you steal?** (Jer 7:9; Mal 3:8; Matt 21:13); (3) **You who say, "Do not commit adultery," do you commit adultery?** (Jer 5:7; John 8:7); (4) **You who abhor idols, do you rob temples?** (Mark 11:15-17; Acts 24:6); and (5) **You who make your boast in the law, do you dishonor God through breaking the law?** (Ezek 22:26; Matt 15:3-9; 23:23). All of these were not new charges but old ones made by the Old Testament and Jesus. And now Paul supports his reason (**For**, *gar*), from Scripture, (Isa 52:5, in the LXX) why the Jew's hypocrisy caused *the name of God* to be *blasphemed among the Gentiles*. The test among God's people may be found not in what they *say* but in what they *do* that will cause others to speak well of God (cf. John 13:35; 1 Pet 2:12).

2:25-27. For (*gar*) used by Paul again explains the previous charge by one of the most important source of pride to the Jew, **circumcision.** On the one hand (*men*), Paul agrees that circumcision **is indeed** valuable, **but** (*de*) only **if** they **keep** ("are doing")

the law. Perhaps, Paul thinks of Jewish tradition that taught no circumcised Jew would ever enter Gehenna (Gen *Rabbah* 48). This ceremony signified to many Jews what baptismal-regeneration signifies for many today. Sinful man has always used religion as an outward ceremony to replace relationship and inward conversion. This then becomes the support system prompting pride and self-righteousness.

Knowing this, Paul tells the Jew that violating the Law will cause them to **become uncircumcised** (lit. in the Gk, "become a foreskin"). This means they are no different than a Gentile. Conversely, **if an uncircumcised man keeps the righteous requirements of the law, will not his uncircumcision be counted as circumcision?** God desires obedience instead of ceremonies or sacrifices (1 Sam 15:22; Matt 12:7). Yet, Paul asks rhetorically: Can the Gentile (**uncircumcised**) who **fulfills** [the spirit of] **the law** (see vv 28-29) **judge** the Jew who possess the **written *code*** (the Law) who ***are* a transgressor of the law?** Of course they can (cf. Matt 12:41-42). Gentiles who please God by practicing the inherent principles of *the law* outdid the Jews with all of their distinct privileges, because what matters to God is the reality (of obedience) and not the ritual (of circumcision).

2:28-29. Concluding this section begun in v 17, Paul gives the reason "**For**" (*gar*) declaring the uncircumcised man circumcised and the circumcised man uncircumcised. Being **a** complete **Jew** was not a matter of **outward** conforming to rituals (circumcision, sacrifices, and ceremonies) or merely belonging to a race **in the flesh** (coming from Abraham chosen of God). Belonging to a race chosen of God, and practicing His mandates, is only part of what being a Jew is all about.

But (*all'*, the strongest contrast in the Gk), Paul states in order to affirm what makes a true Jew: a complete **Jew** is ***one*** who is also

inwardly, and circumcision is supposed to be an outward sign or rite of an inward reality **of the heart, in the Spirit** (*en pneumati*), **not in the letter** (*ou grammati*). The latter phrases may be understood in various ways. (1) It may be better not to capitalize *spirit* (as the RSV) since "the" does not appear both times in the Greek. Thus, one may render the phrase literally as: "in spirit, not in letter." This is then a common way of contrasting the internal spiritual motives as opposed to the external, legalistic Law keeping that simply conforms to an outward exercise (cf. 7:6; 2 Cor 3:6-7). (2) However, various reasons militate against the first option and argue for capitalizing *Spirit*. First, early in Israel's history they were called to display an inner transformation by *circumcising the heart* (cf. Deut 10:16; Jer 4:4; 9:25-26). However, other passages showed that only God could ultimately bring about a changed heart (Deut 30:6; Jer 31:33-34; Jub 1:23; Odes Sol 11:1-3). Second, the context shows that Paul does not use "spirit" in a spiritual sense and "letter" in a literal sense, since in v 27 "letter" clearly refers to the Law of Moses (Moo, *Romans*, 174). Thus, in 7:6 and 2 Corinthians 3:6-7, where Paul contrasts the terms *pneumati* and *grammati*, it refers to the Holy *Spirit* versus the Law. In these latter passages, as here, "the" does not appear in front of *pneumati*, but the NKJV committee decided to add the article and capitalize *pneumati* in the English translation because it captures the meaning of what Paul intended to say best. Paul's contrast of "Spirit" and "letter" is a "salvation-historical one" (Moo, *Romans*, 175; for a definition of salvation-history see Rom 16:25-27). His point is to describe that in times past God's Law played a central role, but he prepares the way for chapter 8 by stating now that the inward circumcision *in the Spirit* is the way to power, please and praise God. A complete Jew then is one **whose praise *is* not from men but from God** (cf. 4:12). Paul may be using a play on words (not apparent in the

English) since the word "Jew" comes from the term "Judah" (*yᵉhûḏâ*) that means, "praise" (*yḏh*). Therefore, contrary to a hypocritical and self-righteous attitude, a spiritual Jew seeks to please and receive *praise* from God, even if it displeases men (cf. John 5:41, 44; 12:43; Matt. 6:2; 23:5-7; Luke 16:15; 1 Thess 2:6). This is commendable because anyone wanting to please the world will become an enemy of God (Jas 4:4).

FROM CONDEMNATION TO JUSTIFICATION

In summary of the entire section begun in 1:18, Paul makes no exception. He debunks the possibility of approaching God by works (2:1-16). Having indicted the Jews of hypocrisy (2:17-29), Paul maintains that sin cannot annul Jewish privilege (3:1-8), even if God uses their sin to enhance His glory (3:1-4). At the same time sin cannot be excused to justify disobedience either (3:5-8). Thus Jews and Gentiles stand condemned under God's wrath and tribunal, a point Paul validates by quoting a number of Old Testament verses (3:10-18). Therefore, Israel, who possesses special revelation is not exempt from God's judgment, since the Law confirmed sin in man instead of justifying the sinner (3:19-20).

The Law was unable to justify, but it pointed people to Christ (3:21, 31) as the only means to obtain the righteousness of God through faith in Christ. No other means are available that puts a person in right standing with God than through Christ's imputed righteousness on our behalf (3:22-30).

3:1. Typical Pauline style (cf. 2:1), he presents an imaginary self-righteous Jewish objector (at least four times in this section vv 1, 3, 5, 7) as in the previous section: **What advantage** (*perisson*, lit. "surplus") **then has the Jew, or what *is* the profit of circumcision?** *What advantage* (*Ti oun*), also translated "what then," appears in Romans twelve times. It is used by Paul as a technical phrase, to transition by raising a question of something previously taught, to further his argument (cf. 3:1, 9; 4:1; 6:1, 15, 21; 7:7; 8:31; 9:14, 19, 30; 11:7). Then a *Jew* could logically think, "Why be circumcised since obedient uncircumcised Gentiles can be seen as being circumcised? Thus, if being a Jew inwardly is what counts, then where is the privilege (cf. 9:4-5) and profit of belonging to a race (2:17-24) and of being circumcised (2:25-29)?" Circumcision was a covenant sign (Genesis 17) indicating the bestowing of many benefits.

3:2. Again, logically, one would expect Paul to say, "None!" Instead he says: **Much in every way!** Why? **Chiefly because to them were committed the oracles** (*logia*) **of God**. The *logion* can refer to: (1) Specific promises to Jews (BDAG, 598), (2) national promises of Messianic salvation, (3) a specific section, particularly the Mosaic Law, or (4) to the entire Old Testament revelation. Perhaps the latter may be Paul's meaning that he unfolds in 9:4-5 (cf. 3:19). To possess God's special revelation was a very high honor indeed.

3:3. Yet, since Paul accused the Jews of being unfaithful (from 2:17-29), he presents the objector's question to advance the argument further: **For what** (*ti gar*) **if some did not believe? Will their unbelief make the faithfulness of God without effect?** Paul uses the phrase "for what" (3:3; 4:3; 11:34) similarly to "what then" (cf. 3:1). The point of doubt is raised against the validity of God's word that reveals His character. Because Jews failed to believe and obey the oracles, what advantage (claims the objector) do the covenant people have since God may renege on His promises?

3:4. Paul answers with the strongest negation in the Greek: **Certainly not!** (*mē genoito*, lit. "by no means," BDAG, 197). This type of emphatic negation appears eleven times in Romans and almost every time God's word, that reveals His character, is at stake (3:4, 6, 31; 6:2, 15; 7:7, 13, 9:14; 11:1, 11; 12:16 [?]).

Man's failure can never dwarf God's promises, purposes and plan. He remains faithful (cf. Deut 7:9; 1 Cor 1:9; Heb 10:23; 11:11; 1 Pet 4:19). *Rather* (may be a better translation, NASB) than **Indeed** (NKJV), **let God be true, but every man** be found **a liar**, even if Gentile insults against God are provoked by Jews (2:24). Paul validates his claim by quoting Psalm 51:4.

3:5-6. Paul's same imaginary objector continues by supposing that if **our unrighteousness demonstrates** God's **righteousness**, to inflict **wrath** on him would be *unjust*. Again, Paul emphatically denies it: **Certainly not!** (cf. v 4). Man's unrighteousness merely shows God's righteous character and right to be their Judge. Wrath here takes on the form of present punishment for the following three reasons (cf. 1:18; 2:5, 8): (1) The Greek article "the" in front of wrath is most naturally understood as an article of previous reference pointing back to the present wrath that began the argument of the book. Here "the wrath" (*tēn orgēn*) then refers back to God's wrath of 1:18. (2) This wrath is part of the present problem within the bigger context of 1:18–3:20, which culminates in the present solution found in 3:21–4:25. Thus, contextually, this wrath must have a present nuance. (3) The term "inflict" (*ho epipherōn*, present tense) has a present force that could be translated "bringing His wrath" (NIV). The meaning then in vv 5-6 is this: God's righteous character (v 4) gives Him the right, now, to inflict wrath on sinners and thereby receive glory by showing His justice that proves His holy character. Thus, God is just. Otherwise, as Jews know, how will He **judge the world** (vv 5-6)? God's future judgment of the world was a common Jewish belief (Isa 66:16; Joel 3:12; Pss 94:2; 96:13).

3:7-8. In these verses, Paul further clarifies the objector's foolishness to what he already mentioned in v 5. Here the sinner objects to God's wrath: **For if the truth of God has increased**

through my lie to His glory, why am I also still judged as a sinner? As a result of corrupt reasoning, the sinner objects to being judged for sin since it enhances God's Holy character. Hence he says, **"Let us do evil that good may come"?** Stunningly, rumor had it that Paul and his companions were **slanderously reported** as teaching this very thing. However, just because God uses man's transgression to enhance His glory and display His grace, it does not mean man should go unpunished. Perhaps the contention "where sin abounded grace abounded more" in 5:20 (and 6:1, 15) originates here in germ. Today, the same slanderous charges of encouraging license to sin are hurled at those who teach God's free grace, as if teaching unadulterated-grace necessarily leads to sin. Unfortunately, in every era, there have always been those who misunderstand or corrupt the meaning of God's free-grace. Just because one teaches grace as Paul taught does not in any way suggest or imply that one should sin. To such a ridiculous charge Paul sees no need to refute. He simply entrusts them to God: **Their condemnation is just**. Obedience is assumed and required by everyone regardless of how God uses disobedience in His sovereign plan (cf. Matt 18:7).

4. The world stands under God's present wrath and future condemnation (3:9-20)

In the entire section, Paul maintains that sin cannot annul Jewish privilege (3:1-8), even if God uses their sin to enhance His glory (3:1-4). At the same time sin cannot be excused to justify disobedience either (3:5-8). Thus Jews and Gentiles stand condemned under God's wrath and tribunal, a point Paul validates by citing a number of Old Testament verses (3:9-18). Thus even those with special revelation are not exempt, because the Law cannot justify (3:19-20).

a. no exception: Jew and Gentiles stand condemned (3:9-18)

3:9. At this point Paul continues with the imaginary Jewish man objecting: **What then?** (cf. 3:1) **Are we better** (*proechometha* appears only here in the NT, lit. "are we better off") *than they* (= Gentiles)? The phrase *than they* does not appear in the Greek text but was added to complete the thought contextually of the objector's comparison between the Jews and Gentiles. After Paul's last statement of v 8 that their condemnation due to sin is just, the Jew may think, "Is there anything that can keep us from experiencing God's wrath and condemnation (2:1–3:8)?" Paul answers: **Not at all. For we have previously charged both Jews and Greeks that they are all under sin.** When it comes to sin, God does not discriminate between Jews and Gentiles.

3:10-12. To validate his point, Paul forms a string-pearl necklace of Scripture by informally quoting from nine Old Testament passages: **As it is written** (from vv 10-18). Sin permeates the human race. First, vv 10-12 explores man's *character deficiencies* illustrated in five statements: **There is none righteous, not even one.** The phrase *none righteous* (*ouk ..dikaios*) is equivalent to the term *adikia* (unrighteous) used by Paul in 1:18. No one in the universe is absolutely perfect. By nature everyone is flawed. Consequently, **none** really have spiritual intelligence. Concomitant to this **none seeks after God,** as result **all have turned aside** ... [and] **become unprofitable.** Logically it follows: **There is none who does good, no, not one** (Ps 14:1-3; 53:1-3; Eccl 7:20, cf. Ps 15:1-3). The all-inclusive language implicating humanity cannot be denied. On the one hand, although man lacks spiritual intelligence, it cannot be proven from these verses that man has *no* spiritual capacity to respond to God's drawing. Unregenerate humanity is not like inanimate rocks that God has to regenerate prior to prompting (a concept absent in Scripture). One then must distinguish between spiritual *intelligence* and *capacity.* If humanity had no capacity they could not be culpable. On the other hand, and equally important, these verses do not teach that man by himself apart from God's prompting ever seeks God as Cornelius and Lydia illustrate. Nowhere in Acts 10:1-48 is Cornelius ever regenerated (or capacitated) prior to believing Peter's message. Equally true, however, Cornelius did not possess spiritual initiative or intelligence, making him a *devout man* and *God fearer* independently of God's prompting through special revelation that he no doubt had. In Acts 10:2, Cornelius' giving "to the people" (*tō laō*, i.e., a common reference to the Jews in Acts) and praying "to God" (*tou theou*, i.e., the God of the Jews) proves, as well as the Ethiopian eunuch of Acts 8:27-28, both had prior knowledge of Scripture. However, Peter had to be sent (Acts 10:9-23) to Cornelius, as Paul was sent to Lydia (Acts 16:9-10) so that both can believe in Jesus, but not apart from God's prior prompting and aid (cf. 10:2; 16:14; 2 Cor 4:1-6).

3:13-18. This second section exposes man's *conduct* and active *depravities.* Through six body parts quoted from the Psalms, Paul proves humanity's total corruption. Total depravity means sin has affected every part of man. Consequently, nothing humanity does can ever commend or justify them before God. However, total depravity does not mean people are as bad as they could be, or that it has totally eradicated the image of God in man.

First, man's **throat is an open tomb**. Their **tongues practiced deceit**, and the **poison of asps is under their lips** (Pss 5:9; 140:3). Throat, tongue and lips are three aspects of man summed up by "speech" that is usually a catalyst leading to actions as the following develops (cf. James 3). Through the **mouth** comes **cursing and bitterness**, i.e., hatred leading to murder as the following quote develops (Ps 10:7). Third, man's **feet** (i.e., their acts) **are swift to shed blood**, resulting in destruction **and misery** because **the way** *of peace they have not known* (Isa 59:7-8; Prov 1:16). What causes humanity to conduct itself this way results in not having a proper respect of God: *There is no fear of God before their eyes* (Ps 36:1). Godly behavior characterized all God-fearers (Job 28:28; Prov 1:7; 9:10; Eccl 12:13), something even the Jews lacked according to vv 10-18.

b. no exception: Justification does not come by the Law (3:19-20)

3:19-20. Lest any Jew thinks this collage of Old Testament quotations refers *only* to pagans, Paul quickly corrects such a thought and even includes himself: **Now we know that whatever the law says, it says to those who are under the law.** *The law (ho nomos)* is a reference to the previous quotations that are drawn from the Psalter, Isaiah, and possibly wisdom literature. Hence, *ho nomos* refers to the entire Old Testament (cf. 2:12; 3:2), since in the strict sense it is not taken from the Pentateuch. No doubt, this implicates the Jews as well since it addresses those literally *under the law (en tọ nomọ,* i.e., "those who possess the law" similar to the use "in the law" in 2:12; Cranfield, *Romans,* 1:195). This makes Paul's previous phrase "all are under sin" (v 9) resonate even louder by silencing the Jews again since **all the world** has **become guilty** (lit., "become accountable") **before God.**

Therefore *(dioti)* Paul deduces, since the Law serves to silence those who wanted to claim its advantage before God, **by the deeds of the law no flesh will be justified in His sight** (cf. Ps 143:2; Acts 13:39; Gal 2:16; 3:2, 5, 10-11). Why? Because one would have to obey it perfectly (cf. Matt 5:48; Rom 2:13), this is impossible to do. Hence no one can ever be *declared righteous* (i.e., *justified* =dikaiōthēsetai,* cf. Thayer, *Greek-English Lexicon,* 150-51) by obeying *the law.* A further reason (**for,** Gk *gar*) why no one can be *justified* by using *the law* is that **by the law** a man becomes *conscious* (NIV) **of sin** (cf. 5:20; 7:7-13). Rather, God intended *the law* to drive men to realize that they need His righteousness (Gal 3:19-24), because *the law* terrified instead of justified.

From 1:18–3:20, Paul firmly established in four sections humanity's need for the gospel. Thus, Gentiles and Jews experience God's wrath and stand condemned in need of God's aid as the following section unfolds (3:21–4:25).

B. The Propitiation for Sinners comes by Way of Sacrifice: Righteousness Comes by Faith Alone in Jesus Christ Alone (3:21–4:25)

Having affirmed that humanity does not possess self-righteousness, Paul establishes how God provides another source of righteousness. Many modern scholars today (e.g., E. P. Sanders, J. D. G. Dunn, and et al.) disagree that Paul tried to teach a *justification by faith alone* that proposes to correct a *salvation by works* that is wrongly attributed to the Pharisees. Instead, this new perspective on Paul believes Jews were already justified by God's electing grace as long as they remain in the Covenant that required man's obedience to God's commandments, "while providing [the] means of atonement for transgression" (Sanders, *Paul and Palestinian Judaism*, 75, 236). This is known as "covenantal nomism" (ibid.). Then, Paul's mission to Jews was only to get them to accept their long awaited Messiah. A further strand of this view suggests that God's rescuing and sustaining actions are not a one-time-event but a repeated-ongoing-event for those who remain in covenant (see Dunn, *Romans 1–8*, 1:lxv-1xvi; Sanders, *Paul and Palestinian Judaism*, 236). This new perspective on Paul, however, subverts and contradicts everything Paul says in Romans 3–5 and 9:30-33 (cf. Carson, et al., *Justification and Variegated Nomism*, 2 vols., for a scholarly treatment exposing the error of this view). For this righteousness of

God is, however, a once-and-for-all event that comes by faith alone in Christ alone as demonstrated in the following section.

1. God's righteousness comes by faith alone in Christ alone (3:21-31)

3:21. But now (*nyni de*) introduces a sharp contrast from what preceded it, and Paul uses it in Romans with a temporal force introducing an explanation that follows (cf. 3:21; 6:22; 7:6, 17; 15:23, 25). Since the Law cannot provide man with his own righteousness, **the righteousness of God** (*dikaiosynē theou*) **apart** (*chōris*) **from the law** (v 20) is the *only* source-of-righteousness able to solve humanity's dilemma. Contextually here, the phrase *dikaiosynē theou* is not an attribute of God but a *status of righteousness* given as a gift to sinners upon faith (1:17; 3:22-25). This *righteousness* that comes from God is not a new concept, but has its roots in the Old Testament, **being witnessed by the Law and the Prophets** (cf. 1:2; 4:1-8; John 5:39). *The Law and the Prophets* was often used to refer to the entire Old Testament (see Matt 5:17; 7:12; 22:40; Acts 24:14; 28:23). Many Old Testament passages linked justification to God's righteousness (cf. Gen 15:6; Pss 7:8-13; 32:1-2; Isa 53:11).

3:22-23. Now Paul transitions (**even**, Gk., *de*) in order to tell *how* one obtains **the righteousness of God**: it simply comes **through** (*dia*, is the *means* not the *merit* by which the gift comes) **faith in Jesus Christ.** The Greek phrase *pisteōs Iēsou Christou* translated *faith in Jesus Christ* may be understood as the NKJV translates it here or as the NET Bible translates it "faithfulness of Jesus Christ," understood as the exercise Jesus provided as the basis for our faith that furnishes the righteousness of God. Either way it does no harm to the sense of the verse. Both are true: *faith in Jesus Christ* is needed to attain God's righteousness and Jesus' faithfulness to God provided the righteousness now available **to all ... who** simply **believe.** Perhaps Paul left the Greek phrase *pisteōs*

Iēsou Christou vague because he wanted to convey both ideas. However, the phrase *to all . who believe* and Paul's similar phrase in Gal 2:16 followed by "in Jesus Christ" argues that in both places is likely that *faith in Jesus Christ* is the point. Furthermore, even if the word *alone* is not used here, the sense of the entire context clearly teaches it (see v 24). First, this *righteousness* is apart from the works of the Law (3:21-31). Second, it excludes works in general as the entire context indicates (3:21–4:25). Thus, faith alone in Christ alone is the sole means to acquire God's righteousness.

Thus, the freeness of this offer must have reminded Paul of humanity's need of vv 9, 19 that reduced everyone to same level of sinners. Hence he says: **For there is no difference.** The reason (**for**, *gar*) is **all have sinned and fall short of the glory of God**. Many people define "sin" by its etymological meaning of "missing the mark." Yet, to impose this meaning on the word is wrong, since this meaning was lost by the New Testament era (cf. Vine, *New Testament Words*, 4:32). Sin came to mean "'an offense in relation to God with emphasis on guilt'" (Grundmann, *TDNT*, 1:273).

The same two Greek words for *all sinned* (*pantes hēmarton*, aorist tense) appear in 5:12. The aorist Greek tense of the verb *sinned* used here leaves the action in some sense undefined. This may convey (as in 5:12) the historical act of Adam's sin, suggesting all sinned in Adam when he sinned as representative of the human race. However, this cannot be taken to belong exclusively in the past, because Paul goes on to use the Greek present tense when he states *fall short* (*hysterountai*). The word *fall short* coveys the idea of climbing an unreachable height, as if God's glory is unattainable. The term *fall short* translated by the Greek *hysterountai* may best be rendered as *lack* (BDAG, 1044) God's glory. This captures Paul's idea contextually best since it expresses a lack in human nature that makes it impossible to attain eternal life through works; a subject

Paul has exhausted (vv 9-20). The same Greek term appears in Matthew 19:20 where the rich-young-ruler wanted to attain eternal life through works (19:16-19). Jesus then challenges him by showing what he lacked (*hystereō*). Consequently, he went away sad (vv 21-22). Man's sin separates him from dwelling in the presence of a holy God, because he lacks His glory as a perfect being.

3:24. Nevertheless, just as *all have sinned and fall short of the glory of God,* all equally qualify to receive what humanity lacks (God's perfect righteousness): **being justified freely by His grace.** Determining the connection of v 24 with the previous context has been widely discussed. Perhaps the participle construction *being justified* (*dikaioumenoi*) *freely by His grace* conveys the universal principle that applies to *all* who *have sinned and fall short of the glory of God.* Not that everyone is justified apart from believing (v 22). Yet, as all humanity is equally lost, all humanity can equally qualify to be *justified freely by His grace,* since "there is no difference" (v 22) among men when it comes to sin.

Justification (*dikaioō*, cf. 1:17) is a forensic (legal) term that means to "declare righteous," or "acquit of guilt" (*not* make righteous, cf. Exod 23:7; Deut 25:1; Acts 13:39) an unrighteous party (cf. BDAG, 249; Thayer, *Greek-English Lexicon*, 150). This distinction is extremely important. When a sinner is justified, his position changes before God, not the condition of his character or practices. Changing one's character is a matter of growth called progressive sanctification. That is why the meaning to "make righteous" is wrong and would imply sinless perfection, which is not the case shown in Scripture (Rom 6–8; 1 John 1:8, 10).

This justification comes *freely* (i.e., without cost to the recipient). If that is not enough, Paul adds the following to make it perfectly clear, lest someone misunderstands: *by His grace* (*chariti*). Hence, one can say justification is a "free grace" gift that comes by faith alone, because it comes without cost and merit to the recipient **through the redemption that is in Christ Jesus**.

Faith by itself does not justify, but faith placed on the proper object does. Christ is the object of one's faith that made it possible by His *redemption* (*apolytrōsis*). The term *apolytrōsis* appears ten times in the New Testament (Luke 21:28; Rom 3:24; 8:23; 1 Cor 1:30; Eph 1:7, 14; 4:30; Col 1:14; Heb 9:15; 11:35) and comes from the Greek word *lytron* ("ransom," cf. Matt 20:28; Mark 10:45) that means, "ransom payment." Thus, *apolytrōsis* diverged in meaning in New Testament times but was commonly used, as here by Paul, of buying back by a ransom payment a slave or captive to be set free (BDAG, 117). Certainly, Paul thinks here of humanity's condemned status under the Law. Redemption from this came through Christ's *ransom payment* at the cross (cf. Matt 20:28; Gal 3:13; 4:5) that freed humanity from the slave market of sin. This price was not only paid for those who will participate of its benefits but includes those who are also lost (cf. 2 Pet 2:1).

The preposition *through* (*dia*) indicates the means *how redemption* was accomplished, and the preposition *in* (*en*) indicates the instrument, *Christ Jesus who* made it possible. Paul elaborates on this last point in the following verses.

3:25-26. These two verses make up a single relative clause, begun with the pronoun **whom**, dependent on *Christ Jesus* in v 24. Thus, Paul explains now in picturesque language how **God** displayed Jesus Christ *as* **a propitiation** that satisfied Him because it redeemed humanity. The Greek term *hilastērion* translated *propitiation* is also the LXX rendering of the Hebrew word *kappōreṭ* that referred to the golden lid covering the Ark of the Covenant in the Tabernacle and later the Temple. This lid is called "the mercy seat" since this was the place where the blood of the sin offering was sprinkled on the Day of Atonement to cover (i.e., atone) Israel's sins (Exod 25:17-22; Lev 16:1-17). The word *hilastērion* appears only here and in Hebrews 9:5, where most translations render it "mercy seat" (NIV, "atonement cover"). Paul alludes to the Old Testament mercy seat where the High Priest entered the holy of holies to meet God annually by means of the blood that was then sprinkled on the mercy seat. Therefore, the blood-sprinkled-mercy-seat was a point of contact between God and sinful-man.

Now, however, **by His blood, through faith** in the person of Jesus Christ (who replaces the place) God and sinful-man can meet, just as the Old Testament mercy seat functioned in covering sins where God and Israel met. Perhaps one does well to render the phrase *God set forth as a propitiation* as: "whom God displayed as a Mercy Seat" (i.e., Jesus Christ is the *person* who replaces where the OT meeting took *place*). This sacrifice not only atones for those who inherit the benefits but also universally for the world's sin (cf. 1 John 2:2). These two phrases *by His blood, through faith* appear in the Greek reversed: *through faith, by His blood*. The NKJV, like other translations, seems to understand *by His blood* to modify *propitiation*, since blood is what was sprinkled on the mercy seat. However, the best and most natural reading appears in the original Greek, which the KJV and NIV also render: "through faith in His blood." This reading is appropriate to the context even if the construction is not found elsewhere. Since *propitiation* is the New Testament reference to the Old Testament mercy seat, then the new concept is that Christ (v 24) becomes that place of contact where God and anyone approaching Him *through faith* can rest assured of God's acceptance because of the efficacy of Christ's *blood* sacrifice. Thus, if anyone approaches God with assurance (*through faith*) that Christ's sacrifice (*by His blood*) was sufficient to cover their sins, He will meet the person at that point as He met those at the "mercy seat" in the Old Testament (Exod 25:22; 30:6, 36). At this point the sinner becomes justified by faith alone in Christ alone.

Christ's death satisfied God, which took place in order **to demonstrate** God's **righteousness** (i.e., His justice, *dikaiosynēs*; cf. 1:17; 2:11) **because in His forbearance God had passed over the sins that were previously committed.** Two things may be noticed here: First, God did not compromise His righteous standards shown in Christ's shed blood. Hence, and second, God's delay in dealing with sin does not mean He forgot, or that bypassing equates justification. God's *forbearance*, connected with the phrase *passed over* in light of Paul's use of "forbearance" elsewhere (Rom 2:4), refers to a period of time before the cross (cf. Acts 14:16; 17:30) when God did not "visit men with wrath commensurate with their sins" but exercised grace (Murray, *Romans*, 1:119). One, however, might think God is soft on sin. Vital to understanding Paul, Moo correctly adduces:

> The sins 'committed beforehand' will not, then, be sins committed before conversion, or baptism, but before the new age of salvation. This does not mean that God failed to punish or 'overlooked' sins committed before Christ; nor does it mean that God did not really 'forgive' sins under the Old Covenant. Paul's meaning is rather that God 'postponed' the full penalty due to sins in the Old Covenant, allowing sinners to stand before him without their having provided an adequate 'satisfaction' of the demands of his holy justice (cf. Heb 10:4). In view of this, it is clear that 'his righteousness' must have reference to some aspect of God's character that might have been called into question because of his treating sins in the past with less than full severity, and that has now been

demonstrated in setting forth Christ as 'the propitiatory' (*Romans*, 240).

Then, *His righteousness* in vv 25-26 does not necessarily mean the same as the righteousness He provides for the sinner upon faith in Christ in vv 21-22. Instead, God's *righteousness* here refers to His "'consistency' in always acting in accordance with his own character" (Moo, *Romans*, 240). God bypassed dealing with sins in full because He anticipated before the cross with absolute certainty the basis of His Son's sacrifice on the cross that justifies all who by faith alone believe in Jesus Christ, or as in the Old Testament, the Seed to come as the object of faith (cf. 4:3). Murray similar to Moo correctly concludes: "It can readily be seen therefore that passing over of sins in the forbearance of God did not make it necessary for God to demonstrate his justifying righteousness, but that the passing over did make it necessary for him to demonstrate his inherent justice and that by showing (to all men in the worldwide proclamation of the gospel) that justification demands nothing less than the propitiation made in Jesus' blood" (*Romans*, 1:120).

Therefore, this demonstrates **at the present time His righteousness, that He might be just and the justifier of the one who has faith in Jesus.** Paul solves this theological conundrum: How can a holy God justify a sinner without undermining His standard and becoming sinful and at the same time demonstrate mercy? God solved the dilemma by sacrificing His incarnate Son, Jesus Christ. Jesus' death demonstrates God's righteous standards (cf. 2:11). Hence, sins were paid as God's justice demanded, but at the same time Jesus' death on behalf of sinners allows God to declare a sinner righteous immediately upon faith in Christ. Thus paraphrasing the last statement captures the sense of Paul's meaning best: *That He might be understood as being absolutely righteous and simultaneously the*

One who declares the sinner, who has faith in Jesus, righteous.

3:27-28. Verses 25-26 are part of a subordinate construction elaborating the principle that "all" (in v 23) are equally justified by God's free grace (in v 24). Sometimes Paul pauses to elaborate (e.g., as he does in the long sentence in Gk of Eph 1:3-14) an extremely important point. He seems to have done that here. Now v 27 returns to the thought of righteousness received upon faith in Christ apart from the Law begun in vv 21-22.

Having shown in vv 21-26 what faith alone in Christ alone includes, from vv 27-31, Paul now shows what it excludes. Through five rhetorical questions (in Gk), Paul surfaces various issues that his audience might raise: The first two questions are found in v 27, the other two in v 29, and the last one in v 31. Question no. 1: **Where is boasting then?** Perhaps Paul recalls the previous discussion (2:17-29), since Jews were known to boast because of their privileges. This thought, however, also includes humanity in general, since everyone suffers from pride that appeals to salvation by works (Rom 4:1-4; Eph 2:8-9). Paul's answer comes suddenly: **It is excluded** (*exekleisthe*, aorist passive, occurs elsewhere only in Gal 4:17). The aorist passive tense of the verb seems to conceal the divine action of God, accomplished in Christ, that excludes any possible merit. Paul's desire to supply the answer lies behind the intent of asking question no. 2: **By what law? Of works?** (The latter is not a separate question in the Gk). He answers: **No** (*ouchi*, lit. it emphatically means "no, not indeed"), **but** (*alla*, strongest contrastive conjunction in Gk) **by the law of faith.** The idea of the *law of faith* is vital to man's relationship to God. It must be understood as a governing principle establishing man's *initial relationship* with God (as here; see also Gal 2:16; 3:11-12, 22-24), and man's *ongoing fellowship* with Him (Rom 14:23; Gal 2:20; Heb 11:1, 6). As *the law* of *works* brought condemnation, the *law of faith* brings justification. That is why Paul concludes **that a man is justified by faith apart from the deeds of the law.** God never gave the Mosaic Law with the intent to justify anyone, but men misappropriated it.

3:29-30. Logically, Paul infers that God is the God of the Gentiles also by asking question no. 3: . . . **is He the God of the Jews only?** That is, if the Law is essential to justification, God would restrict Himself to being a solely Jewish God since the Jews were the only ones entrusted with it (9:4). Yet, Paul anticipated a "no" answer here; but in question no. 4 he anticipates a "yes" answer: **Is He not also the God of the Gentiles? Yes, of the Gentiles also.** Jews believed God was the God of the Gentiles but only by virtue of the creative order (Exod *Rabbah* 29:4). Though Israel occupied a special place in God's purposes (cf. 1:16; 2:9-10; 3:2; 9:4; 11:1, 17), Paul understands **since *there is* one God who will justify the circumcised by faith and the uncircumcised through faith** He is equally the God of both groups. Perhaps Paul establishes his defense on two grounds. Accepting the Law was the only way Gentiles could ever become related to God like the Jews. However this barrier was now gone (cf. Eph 2:14-15, see Moo, *Romans,* 251-52). Furthermore, *since there is one God,* understood from Israel's creed of the great "Shema" of Deuteronomy 6:4, then logically Gentiles cannot really look to any other God by whom they can be justified.

3:31. By now (having dealt a blow to the Law as a means of justification) Paul anticipated what some Jews were probably thinking by question no. 5: **Do we then make void the law through faith?** To which he strongly replied: **Certainly not!** (*mē genoito,* see 3:4). Contrary to popular opinion, justification by faith alone in Christ does not *void the law* or make it meaningless. Conversely, Paul (**we**, an editorial plural; cf. 1:5) knew that *faith* (understood contextually) **establishes the law**. This is seen in two ways. First, *faith* does not allow one to lower the righteous standards of the Law. If anyone taught the Law must be kept to be justified, the Law's integrity would be damaged since any efforts to obey the Law perfectly, even by Christians, are fraught with failures. Trying to accomplish this feat will cause one to lower the standards of the Law, which Jesus did not permit (5:19-48; Jas 2:10). Only the doctrine of justification *by faith apart from the deeds of the law* establishes the complete and holy standards of the Law. Christ's death satisfied God's justice with regard to man's infraction of the Law. One should never think that flawed obedience to the law can justify anyone. Second, the purpose of God's law was to bring people to faith in Jesus Christ *not* to replace the person of Christ (cf. Gal 3:23-25) and was used as means of sanctification (Lev 18:5; cf. Rom 10:5-8). Hence, if one understands the intent of the law one must conclude that faith alone in Christ *establishes the law.*

Thus, Paul affirms in this section that although the Law pointed people to Christ (3:21, 31) the only means to attain the righteousness of God was by grace through faith in Jesus Christ. No other avenue exists that puts a person in right standing with God than through Christ's imputed righteousness on our behalf (3:22-30).

THE SCRIPTURE'S WITNESS TO JUSTIFICATION

2. God's righteousness by faith alone in Christ alone existed in the Old Testament as illustrated in Abraham (4:1-25)

Since the gospel establishes the law by not vitiating its standards (3:27-31), the reverse is also true. Paul already affirmed that the Old Testament establishes his gospel (3:21-22), but now he elaborates fully. Typically in Romans, Paul gives validation from the Old Testament, to extricate possible misconceptions, lest anyone think his teachings are innovative (cf. 1:2). Hence this is a pivotal chapter in establishing justification by faith alone in Christ alone, derived from the Old Testament.

4:1. What then (*Ti oun*, cf. 3:1) **shall we say** is Paul's way of transitioning from something just taught to what he would now elaborate further. Abraham becomes Paul's primary example, drawn from the Old Testament section of the *Torah,* to illustrate that justification by faith alone in Christ is not innovative news (cf. 1:2; 3:21-22; 4:2-5). Thus rhetorically, Paul raises a question a Jewish reader might have: What **shall we say Abraham our father has found according to the flesh?** The term *father (patera)* appears in the Majority Text and is the common designation for Abraham in the New Testament (cf. Luke 16:24, 30; John 8:35; Acts 7:2; Rom 4:12). Conversely, the term *forefather (propatora)* appears only once in the LXX and here in the Neutral Text (i.e., the name for the mss derived predominantly from Aleph and B by Westcott and Hort when in 1881 they first published their eclectic two-volume Gk text) of the New Testament. Paul need not distinguish the physical from the spiritual ancestry here since he develops it later in 4:11-12, 16-18. Although *according to the flesh* (*kata sarka*, cf. 9:3) may further describe Jewish lineage, this seems redundant (see how *kata sarka* is used in 1:3-4) since the entire context points this out. A group of Greek manuscripts place the infinitive *has found* (*heurēkenai*) after *shall we say,* allowing *kata sarka* to modify *our father* (or "…Abraham, our forefather according to the flesh," as the NASB or even the RSV translates it), indicating ancestry, "father by race." Another group of Greek manuscripts places the infinitive *heurēkenai* after *our father,* in which case it modifies *kata sarka* ("… our father has found according to the flesh") understood as "by his own labors [or] powers." Verse 2, and the overall context, supports understanding *kata sarka* as "according to his own efforts" (see Godet, *Romans*, 1:168).

4:2. For (*gar*) explains the last phrase of v 1 by describing what role Abraham's works play in justification. It would not be misleading to think Paul corrects Jewish legalism, evident in their literature. Contra Schreiner (and the new perspective on Paul view; cf. intro to section 3:21–4:25), who although states, "All Jews believed that Abraham's works flowed from God's grace," incorrectly concludes: "Paul would not deny that works are necessary to obtain eternal life" (Schreiner, *Romans*, 216-17). Since Jews widely held that Abraham's status before God was meritorious (see 1 Maccabees 2:50, 52; Jubiless 15:1-10; 16:20-26; 17:17-18; 23:10; 24:11; Sirach 44:20-21; Kiddushin 4:14; Prayer of Manasseh 8), Paul needs to correct this issue. It is important to note that Paul uses the Greek first-class-condition **if** (*ei*). This type of condition that *assumes something is true for the sake of argument* allows one to conceive that Paul thought works could have **justified** Abraham. Hence, he follows this thought closely by stating: *if* works *justified Abraham,* **he has *something* to boast about.** Paul does not regard all forms of boasting sinful or perhaps a type of false-humility. Instead, Paul viewed spiritual boasting as something valid (cf. 2:17, 23; 5:3; 1 Cor 9:15-16; 2 Cor 5:12; 9:2; 10:8, 13, 16; 11:16, 18, 30; 2 Thess 1:4) without excluding God's indispensable enabling and function in the matter (1 Cor 15:10; 2 Cor 1:12). Therefore, Paul does not deny boasting in an absolute sense, **but** (*all'*, the strongest Gk contrast) when it comes to legal-justification in declaring a sinner righteous boasting could **not** occur **before** (*pros*) **God.** The fact that one may translate the preposition *pros* "in the direction of" (BDAG, 873) or "toward" (NIV) leaves room for Paul's understanding of another type of justification, by works, *in the direction* seen by men as mentioned in James 2:21, *but not in the direction of God.*

4:3. For what (*ti gar,* cf. 3:3) explains the last phrase in v 2, "not before God," by citing a well-known **Scripture** from Gen 15:6: ***"Abraham believed God, and it was accounted to him for righteousness."*** However, what exactly did Abraham believe about God? It may be too much to claim that Old Testament saints knew that their object of faith was named Jesus Christ, called the Lamb of God, and that He would be crucified with all of its implications. Likewise, it may be too little to claim that Old Testament saints were merely theists (see Kaiser, *Toward Rediscovering the Old Testament,* 122-25).

If God was the sole object of faith in the Old Testament and Christ the sole object of faith in the New Testament, then a major disagreement exists in the method of personal justification between the two Testaments. Though many believe this, it does not seem to fit the biblical data. The context of Genesis 15:6 refers to Abraham's belief in God that He will provide a seed (vv 4-5). Since this reiterates by renewing the promise God made to Abraham in Genesis 12:1-3, this promised-seed must entail more than an immediate progenitor, since it includes the worldwide blessings promised in the earlier passage (Moo, *Romans*, 261-62; Leupold, *Genesis*, 478; Calvin, *Genesis*, 406). Romans 3:21-22 claims the Old Testament bore witness of God's righteousness and that righteousness directly involved Jesus Christ. Paul's faith alone in Christ doctrine, taught in 3:21-31, defended and elaborated in chapter 4 as an Old Testament derived doctrine does not make sense if the same object of faith was not understood. Other passages like Luke 10:24; 20:41-44; 24:25-27; John 5:39, 46; 8:56; Acts 2:14-36; 8:32-33; Galatians 3:8, 9, 29; 1 Peter 1:10-12 explicitly suggest Old Testament believers knew of a coming deliverer. Even if the future would reveal all of the details concerning this Deliverer, Old Testament saints knew enough to believe God's promise of a coming Savior.

Quoting Genesis 15:6 becomes important for Paul (not only because it is the first mention of *believe* [*'mn*] and righteousness [*ṣᵉḏāqâ*] in the Hebrew Scripture) since the Jews (see above) used this text to establish Abraham's meritorious works of faith. Thus, he cites this passage with a polemic purpose to prove that Abraham's trust in God's promise was unmeritorious. The *righteousness* Abraham obtained was *accounted* (*elogisthē*, or as the NIV translates "credited") by God, as the passive voice indicates. This word *elogisthē* (from *logizomai*, appears 19 times in Romans out which 11 of them are in chap 4) was an accounting term used in New Testament times for keeping records of commercial accounts involving debits and credits (MM, 377-78). This bookkeeping term was applied figuratively to human conduct (2 Sam 19:20; Ps 106:31;

1 Macc 2:52; Phlm 18). Thus, when Abraham believed God's promise, his debit account of sin was wiped clean and God credited (or *imputed*, as in v 6 in the NKJV) his account with *His righteousness.*

4:4-5. No other verses are more essential to defining the exclusion of works, in relation to justification by faith, than these. Paul's polemics against faith being a meritorious **work** continues here since **the wages are not counted** (*logizetai*, see v 3) **as grace** (*charin*) **but as debt** (*opheilēma*). The term *opheilēma* can also be rendered "obligation" (NIV) just as the term *charin* can be rendered "favor" (NASB). An employer is obligated to pay wages to someone who earns it. However, Paul specifically qualifies v 3 by singling out that meritorious works (found vv 1-2, 4-5) play no part (since no one has what it takes to earn it, cf. 2:5-13; 3:10-12, 20, 23) in obligating God since justification by faith is a matter of unmeritorious favor. That is why Paul unequivocally contrasts (**But**) those **who** do **not work** with those who simply believe **on Him who justifies the ungodly** (*asebē*, cf. 1:18; see Josh 24:2 where ungodly Abraham appears) by **faith**, and as a result (*eis*, BDAG, 291) God imputes **righteousness.**

Many have tried to argue that even a person's faith must be a gift of God or else one can claim credit since faith may be considered a work (cf. Wallace, *Greek Grammar*, 334-35, who refutes that faith is a gift in Eph 2:8-9). No other verse (which Paul refutes similar Jewish exegesis of Genesis 15:6, cf. 4:2, Jeremias, *TDNT*, 1:8; Str-B, *NT and Talmud*, 3:34, 186, 204) argues more strongly against considering faith a meritorious work than these. Paul, logically, never thinks of faith as a meritorious work when connected to justification or else he would never contrast it with works of the Law (as in 3:27-28 and in Gal 2:16; 3:2-5, 9, 10).

4:6-8. Paul's explanation of justification by faith alone continues by following Jewish Law that settled an issue by having at least two witnesses (Deut 19:15; Matt 18:16; 2 Cor 13:1). Having cited Abraham as a witness from the Law, Paul now cites David as a representative of the Prophets (cf. 3:21; in Acts 2:29-30 David is called a prophet) to bear witness of the free-grace offer of the gospel (3:24) found in the Old Testament.

Prior to quoting David's words in Psalm 32:1-2, Paul interprets David as **describing the blessedness of the man to whom God imputes** (*logizetai*, cf. vv 3-5) **righteousness** by faith **apart from works**. The term *logizomai*, appearing in both passages (Gen 15:6 and Ps 32:1-2) cited in vv 3, 7-8, establishes a link that helps interpret how the verb was used. Perhaps Paul uses a common rabbinical method of exegesis (called *g^{e}zêrâ sâwâ*, "equal category") that encouraged interpretation of one passage in light of the other.

As in Abraham's case, Paul quotes Scripture to stress the free grace offer. However Paul takes it a step further with David, as expressed in an important two-part blessing. **Blessed** (*makarioi*), **lawless deeds** (*anomiai*), and **sins** (*hamartiai*), all of which appear in the plural form, imply that David thinks of more than one type of happiness. To these types of *sins,* the verbs *forgiven* (*aphethēsan*) and *covered* (*epekalyphthēsan*) are employed. **Blessed** (*makarios*) of v 8, appearing in the singular, however, expressed through the verb *impute* (*logisētai*, cf. vv 3-6), is a matter of greater glory because it describes the man who God will not credit with a single **sin** (*hamartian*). David describes in a staircase manner transitioning from the lesser to the greater (cf. 5:6, 9-10; 8:32 where the *fortiori* argument is reversed from the greater to the lesser). The lesser of the blessing is supported by the context of Psalm 32:3-4 that shows how sin causes one to lose joy (v 7). Thus, to enjoy the experience of continual forgiveness of sins, one must understand the greater one-time-act of justification (vv 6-8).

4:9-12. Paul illustrated justification apart from works from the two greatest figures in Jewish history: Abraham the father of the race and David the greatest king. However, through a rhetorical question, Paul surfaces a common concern that his Gentile audience might raise: Can **this blessedness** of imputed righteousness described by David *come* **upon the circumcised** (Jews) *only,* **or** can it come **upon the uncircumcised** (Gentiles) **also?** To which Paul astutely responds by pointing to Abraham's imputation of **righteousness** on the basis of faith, since he was **uncircumcised** twenty-nine years before (according to Jewish chronology, Gen 15:6) **he received the sign of circumcision** (Gen 17:10-11). If he received this **seal of the righteousness of the faith** much later, then clearly the **uncircumcised . . . who believe** can expect this **righteousness** to be **imputed to them also.** Though many people were justified by faith before Abraham (Heb 11:4-7), the Hebrew Scripture does not specifically record it. Since Abraham was justified prior to being circumcised and Scripture records it, he serves as the perfect archetype father to the uncircumcised Gentiles who are similarly justified by faith.

Furthermore, since Abraham was circumcised later, he also became an archetype father (cf. 4:1) for the circumcised; **but** (*alla,* strongest Gk contrast) Paul seems to believe Jews cannot claim ancestry in a spiritual sense apart from **also** walking **in the steps of** Abraham's **faith** (Matt 3:9-10). Circumcision only served as a *sign* confirming the reality of something else (Rom 2:25-29). Paul illustrates this concept elsewhere by describing his converts as a "seal" authenticating the reality of his apostleship (1 Cor 9:2). Thus following Abraham's physical circumcision, his *walk* (= life, cf. Heb 11:8-10; Jas 2:21-23) was consistent with *the faith he **had** while* ***still* uncircumcised**. Perhaps Paul anticipates the Christian life section coming in chapters 5–8 that equally apply to Jews and

Gentiles who are justified by faith and who *walk in the steps* of this *faith* (by living resurrection lives).

4:13-15. For (*gar*) begins Paul's explanation of why, in the previous context (vv 9-12), there was no mention of the Law. Jewish theology was steeped in thinking the deliverance of the Lord came to Israel who inherited the promises of the Lord (Ps Sol 12:6) and excluded Gentiles since they did not possess the Law. Paul's interpretation militates against the rabbinic understanding that all of the Abrahamic promises were made to him prior to having the Law that he somehow knew and kept (Kiddushin 4:14). Rabbis cite Genesis 26:5 in the Kiddushin to prove Abraham's obedience to God's Sinai commands. Yet Abraham's obedience cited in Genesis 26:5 does not support this view. God gave Abraham many commands from chapters 12:1–25:9, but those given at Sinai were not part of these. Hence this is illogical (as well as unbiblical) since chronologically **the promise** (*epaggelia*, singular) **that** Abraham **would be the heir of the world,** given also to **his seed** (*tō spermati*, a collective singular), came 430 years before **the law** (Gal 3:17).

Important to note here, the word *promise* is singular and appositional to the phrase *that he would be the heir of the world* that *his seed* would partake explains this promise. That is, going back to Abraham's promise in Genesis 12:3, "and in you all the families of the earth shall be blessed," helps one see the universal dimension of the promise. Hence Paul understood, as already seen contextually from 4:9-12, that "the Scripture foresaw that God would justify the Gentiles by faith" (Gal 3:8, NIV). Logically, partaking of this facet of the Abrahamic Covenant *promise* comes to all (Jew or Gentile) who are justified by faith. The literal Greek translation makes this point even stronger by its use of the preposition *dia* ("through") as a contrast, pointing to the means of how one attains this *promise*:

not **through** (*dia*) **the law** . . . **but** (*alla*, strongest Gk contrast)
through (*dia*) **righteousness of faith.**" **For** (*gar*) is again used by
Paul to further clarify the previous point: That **if** this *promise* could
be obtained by **the law,** by making one **heirs,** then **faith is made
void** (from *kenoō*, lit. "to render powerless") **and the promise**
(*epaggelia*, singular) **made of no effect** (from *katērgetai*, lit "can-
celled"). Hence, this singular *promise,* contextually, does not refer
to any of the other Abrahamic promises made directly to national
Israel (e.g., land, circumcision, etc., cf. Gen 12:7; 13:14-17; 15:18-
21; 17:6-8; 22:17), but to the *promise* of justification by faith blessing that along with Israel everyone was meant to share (Gen 3:15;
12:3; Gal 3:7-8).

Since a close relation exists between the *seed* of v 13 and
Abraham's "Seed" in Galatians 3:17 (Christ), one may understand
a similar meaning here. Grammatically, *sperma* is a collective singular that could either refer to descendants or Christ. Here the
context must be decisive in determining, unlike Galatians 3:17 that
clearly reveals Christ as the Seed. Contextually, justification by
faith, coming to Jews and Gentiles apart from circumcision and the
Law, is the subject matter. Thus, the collective group of Jews and
Gentiles are in view, not Christ. Furthermore becoming an *heir of
the world* based on justification by faith pertains to someone other
than Christ, since He kept the Law, does not need justification by
faith and provides the basis for the believer's faith. Therefore, it
seems more natural to understand *seed* here as way of referring to
all whom by faith become Abraham's children.

It follows that Abraham's children by faith that become the *heir*
(*klēronomon*) *of the world* means nothing more than becoming
"heirs of God" by faith alone (cf. v 14; 8:17a; Gal 3:29; 4:1). This
contrasts with those who become co-heirs with Christ to reign in
the kingdom conditioned on suffering and obedience (8:17b; 2

Tim 2:11-13; Rev 2:26).

The explanatory conjunction **because** (*gar*) indicates (by its third consecutive use) that Paul follows a logical train of thought begun in v 13 (that lit. in the Gk reads "not through law"). Hence, to void the promise by faith of v 14, by attempting to claim it through the Law, will result in doom, *because* **the law brings about wrath** since no one keeps it flawlessly. The phrase "*because the law brings about wrath*" should be taken negatively, even though Paul states that the Law in itself is "holy," "just," and "good" in 7:12. However, if one tries to use *the law* to earn God's righteousness, which Paul's Jewish contemporaries believed that they could do (2:1–3:20), they will remain in a state of wrath (John 3:36).

Paul refers to the negative affects that *the law* brings in contrast to the promise of a faith-based-righteousness. For those who are not of the promise, *the law* is continually at work and wrath continues to be upon them (1:18–3:20). Furthermore, the word *brings* (*katergazetai*, i.e., works) appears in the present tense and is used throughout the book referring to a current experience (cf., Lopez, *Wrath of God*, 61). Contextually then, Paul refers to the present experience *the law* brings if one tries to keep it—wrath. Since transgressing *the law* is a present experience contextually, this *wrath,* as a result of a present transgression, brings current consequences. Hence, here *wrath* refers to the present experience of wrath begun in 1:18, since the Greek article "the" in front of wrath is most naturally understood as an article of previous reference. Thus, the outcome must by necessity be referring to present experience, and as the context indicates, it is not referring to eternal judgment.

Conversely, Paul explains **for** (*de*, also used at times like *gar* for explaining) **where there is no law** *there is* **no transgression**. That is, since the Law cannot be kept perfectly, those who claim the promise through justification by faith are not in peril of transgressing it, because the Law issue is not germane. Paul does not mean that where there is *no law* there is no sin (cf. 5:13). Instead, the presence of the *law* reveals clear lines that when crossed turn sin into *transgression* (*parabasis*). For example, a husband may curse his wife, which is sinful, but not illegal. Biblically, since God knows man's deceitful heart (Jer 17:9), it is possible for man to sin and not realize it. Hence Paul always uses *parabasis* as a violation of a legal command stated by God (2:23; 4:15; 5:14; Gal 3:19; 1 Tim 2:14), so that sin may not appear vaguely, but for what it really is, a *transgression* of God's Law.

4:16-17. Therefore (*dia touto*) draws a conclusion from the previous in what follows. The Law produces wrath, and the inability to possess the promise of justification, since no one can ever keep it. This is why the promise *is* **of faith**. It guarantees the result **that** (*hina*) it will never be lost since it is understood as a gracious **promise** unable to be earned. All **of the law** (Jew) and **of the faith** (Gentiles) who accept this *promise* by *faith* qualify to call Abraham their **father** in the spiritual sense. This, in fact, corresponds to Scripture: *"I have made you a father of many nations"* (Gen 17:5). This all came about because Abraham fulfilled one condition: **in the presence of Him whom he believed—God.** Perhaps this phrase should be translated as: "In whose presence he believed, namely, God's presence." Abraham simply *believed* God could **give life to the dead and calls those things which do not exist as though they** did. Contextually, Paul's idea here refers to Genesis 17:15-21, where against all odds, beyond the childbearing years of Abraham's dead body (i.e., sterile from old age) and Sarah's dead womb (i.e., barren), through God's power, they conceived (cf. v 19). Thus, if God can create life (out of nothing, *creatio ex nihilo*) in a barren womb, one can be absolutely certain that justification by faith guarantees the promise of God's imputed righteousness to sinners that John calls eternal life.

4:18. Paul further strengthens his argument through Abraham, **who contrary to hope, in hope believed** God (cf. 4:3 for the content of Abraham's faith), and as a result (*eis*) **became the father of many nations** (cf. v 17). The phrases of *hope* appear in Greek next to each other, indicating that Abraham's *hope* (=faith) was *contrary* to anything that can possibly be achieved on a purely human level. That is, Abraham's faith to have a child was "beyond" reasonable "hope" if it rested on his physical ability. But since his *hope* rested *on* God's promise, his hope was secure (cf. v 19-21).

4:19-22. Thus, Paul elaborates in the following three verses the reason for Abraham's "hope" in v 18. Abraham **was not being weak in faith.** To be *weak in faith* does not mean to believe doubtfully, because this would be contradictory. That is, one either does or does not believe. Instead, the phrase means to be able to rise to the occasion and embrace something that defies human logic, like Abraham did. Beyond human logic, since the reproductive functions of Abraham and Sarah were **already dead** (*nenekrōmenon*, perfect passive participle), Abraham believed. The perfect tense of *dead* implies a previous and presently existing state of affairs well beyond the reach of human fulfillment **(since he was about a hundred years old),** because of the **deadness of Sarah's womb**. This means God waited until it was humanly impossible to fulfill the promise in order to exclude any possible human merit.

Conversely from works, Abraham's faith rose to the occasion. Although his faith was stronger at times more than others (17:17, 23-27), he remained faithful to the end (Gen 22:1-18). **He did not waver . . . but was strengthened** (*enedynamōthē*, aorist passive) **in faith**. One may understand this in various ways: (1) The phrase *was strengthened in faith* may be taken to mean that God answered Abraham and Sarah by empowering them (indicated by the passive voice, *strengthened*) to have children *by means of their faith*. (2) Or it could mean that due to Abraham's unwavering faith he became stronger (by God's help indicated by the passive voice, *strengthened*) *in faith*. That is, by God's help Abraham became more confident in the fulfillment of the promise that he already believed (cf. v 21). The context seems to favor the latter (Cranfield, *Romans*, 1:248).

God perhaps waited until it was absolutely impossible (cf. v 19 above) for both of them to have children in order to challenge and cause Abraham's faith to grow and bring **glory to God**. This may be a paradigm of how God works with people to strengthen their faith (cf. Jonah's experience, Job, Israel's Babylonian captivity experience, the prophets prediction of future restoration of Israel and Jesus' crucifixion and resurrection [a form of Sarah's dead womb brought to life by God] that brought strength to the apostles).

Finally Paul defines Abraham's faith as **being fully convinced** (*plērophoreō*). Important to note here is how Paul defines "faith" following upon v 20. The term *fully convinced* may not be the best translation since it implies the possibility of varying degrees of assurance (99%, 90%, 80%, etc...) in believing the promise initially. This idea, of course, is unbiblical, since the Scripture knows of only two options when it comes to believing God's promise of supplying a Savior (known today as Jesus) that will come through Abraham: either one *is* or *is not* convinced of the truth that Jesus Christ gives eternal life (cf. John 11:25-27). The Greek term *plērophoreō* basically means: to be *assured*, or to be *certain* (BDAG, 827). The entire context refers to faith in the promise of God. Paul, now, clarifies Abraham's faith as fundamentally being "assured" or "convicted" of God's declared or **promised** seed. Clearly this is not an "act of the will" exercised by Abraham but rather a "conviction" or "persuasion" that what God *promised* is true. No one can ever become convinced by an act of the will if they *mentally* believe something is false. Even at a basic human level faith is a conviction that something is *certain, reliable,* or *true* (cf. BAGD, 660-62; BDAG, 816-17). Hence, at the very moment of faith, God illuminates a person's mind allowing one to become *persuaded* or *convinced* of the truth (cf. Acts 16:14; 2 Cor 4:6). Thus, in one sense, it is incorrect to speak of the exercise of simple *faith* as "intellectual assent" because it carries the connotations of being *disinterested* or *detached,* and carries pejorative connotations. However, in another sense, defining the exercise of simple *faith* as "intellectual assent" technically speaking is correct, because *intellect* means, "the capacity for rational or intelligent thought" and *assent* means, "to agree." Putting both of these together implies that if one *intellectually assents*, he has thought intelligently about God's promise and afterward agreed that it is true by faith. If the object of one's intellectual assent refers to believing God's promise to attain His righteousness, then by intellectually assenting a person complied with the necessary condition to obtain that promise. Obviously, **He** (God) is powerful enough to **perform** the incredible promise of supplying a Savior from Sarah's dead womb and Abraham's dead body. This is exactly what Abraham became convinced/believed (vv 17-20), and **therefore** (*dio*, indicates an emphatic marker of result) because Abraham complied with God's sole condition for justification: *"it was accounted to him for righteousness"* (cf. 4:3-5).

4:23-25. As as a good teacher, Paul concludes the justification-by-faith section (3:21–4:25) in the following three verses by applying Abraham's account to the present-day-saint. That is, the faith account in Genesis 15:6 **was not** *just* recorded solely **for** the **sake** of preserving Abraham's memory and stupendous story of faith (Sirach 44:19; Heb 11:8), **but also for** the present-day-person. This has been Paul's point in the entire chapter (4:3, 5-6, 9-11, 23-24).

At this point one comes to the crux of Paul's argument for writing chapter four. The Old Testament records Abraham's justification-by-faith account to show that everyone today receives God's **imputed** righteousness **who believe in Him** in the same manner. Paul did not invent the doctrine expounded in 3:21-31. It appears in the Old Testament too as 4:1-25 delineates.

The object and basis of Abraham's faith in Genesis 15:6 are in God's power to produce the promised Seed from Abraham's dead body (cf. 4:3). Now Paul reveals this same object and basis of the believer's faith as **Jesus our Lord** *resurrected* **from the dead**.

Paul continues in v 25 to develop Jesus' central function in God's plan to justify sinners by faith from v 24: **who** (relative pronoun refers back to Lord) **was first delivered up because of** (*dia*) **our offenses, and was raised because of** (*dia*) **our justification.** Perhaps Paul thinks of Isaiah 53:6, 12 here, since the same concept and Greek verb in the LXX *paradidōmī* (= *delivered up*) appears there with the word "death," which no doubt his readers understood here since it does not appear in the Greek text (which the NIV and RSV include). The term *paradidōmī* appears in the New Testament with reference to Jesus' crucifixion (Matt 26:2) of being *delivered up* by Judas (26:15-16), and it is also used of God delivering up Jesus to be put to death (Rom 8:32). Here being *delivered up* means to die.

Finally, Paul concludes the chapter by explaining Jesus' function in God's justification-by-faith program: He *was first delivered up* "*because of*" (*dia*) *our offenses.*

The first use of the preposition *dia*, linked with *our offenses* (i.e., sins), could be understood, though it rarely is, prospectively (as an event looking forward): Jesus was slain "with a view to" our sins. Using "*because of*" or "*on account of*," understood retrospectively (as an event looking back), makes more sense and allows the normal rendering of *dia*: Jesus was slain "on account of" our sins. Thus, Christ's death was required due to human sin that could not be atoned without the shedding of *His* blood (cf. 3:25; Heb 9:22; Isa 53:11-12).

The second use of *dia* may also be used retrospectively: Jesus *was raised* "because of" or "on account of" *our justification*. This would mean justification, in a sense, caused Jesus' resurrection. This implies our sins killed Jesus, but our justification raised Him in the sense that it was a "necessary effect" since God accepted His sacrifice (Godet, *Romans*, 1:184-85). While this is true, Moo correctly suggest that "it is difficult to see why this may be so," since Paul has used *justification* "with reference to the subjective appropriation through faith. Accordingly, we can give the preposition a 'prospective' reference—'because of' in the sense of 'because of the need to,' 'for the sake of'" (*Romans*, 289). Hence, *dia* may be used prospectively in the sense: Jesus *was raised* "with a view to," "for the sake of," or even "in the interests of" our justification; all of which are valid translations and are less forced than the previous. This would mean that Christ's death sets God's seal of approval on His sacrifice for sins on the cross (John 19:30). Thus one can say God's legal declaration, before His tribunal, finds its legal basis on Christ's resurrection since God accepted His sacrifice.

Perhaps translating the preposition *dia* retrospectively in the first part of the clause and prospectively in the second may be the best way to interpret it (Cranfield, *Romans*, 1:252-53; Käsemann, *Romans*, 129): Jesus *was slain because of* our sins [i.e., causally "because we are sinners"], and *was raised* "for the sake of" *our justification* [i.e., finally "in order to secure our justification"] (Moo, *Romans*, 289). One, however, must be cautious in taking the resurrection to mean that it was the *only* cause of justification. Hence Paul can say in one place that we are "justified by His blood" (5:9), and in another place that believing "in the heart that God has raised Him from the dead" results in justification (cf. 10:9-10).

Clearly, Paul achieved his goal in chapter four by establishing that the justification by faith alone in Christ alone existed in the Old Testament: Romans 4:1-8 demonstrates that justification-by-faith cannot be earned by works but comes by God's free-grace. Verses 9-12 show that Abraham's justification came before circumcision; hence circumcision is unnecessary for justification. Verses 13-17 argue that Abraham was justified before the Mosaic Law. Therefore the Law is not the basis of justification. Finally vv 18-25 summarize Paul's argument: Abraham was justified by *simple* faith in God's power to provide the promised Seed, whose name and function is now clearly known.

5
LIFE REIGNS OVER DEATH

C. The Power of the Gospel Delivers: Only the Righteous Can Experience Life and Expect Ultimate Deliverance (5:1–8:39)

From 3:21–4:25, Paul presented God's solution to humanity's condemnation (see 1:18–3:20). Thus, the basic exposition of justification by faith alone in Christ has now ended. Now Paul, in chapters 5:1–8:39, presents how the gospel furnishes power to affect a radical new life to the justified. Considerable debate exists in determining whether chapter 5 extends the justification section, transitions it, or belongs exclusively to the sanctification section as a whole. Chapter 5 functions as a transition pointing to chapters 6–8, and may be seen as belonging to it. Since the term "life" and its derivatives appear a mere three times from chapters 1–4 (1:17; 2:7; 4:17) and twenty-five times in chapters 5–8 (5:10, 17-18, 21; 6:2, 4, 10 [2x], 11, 13, 22-23; 7:1, 2, 3, 9, 10; 8:2, 6, 10-11, 12, 13 [2x], 38), this indicates the noun "life" and the verb "live" bind chapters 5–8. Furthermore, the theme of "hope" in 5:2 reappears and climaxes at the end of the section (8:17-25), unifying the entire section. Other phrases that link 5–8 as one unit of thought appear six times in four chapters (at the beginning, middle and end): "through our Lord Jesus Christ" (5:1, 11), "through Jesus Christ our Lord" (5:21; 7:25) and "in Christ Jesus our Lord" (6:11; 8:39; cf. Cranfield, *Romans*, 1:254). Hence what follows can accurately be referred to as the "Christian-life-section."

1. Justification endows one with sanctifying-power to be delivered from God's wrath to experience life (5:1-11)

5:1-2. Therefore (*oun*) is an inferential connector concluding the previous section and introducing the experiential results of the justified. As a result of **having been justified** (*dikaiōthentes*) **by faith, we have** (*echomen*) **peace with God**. This is the greatest benefit believers receive at the moment of justification that comes **through our Lord Jesus Christ** (cf. 4:25). This once-for-all act is indicated by the aorist participle *dikaiōthentes* that suggests antecedent time to that of the main verb *echomen*. Hence the present active indicative verb translated *we have* refers to a present possession stemming from what God effected from 3:21–4:25. Some of the earliest Greek manuscripts record the subjunctive verb *echōmen*, meaning, "Let us have peace with God," instead of the indicative verb *echomen* that means: *we have peace with God.* However, the subjunctive verb's meaning here is totally foreign to the context (Wallace, *Greek Grammar,* 464), since it implies one can choose to have peace with God after being justified. This is *not* a subjective peace *of* God that one enjoys when obedience to His mandates take place but an objective reality. The other indicative verbs in the context also favor the present tense: "we have" (*eschēkamen,* v 2), "we stand" (*hestēkamen,* v 2), "we were reconciled," (*katēllagēmen,* v 10), and "we have" (*elabomen,* v 11). Thus, *by faith through Jesus Christ,* the believers begin a relationship with God and are no longer at enmity with Him.

Paul connects verses 2 and 1 by stating that the One **through** (*dia*) **whom we also have access by faith into this grace in which we stand** is the same *Jesus Christ through* (*dia*) *whom we have peace with God.* Both prepositions *dia* denote agency, first through whom one becomes a believer and second how a believer can then

approach God (cf. 4:25 for a different meaning of both prepositions *dia* within the same verse). That is, Jesus makes it possible to
not only have peace with God *by faith*, but also to have access into
this grace *by faith*. The imagery here reflects the thick curtain
between the holy place and the holy of holies in the temple that
separated man from having access to God that has now been
removed by Christ's death (Matt 27:51). Clearly the conjunction
also, referring to the *access* spoken by Paul, is something additional
to justification. The Greek word *access* (*prosagōgē*) appears in only
two other places in the New Testament (Eph 2:18; 3:12). In both
of these texts, as here, the reference is to the believers' privilege of
approaching God's throne. As peace with God came *by faith* so also
access to God's throne, to praise, pray, or petition Him, comes also
by faith. Paul's last mention of *faith* here (in chaps 5–8) refers to the
justifying faith of v 1 rather than the faith exercised in Christian
living (Gal 2:20). Conversely, *this grace* where believers *stand*
(*hestēkamen*, as the perfect tense suggests an accomplished permanent position with ongoing ramifications) is the same grace by
which God justifies (cf. 3:24) and also furnishes to believers to
experience life (5:17, 21).

These are all good reasons for Christians to **rejoice**
(*kauchōmetha*). The tense for *kauchōmetha* may be indicative or
subjunctive because the Greek form is the same in both cases. The
indicative refers to the reality of the action: "we rejoice." The subjunctive suggests contingency: "let us rejoice." In either case, the
Christian is to rejoice in God. Thus, after Paul shares the wonderful truths of the believers' past justification *by faith* and present
access by faith into this grace, he knows believers can *rejoice* now **in
hope** of the future sure expectation in participation **of the glory of
God** (8:30), a *glory* lost to unbelievers due to sin (3:23).

5:3-5. No sooner than Paul points ahead, **and not only that,**

but (*alla*), he uses a strong contrast to bring the Christian back to the grim realization of suffering that surrounds him: **we also glory** (*kauchōmetha*) **in tribulations**. The word *glory* is the same word translated "rejoice" in v 2 that actually means "exult," "to take pride" or "boast" (BDAG, 536). Paul means that there are two types of valid boasting before men (cf. 4:2): The future one in God (v 11; 1 Cor 1:31) and the present one through *tribulations* that build our character (vv 3b-5, see 2 Cor 12:9-10). Also James referred to this last idea in 1:2-4, 12.

Tribulations should then produce three character building qualities that potentially produce good fruits (by adding *hē de* in the Gk): **perseverance . . . character . . .** and **hope.** (1) *Perseverance* refers to the continued capacity to bear-up under difficulties. (2) *Character* refers to "a test that promotes and validates the character of the one undergoing it" (BDAG, 256). (3) *Hope* is a result of successfully bearing up under tribulations (ibid.), and the expectation of an enhanced glory based on suffering (8:17-39).

Paul further adds (by using *hē de* as in 5:4) that this **hope does not disappoint** (*kataischynei*). The present form of the verb *kataischynei* means "put to shame." Hence the *hope* produced by suffering (vv 3-4) will not presently allow us to be put to shame (see Paul's use in 9:33; 10:11). From 5b-10, Paul explains why Christians can be confident through the use of the causal clause: **because** (*hoti*) **the love of God has been poured out in our hearts by the Holy Spirit who was given to us**. Paul's point contextually refers to the internal realization of "knowing" (v 3) God's love, discovered by those who experience tribulations (vv 3-5; cf. Jas 5:11). This realization comes by means (*dia*) of the *Holy Spirit given to us* at the moment of justification (8:9), but He aids us in life and suffering (8:1-39). Thus vv 1-5 serve as a seed-plot from which the Christian life section will be developed in chapters 5–8.

5:6-8. **For** (*gar*) is an explanatory conjunction used by Paul to clarify **when** God's love in v 5 reached out: *when* **we were still without strength.** By inference of the Holy Spirit's arrival, the condition of helplessness became resolved. God provides the power to believers now, to live resurrection-life (6:1-14; 8:10-13). Paul uses a well known (*fortiori*) rabbinic device that argues from the greater to the lesser (though the *qal wayyōmer* argument can also function from the lesser to the greater as in 4:8; cf. Moo, *Romans*, 309-10, fn 87) throughout this section (usually indicated by "much more," 5:9-10, 15, 17, 20). He first argues from the greater: **in due time** (cf. Mark 1:15; Gal 4:4) **Christ died for** (*hyper* "on behalf of") **the ungodly** (cf. 3:25; 4:25; 6:10; 7:4; 8:32; 14:15). Later he argues to the lesser: If God did the greater work through Christ for sinners, much more will He provide the power necessary for Christians to live victoriously, as the culmination of the immediate (5:9-10, 17, 21) and overall section shows (chaps 6–8).

For (*gar*) Paul further explains v 6 by describing the immense nature of God's love through Christ's death by contrasting v 7 with v 8: **scarcely for a righteous man will one die; yet perhaps for a good man someone would even dare to die.** The relationship between these two clauses is unclear. Some have seen no distinction between *a righteous man* and the literal phrase *the* (instead of "**a**" translated by NKJV) *good man* (e.g. Bruce, *Romans*, 117), since in the New Testament where the words are used together no distinction occurs (Matt 5:45; Luke 23:50; Rom 7:12). However, Paul could be making a distinction between any *just* man in general, which few may be inclined to die for, instead of a specific (hence the definite article appears in front of) *good man* with whom one may have a personal relationship (Moo, *Romans*, 308).

In either case compared to the best human love, God's **love** is overwhelming. He displayed it **in that** (*hoti*) **while we were still**

sinners, Christ died for us. The *hoti* clause is epexegetical (Wallace, *Greek Grammar*, 460). That is, the clause explains the extent of God's love in two ways: First, God's unconditional *love* expresses itself by reaching out to sinners while they were *still* going the opposite direction. Second, God's *love* also expresses itself in the historical act of Christ's death. For Paul, Christ's death is the ultimate tangible manifestation of God's love. Incredibly, no other verse, except John 3:16, shouts more clearly than this one of God's amazing grace! No amount of human justice or goodness can begin to compare.

5:9-10. Since God extends His love "while we were still sinners," Paul echoes how, **Much more** (indicative of the rabbinic *qal wayyōmer* argument: from the major [since Christ died for our justification] to the minor [how *much more* will God not give believers the means of sanctification that will deliver them from the power of sin that incurs wrath]; cf. v 6; Moo, *Romans*, 310) now, **having been justified** (*dikaiōthentes*) **by His blood,** we should expect His love to be manifested in the lesser of the two acts: **we shall be saved** (*sōthēsometha*) **from wrath through Him.** The aorist passive participle *dikaiōthentes* reverts to the idea of v 1, "Therefore, having been justified." This phrase drew a conclusion from the previous section 3:21–4:25, and anticipates vv 9-10, which are key hinge verses in Paul's central argument of Romans. In a similar form the term *dikaiōthentes* anticipates, and is further distinguished from, salvation from wrath. The Greek phrase *tēs orgēs* has the definite article "the wrath," known as the article of previous reference. Some see this reference as the wrath of 2:5, 8, which they interpret as eternal judgment (Murray, *Romans*, 1:171; see Dunn, *Romans 1-8*, 258). However, this is unlikely. Five reasons argue for interpreting *we shall be saved from wrath* as a present experience, from the power of sin, intended for believers as chapters

6–8 discuss: (1) Since the wrath referred to in 2:5, 8 occurs in the section governed by the present experience of wrath (1:18–3:20), the most natural reference is to "the wrath of God" begun in 1:18-32 (cf. 2:1, 5, 8). (2) The phrase *saved from wrath* "*through Him*" and "*by His life*" (v 10) are parallel phrases which demonstrate the concept of life. Contextually the word *life* appears overwhelmingly in sections that deal with the present experience of life (Rom 5–8; 12–15, see intro. to section above). Thus Paul intentionally uses "life" or "live" in an experiential manner (Rom 6:2, 11, 13; 7:1, 2, 3; 8:12-13) to which the verses of this section belong. (3) The "death-life" motif also appears together in eight verses in chapters 5–8 where the contrast is between experiential life and death. (4) The future tense *we shall be saved* (*sōthēsometha*) may be understood as a predictive future that can have either of two nuances: A strict-future fulfillment (from the presence of sin) or an immediate-future fulfillment (from the power of sin), understood as a "logical" future that states what is natural and expected (see Moo, *Romans*, 340). The context must determine. The immediate context has constantly referred to *the present experience of the believers,* a concept Paul strengthens by his graphic description of God's love (vv 3-8) to motivate believers. In chapters 5–8, twenty-three future verbs appear. Out of these, fifteen passages (including 5:9-10) use an immediate-future tense that states what is naturally expected now: "those who receive abundance of grace . . . righteousness will reign in life" (5:17), "How shall we who died to sin live any longer in it?" (6:2), and "we also shall be in the likeness of His resurrection" (6:5, cf. 5:19; 6:1, 8, 14; 7:3; 7:7, 24; 8:11, 13, 33). One should understand Paul's use of the future tense *sōthēsometha* as a logical future emphasizing something naturally expected to transpire upon the believer's obedience. (5) Hence the salvation theme has not recurred since 1:16, because Paul chooses to reserve the term to express deliverance from wrath resulting from Christians who "walk in newness of life" (6:4) experienced upon obedience (6:11-13; 8:1-13). That is why Paul does not use "save" (*sōzō*) and "salvation" (*sōtēria*) in the justification section (3:21–4:25). Unfortunately this has gone relatively unnoticed. Instead Paul uses the word *justified* (*dikaioō*) to connote judicial acquittal. Thus to say that to be *saved from wrath* indicates deliverance from future eternal judgment would be redundant since this was expounded to the fullest extent in 3:21–4:25.

Paul understands wrath as something Christians can still experience post-justification (cf. 13:4-5) if they choose to continue in "ungodliness and unrighteousness" (1:18). Therefore, deliverance from the power and experience of sin comes "through Him . . . by His life" (i.e., living the resurrection-life of Christ found in the following section concerning sanctification, Rom 6–8).

In v 10 Paul reiterates, with a new emphasis, the proposition of v 9. **For** (*gar*) acts as an explanatory particle that further explains the previous verse, and further clarifies v 9 by making Paul's argument more evident and forceful: (1) He adds the term *enemies*, which makes the *fortiori* "much more" argument more striking; (2) he substitutes *justified* with the term *reconciled,* corresponding better with the term *enemies*; (3) he personalizes it more by stating the atonement work was accomplished *through the death of His Son* instead of the less personal term *by His blood*; (4) finally, he clarifies *through Him* by using a more exact expression *by His life* (Godet, *Romans*, 1:195).

It is important to note that the new term *reconciled* that Paul introduces is parallel to the term *justified.* Although both terms are related conceptually, they have a distinct nuance. Justification is a legal term which pictures the believer being declared righteous by a judge (cf. 3:24). Reconciliation is a relational term that occurred

through Christ's death, which Paul explains in 2 Corinthians 5:20-
21. Thus, by Christ becoming "sin for us," we became "the righteousness of God in Him." Only to this extent can reconciliation
parallel the righteousness of God as vv 9-10 show (Büchsel,
TDNT, 1:255). On the other hand reconciliation (*katallassō*)
refers to repairing an estranged relationship, or removing a barrier,
between hostile parties. Thus reconciliation terminology is relational in nature. The term reconciliation is not normally attested in
Hellenistic secular or cultic usage, because it was inappropriate to
think there could be a personal relationship between man and
deity. Reconciliation is used strictly by Paul in the New Testament
(v 11; 1 Cor 7:11; 2 Cor 5:18, 19, 20, see also Eph 2:16; Col 1:20-
22), and it carries two aspects that occur at different times: (1)
When Christ died on the cross "God was in Christ reconciling the
world to Himself" by "not imputing" sinners' "trespasses to them"
but to Christ instead. Thus, God reconciled the world by removing the universal sin barrier whether or not people become believers. In short, God's universal reconciliation makes people savable.
This could *not* be said of justification since God did not justify the
world. (2) When sinners believe God's reconciliation message of
the cross of Christ (Rom 3:25; 2 Cor 5:20, 21), they personalize
the universal scope of God's reconciliation. Hence, after God reconciled the world to Himself, the only barrier left between men
and God is "unbelief." Therefore one has to hear and believe this
message in order to be justified (2 Cor 5:20-21; Rom 3:25-26).
Thus, Paul's use of reconciliation here constitutes the full two-fold
experience that strengthens the *fortiori* argument. The expression
when we were enemies we were reconciled to God refers to His
universal reconciliation, similar to the concept found in 5:8 (cf.
John 3:16-18; Rom 3:25; 1 John 2:2); the use of the participle
expression **having been reconciled** (*katallagentes*) parallels the

participle "having been justified" that describes those who appropriated the message. Paul's full experience (or both aspects) of "reconciliation" is expressed in Col 1:20-22.

Thus, after being reconciled, one can expect in the immediate future to be **saved** (*sōthēsometha*) **by His life.** The future tense *sōthēsometha* "through Him" and "by His life" refers to Paul's thought already expressed in v 9. That is, Christians who avail themselves of the resurrection-power found in *His life* (=*through Him* that is resident in the gospel, 1:16) will find deliverance from wrath (v 9), but only if they "walk in newness of life" (6:4) which Paul explains in chapters 6–8.

5:11. And Paul continues from the previous thoughts, **not only that** (i.e., not only are believers to be "saved by His life"), **but we also rejoice in God.** Paul closes the section of vv 1-11 by stressing the recurring theme of rejoicing from "tribulation" in vv 2-3. This close connection, of being able to "exult" or "boast" *in God* comes as a result of being "saved by His life." Christians who do not present themselves as "instruments of righteousness to God" (6:13) will not be able to *rejoice in God.* Because true Christian joy, even in tribulations (cf. Jas 1:2-12), comes by knowing God's love for us (vv 3-8) and by living resurrection-lives (vv 9-10), this is how Christians can experience the full joy of having **now received the reconciliation** (cf. v 10).

2. Grace-righteousness reigns in life over sin's reign of death (5:12-21)

5:12. Therefore (in Gk lit. "because of this") Paul's conclusion, drawn from vv 1-11 and linked to vv 12-21, must be understood in order to follow his flow of thought leading into the sanctification chapters 6–8. In vv 1-2 Paul affirmed justification was accomplished, but in vv 3-4 he stresses that suffering is still a present reality. Hence clarifying God's love, in vv 5-8 through the greatest act

(Christ's death for us), indicates He will do the lesser act and empower Christians to be delivered from wrath by living resurrection-lives in vv 9-11. Thus the comparison of Christ and Adam, in vv 12-21, serves to assure Christians of the realm change (from the old to the new nature) necessary to overcome sin and experience the life that chapters 6–8 so marvelously unfold.

As Paul began to draw parallels between Adam and Christ, by stating **just as**, for fear of being misunderstood (Cranfield, *Romans*, 1:269), he never completed his thought until v 18 (with "even so"). Paul explained that **through one man sin** (lit., "the sin" indicating original sin) **entered** (lit., "entered into" as if Adam became the door of) **the world**. Though Eve sinned first (Gen 3:6), Adam was endowed with headship over humanity (Gen 2:7-23; 1 Cor 11:3). As a result of one man's sin **death through sin** immediately arrived on the scene; **thus death spread** (from, *dierchomai*) **to all men, because** (*eph' ōh*) **all sinned** (*hēmarton*). The term *dierchomai* implies going "through an area" (BDAG, 244). The idea then is quick permeation of a complete area as smoke permeates an entire house. Considerable debate exists about the antecedent (and hence the meaning) of the preposition and relative pronoun *eph' ōh* (cf. Cranfield, *Romans*, 1:274-81). Yet the phrase should be interpreted as a causal conjunction. Greek of antiquity interpreted *eph' ōh* to usually mean "on condition that," but by the New Testament era it was used as a causal conjunction "because" (Robertson, *Grammar*, 963; Wallace, *Greek Grammar*, 342-43). Besides it makes perfect sense contextually, from the reading of vv 13-14, to translate it thus here, and also because of its ample usage in the papyri (MM, 234) and Paul's use elsewhere (2 Cor 5:4; Phil 3:12). The Greek aorist (implying past) tense of *hēmarton* appears in all three verbs of v 12 (*entered* and *spread*). Hence Paul views the history of humanity as having sinned in Adam (cf. Rom 3:23, where the aorist *hēmarton* also appears).

At the inception of this section two things must be noted to further understand Paul's argument from vv 12-21: (1) God's penalty for Adam was physical as well as spiritual death, which severed the relationship and experientially meant losing fellowship with God (Gen 2:16-17; 3:8-10, 22-24). Hence one should not understand Paul to be speaking only of physical death but also of experiential death as a reigning power (5:14, 17, 21), both of which accompany sin (cf. 6:23; 7:13; 8:12-13). (2) Various views exist to explain humanity's participation in Adam's sin. First, the example view understands that men sinned independently of Adam but follow Adam's example. This view does not fit because of the aorist tense usage (see above), and it does not do justice to other passages (cf. 3:10-12; 3:23) or to the context that links Adam's sin as the cause of all human death. Second, the fallen nature view interprets *all sinned* to refer to individual sin, but also as a result of inheriting Adam's fallen nature. This is sophistry since one can only act according to one's nature (e.g., lions roar, eagles soar and dogs bark because it is their nature). Third, the federal headship view considers Adam legal role as the federated representative of the human race. Thus, when Adam sinned by virtue of violating his covenant of works with God, all inherited the legal penalty that was judicially imputed to the human race (1 Cor 15:22). Two things plague this view: Scripture knows of no such covenant of works, and it seems unfair that all people, though not personally present, must pay for Adam's sin. Fourth, the seminal headship view understands Adam as the federated head of humanity, but recognizes that seminally (i.e., biologically and spiritually) all of humanity was in Adam. Hence, when the first man sinned, God considered everyone to be a participant in Adam's act. Contextually this fits well in vv 12-21 and other passages. For example, the author of Hebrews, while arguing the superiority of the Melchizedekian priesthood over that of Aaron, said: "Even Levi, who receives tithes, paid tithes through Abraham, so to speak, for he was still in the loins of his father when Melchizedek met him" (Heb 7:9-10). Then Paul can say that even if all of humanity was not *legally* culpable by judicial implication of Adam's sin, all humanity was *actually* culpable because they were present in Adam and thus participated with Adam in his sin.

5:13-14. Perhaps Paul thinks someone will object to the universal doctrine of original sin, since it was not taught in Jewish theology (Fitzmyer, *Romans*, 409). Furthermore, an objector may think of Paul's earlier statement: "for where there is no law *there is no transgression*" (cf. 4:15). Hence Paul feels the need to explain v 12: **For** (*gar*, explanatory particle) **until the law** was given, in Exodus 20, **sin was in the world.** The existence of sin's presence and power is evident in Genesis and Exodus 1–19. However **sin is not imputed when there is no law.** This does not mean people who lived after Adam without the *law* will not be held accountable since Romans 2:11-16 asserts that all will be judged likewise. Even less can it mean based on Revelation 20:11-15, that God does not have a record of everyone's sins. Paul means in relation to the Mosaic Law no "record" (from *ellogeō* translated *imputed*) exists, because the law was not yet in effect. This does not mean that records related to other God-given-mandates not recorded in Scripture, did not exist (e.g., in Gen 4:3-5 Cain and Abel's mandate to sacrifice is nowhere recorded in Scripture, yet unless God commanded it how did they know?). Thus Paul reasons: **Nevertheless** (*alla*), by using the strongest Greek contrast, **death reigned from Adam to Moses.** That is, proof that sin existed before the Law is evident by death reigning *from Adam to Moses.* Paul adds: **Even** (*kai*) **over those who had not sinned according**

to the likeness of the transgression (from *parabasis*) **of Adam**. The clause introduced by *kai* (a coordinating conjunction) suggests there are no exceptions (Morris, *Romans*, 233), since *kai* links all of Adam's descendants who sinned after the Law given to Adam and before the Law given to Moses. The term *parabasis*, employed in 2:23 and 4:15, refers to a violation of the Law. Adam's *parabasis* was a violation of a direct command of God (Gen 2:16-17), which if given by God is law, but not the Mosaic Law that was given later at Sinai. Thus Paul means that Adam's descendents do not commit the same direct *transgression* of eating from "the tree of the knowledge of good and evil," because that specific mandate was not given to any that followed. Yet they still sinned which proves two things: (1) Those who came after Adam still violated other direct mandates (cf., from Genesis to Exodus 20). (2) Since Adam represents all of humanity and sin and death ruled stemming from him (vv 15-19), it proves that they followed Adam by sinning in their own way, or in a sense that all sinned in him when he sinned (cf. v 12; cf. Murray, *Romans*, 1:191, fn 23); either way it makes Adam a pattern of those who followed (Morris, *Romans*, 233-34).

Consequently, Paul confirms even more Adam's representation of humanity by making a comparison (though the antithesis is not yet apparent, cf. vv 15-17) to Christ **who is a type of Him who was to come.** As Adam became the pattern for those who suffered sin and death, so Christ became the pattern for those who receive and experience life (v 17, 21).

5:15. But (*all'*) Paul begins with a sharp contrast here in order to qualify the types. In vv 15-17, he begins to show vast distinction between Adam and Christ, before making a formal conclusion in v 18 (by the words "even so," cf. Cranfield, *Romans*, 1: 284, 289) of the incomplete comparison begun in v 12 (by "just as"). Paul's brief excursus in these verses serves to clarify a possible misunderstanding, arising from the ambiguous comparison between Adam and Christ, made at the end of v 14.

But, Paul says to clarify: **the free gift** (*charisma*) **is not like the offense** (*paraptōma*). Contextually there may not be much difference between the term *paraptōma* (which means "false step," possibly synonymous to Adam's one sin [v 16]), and the term *parabasis*, (implying a direct violation of God's command, [v 14]). Hence **the one man's offense**, "sin" or "disobedience" (all appear in the Gk singular form in vv 15-19) refers to Adam's one transgression of God's command (vv 12, 14). Paul may have switched words to create phonetic parallels (see Gk words above) so they all end with-*ma* that follow from vv 15-19 (Dunn, *Romans 1–8*, 279).

The first contrast between Adam and Christ is a matter of degree: **For if by the one man's offense many** (*polloi*) **died, much more the grace of God and the gift** (i.e., "the gracious gift of God," as a *hendiadys* referring to two formally coordinate terms expressing a single concept in which one of the components defines the other) **by the grace of the one Man, Jesus Christ abounded to many** (*pollous*). The marker *much more* shows the degree. Thus Adam's one act resulted in death for the human race (i.e., the meaning of *polloi*). By contrast, because of *the grace* (i.e., the one righteous act mentioned in v 18) of Christ, *many* who received it (i.e., *pollous* means believers who receive this gift as v 17 shows) abided in a sphere of great abundance. Hence the abundance of grace is always better than the lack caused by sin (3:23) since it produces the resurrection-life that Paul will soon develop (6:1-23).

5:16. Paul begins to develop the contrasting results of each party: **And the gift** (*dōrēma*) **is not like that which came through the one who sinned.** Here the word *dōrēma* means something "granted," different from what resulted from Adam. Paul explains these results in two contrasting statements: **For the judgment**

(*krima*) is what **resulted in condemnation** (*katakrima*)**, but the free gift** (*charisma*, i.e., grace) **...** is what **resulted in justification** (*dikaiōma*). The word *krima* refers to the sentencing point of Adam that parallels the starting point of the *charisma* recipients. Each of these starting points issue in different results: Adam's sin issued in *katakrima* (occurring elsewhere only in v 18; 8:1), which means the result of the sentence or the penalty itself that follows the sentence (= "penal servitude," MM, 327-28). That is, Adam's judgment led to everyone's enslavement which places people in a position to sin as Romans 1:18–3:20 describes. By contrast the result issuing from the grace recipients is *dikaiōma*, which means right actions or behavior as used immediately in v 18; 2:26; 8:4, and in 1:32 where "rules to obey" is the meaning. Hence the common meaning here of justification is wrong and unparalleled anywhere in the New Testament. Thus Paul's contrast refers to the sphere of enslavement unbelievers find themselves in, issuing in sinful acts (*katakrima*), versus the sphere of liberation believers find themselves in, stemming from God's gift (*dōrēma*), issuing in righteous actions (*dikaiōma*).

5.17. For (*gar*) is an explanatory conjunction that Paul uses to further clarify the parallels, of the consequential truth, taught in the previous verse. Adam's sin in Genesis 2:17 became **the one man's offense** by which **death reigned** (*ebasileusen*). The Greek aorist past tense verb *ebasileusen* and its meaning here views death's reign as a tyrant-king that "ruled" from the time of Adam's first sin until now. Therefore men were ruled by death through the power of sin in their lives that resulted in a death-oriented-experience (6:23). Men are therefore under the *katakrima* (penal servitude) of sin mentioned in v 16.

By contrast **much more** (see *fortiori* explanation in 5:6, 9) **those who receive abundance** (cf. v 15) **of grace and of the gift**

of righteousness will reign in life through the One, Jesus Christ.
Since death had automatic dominion over those born of Adam Paul
did not say that the subjects of death reigned in death, because
death exercises dominion over them (Murray, *Romans*, 1:197). Yet,
those who *will reign in life* are only those who *receive the gift of righteousness.* This is important. In Romans 3:21–4:25 Paul stressed the
importance of responding to God's righteousness through faith in
Christ. Thus only those who *receive* Him are the recipients of grace.
As a result of this, universalism receives the death knell. Since men
are under the "penal servitude" due to their unrighteousness, God
must supply His righteousness if humanity will ever escape their
enslavement to sin. Hence only those who receive the free gift of
eternal life (5:15) *will reign in life.* Contextually the future reign
here does not necessarily refer to the saints' future reign with Christ,
but to a "logical" future (Moo, *Romans*, 340) of the present experience of life that Paul developed earlier by the phrase "through Him"
and "by His life," in 5:9-10. This is precisely what Paul surfaces here
and in chapter 6. The means by which this *reign in life* manifesting
righteous acts comes is *through ... Christ.* This is nothing less than
the resurrection-life experience that Paul begins to develop here but
completely discloses in 6:1-23.

5:18. Therefore (*ara oun*, lit. "so then") is Paul's way of
summarizing the basic argument he began in v 12. He clarified
other related issues in vv 13-14, and finally elaborated the parallel
between Adam and Christ in vv 15-17. Now he basically repeats
the same truth expressed in v 16 that he elaborated in v 17. Because
of the **one man's offense** ("false step," cf. vv 14-15) **judgment
came to all men** (resounding the truth of v 12), this resulted in
condemnation ("penal servitude," cf. v 16) issuing in disobedience. By the contrasting use of "just as" begun in v 12, **even so**
completes this parallel between Adam and Christ that Paul will

carry to v 19 (Dunn, *Romans 1–8*, 282-83; Cranfield, *Romans*, 1:284, 289). Two things are noted here as this section comes to a climatic end: (1) The **one Man's** (Christ as in vv 15, 17, 19) **righteous act** (*dikaiōmatos*, cf. v 16) may refer to Christ's complete life of obedience (Schrenk, *TDNT*, 2:221-22) that culminates and makes His atonement valid. Although this is theologically true, however, *dikaiōmatos* appears in the singular form implying one act, not numerous acts, as the plural form would suggest. In addition, to conclude that this refers to Christ's obedient life weakens Paul's parallel maintained throughout between Adam's one trespass (vv 15-19) and the one sacrificial act of Christ in Romans 3:24-26 (Dunn, *Romans 1–8*, 283). This dovetails perfectly with Christ's *righteous act* termed "obedience" (v 19) also in the singular form. Thus, Paul refers to Christ's work at the cross as the *righteous act that furnishes wha people must receive, the **free gift** that supplies life.* (2) Paul's last point is that **justification of life** (*dikaiōsin zōēs*), in the NKJV, could be translated as "righteousness that leads to life" known as a genitive of result (cf. BDF, 166). This captures the contextual thrust best (of vv 9-10, 16-17) and echoes Paul's point again of the righteousness received that supplies the ability to live the resurrection-life.

5.19. For (*gar*, explanatory particle) Paul elaborates further what he just said in v 18. Adam's **disobedience** that caused **many** to be **made sinners** parallels Christ's **obedience** that **many will be made** (*katastathēsontai*) **righteous** (*dikaios*). As *disobedience* expresses Adam's one act (of Gen 2:17), *obedience* expresses Christ's one act at the cross (of John 19:30). While the *many* in Adam correctly refers to all humanity (cf. first part of vv 15, 18), the *many* in Christ refers only to "those who receive … the gift of righteousness" (v 17, cf. second half of vv 15-16). Finally, Paul may mean by the future verb *katastathēsontai* that many people *will be made* *righteous* forensically, by faith, "throughout future generations" (Murray, *Romans*, 1:206). This is unlikely for three reasons: (1) Although the term *dikaios* in 1:17 expresses the forensic concept, in 5:7 Paul uses it with its other customary meaning of an upright person who behaves properly. (2) The usual Greek word used by Paul in Romans of declaring a person righteous is *dikaioō* (3:24, 26, 28, 30). (3) Contextually one should interpret *katastathēsontai* as a logical future (cf. 5:9-10, 17; Fitzmyer, *Romans*, 421). Paul views believers, by virtue of receiving the gift of righteousness, as those who *will be made righteous* (as in vv 17-18) as behaving righteously by the process of sanctification as they live the resurrection-life mentioned in chapter 6.

5:20-21. In case some are wondering about the **law**, Paul said it **entered** (*pareiserchomai*) **that** (*hina*) **the offense** (cf. vv 15-19) **might abound**. The term *pareiserchomai* should be translated "come in beside" (BDAG, 774). Galatians 2:4 is the only other place where the term appears carrying a negative connotation as it usually does in the New Testament era. Thus Paul implies that the Law "as a side issue" has no "primary place in the divine plan" (cf. BDAG, 774) because it could not change Adam's situation. Similarly, Galatians 3:19 emphasizes the same purpose. That is, the *law* came along side with the purpose (hence the *hina* clause) that the *offense* (i.e., *paraptōma* means "sin"; BDAG, 770) might *abound* (lit. "increase") and give people knowledge of sin (cf. 3:20; 7:13), since it could not change man's disposition but disclose it. **But where sin** increased, **grace abounded much more** (*hyper-perisseuō*). The word *hyperperisseuō* means "to be very high on a scale of amount" (BDAG, 1034). Sin can never begin to match God's immense grace found in Jesus Christ.

So immense and powerful is God's grace described in 20*b* **that** (*hina*, introduces a purpose clause with the goal to depose sin's reign by grace's reign) **as sin reigned in** (*en*) **death . . . grace might reign through righteousness**. Paul spoke, in vv 14, 17, of death reigning, but now refers to sin's reign as a king *in death*. The ambiguous *en* may be rendered in various ways: "sin reigned with death" (i.e., accompaniment), "sin reigned through death" (i.e., instrumentally), or "sin reigned in the realm of death" (i.e., sphere). The latter seems best since the sphere where death reigned, in vv 16-17, is the same where sin reigns as king. Nevertheless, God's immense grace as a powerful king establishes its throne **through** (by means of) **righteousness** (*dikaiosynē*) in the lives of believers by overthrowing sin's monarchy. However, although this over-throwing of sin occurs in one sense at justification, Paul's idea here refers to the grace-rule that believers will manifest in living right-eously as chapter 6 shows: "present . . . your members as instru-ments of righteousness to God" (v 13), "obedience leading to right-eousness" (v 16), "slaves of righteousness" (v 18) and "you were free in regard to righteousness" (v 20). Hence, the purpose of believers is **to** (*eis*, preposition indicating purpose) experience **eternal life** similar to the purpose in 6:22 that shows believers being set free from sin "leading [*eis*] to sanctification, and the end is eternal life" (NET). Thus Paul concludes by showing how all of this is possible **through Jesus Christ our Lord** (cf. the phrases "through Him" and "by His life" in 5:9-10) as chapter 6 develops.

6

RESURRECTION POWER THAT THRIVES

3. Justified believers should live resurrection lives (6:1-23)

The typological parallels of Adam with Christ from 5:12-21 were foundational. Paul's groundwork served to assure Christians of the realm change necessary to overcome sin and experience the life that the sanctification of chapters 6–8 will unfold. Thus God's provision of righteousness involves much more than a righteous declaration of freedom from the penalty of sin through Christ (5:6-8). It also provides the strength to overcome the resident power of sin through the Holy Spirit (5:5) to fulfill God's demands (8:4). Paul does not mention the Spirit until chapter 8, because he chose to conceal any mention until his readers fully realized their severe need of aid to fulfill God's demands. With that need in mind, chapter 6 serves as a prelude to bring believers to the realization of the resurrection life in them that chapter 8 covers.

Chapter 6 divides logically into two sections, vv 1-14 and vv 15-23, signaled by the rhetorical question, "What then" in v 1 and v 15. This section contains seven key concepts: *Sin* (6:1, 2, 6 [2x], 7, 10, 11, 12, 13, 15, 16, 18, 20, 22, 23) *die* or *death* (vv 2, 4, 7, 8, 9 [2x], 10 [2x], 11, 13), *know* (vv 3, 6, 9, 16), *reckon* (v 11), *present* (v 13), *slaves* (vv 6, 16 [2x], 17-18, 19 [2x], 20, 22), and *righteousness* (vv 13, 16, 18, 19, 20). Also, chapter 6 may be divided thematically: vv 1-11 stress positional deliverance from the realm of sin's power and vv 12-23 develop the practical duty to become slaves of righteousness to God. This explains the indicative/imperative verb combinations stressed in these verses, e.g., "he who has died has been freed from sin" and "do not let sin reign in your mortal body" (6:7, 12).

6:1. What shall we say then? In typical Pauline style, the author transitions from a previously taught truth by raising (through an imaginary objector) a question to further his argument (lit. Gk "What then, shall we say?" cf. 3:1; 6:15). Paul, after having taught in v 20 that if sin "abounded" God's grace "abounded much more," suggests someone might ask: **Shall we continue in sin that grace may abound?** Perhaps legalistic people spread rumors that Paul's teaching of God's free grace gave people a license to sin more (3:7-8). Hence libertarians could have reasoned, "Why not sin more if it results in experiencing more grace?"

6:2. Paul emphatically rejects such absurd logic: **Certainly not!** This strongest denial in Greek expresses shock and occurs frequently (cf. 3:4) in Romans, and Paul always uses it after a ridiculous question. The thought that God's free grace gave license for Christians to sin was detestable to Paul. Hence he replies rhetorically: **How shall we who died to sin** (i.e., with reference to sin's realm; cf. Wallace, *Greek Grammar,* 145) **live any longer in it?** Christians, dying to the realm of sin, becomes Paul's main theme in vv 2-13. He personified death or sin as a reigning king in 5:14, 17, and 21 that rules unbelievers. Through vivid imagery Paul pictures how believers died to sin's dominion at the point of justification (v 7). Therefore as death transfers one to another realm, believers' are transferred from the realm of sin and death's dominion (vv 6-7, 9-12, 14, 17-22) to a new realm of power found in resurrection-life (cf. vv 4-5, 8, 10-11, 13, 18-20, 22-23).

Yet, Paul's rhetorical question (*How shall we . . . live any longer in it?*) raises other questions. Does Paul mean: (1) Christians *cannot* sin *at all*, (2) Christians *do not habitually* sin or (3) Christians *must not* sin? The options are: (*a*) Christians *cannot* sin because they no longer live *positionally* in the realm of sin and death. Yet persisting in sin (as Scripture and experience widely supports) is not the same as living in its realm. That is, a foreigner may practice habits customary in his home land while living in another land. Therefore removal from a realm does not necessarily result in relinquishing all old habits. (*b*) Adherents to the first view go on to acknowledge two realities: Paul addresses believers in chapter 6 and *true* believers cannot live as if sin *continually* rules (Moo, *Romans*, 352, 358). Thus Christians *do not habitually* sin. Such a view is fraught with difficulties. For one it strips Paul's use of imperatives of any real significance (vv 12-13). Why command holy living if it will automatically occur? It also introduces a distinction (*committing sin habitually* vs. *committing sins*) foreign to chapters 6–8. In fact, if one believes Christians cannot go one day without sinning, what else can it be called but habitual sin (1 John 1:8, 10)? (*c*) The last option fits best. Paul suggests that to deliberately continue sinning is abhorrent and unimaginable. It is inconceivable to think grace encourages sin. Sin is never an authentic Christian experience. The fact that one can abuse grace is real (or else why pen chaps 6–8) but repugnant to Paul. Christians *should not* and *must not* sin as a pattern! This view gives the only logical reason why Paul warns against abusing grace (in 6:1) and why he commands (in 6:12) that Christians must not sin. Why say this if Christians could not repeatedly practice old habits?

6:3-4. Paul elaborates fully here the positional reality believers find themselves in expressed by the idea of "died to sin" introduced in v 2. In fact, Paul probably expects them to **know** (as in 6:16; 7:1; 11:2) since he asks rhetorically: **do you not *know* that as many of us as were baptized** (from *baptizō*) **into Christ Jesus**

were baptized into His death? *Baptizō* means total immersion
with a reference to dying something completely different (Oepke,
TDNT, 1:529-30). However, what did Paul mean: (1) Water baptism, (2) metaphorical use of baptism, or (3) Spirit baptism?

(*a*) Few scholars deny the imagery of water baptism. Paul uses
water baptism in 1 Cor 1:13-17; 15:29. Since numerous New
Testament examples exist showing that when people believed they
were immediately water baptized (Acts 2:37-38; 8:13, 35-36;
10:43-47; 16:14-15, 31-34), Paul may use this imagery to indicate
the reality. Yet, the context indicates a real death for Christians, not
merely a water rite, but a judicial act that occurs at death "with
Christ" (see view 3). This would imply water baptism judicially
saves, a view unfounded in the New Testament. Close similarities
appear in Col 2:11-12 where the phrase "made without hands"
prevents the water baptism view.

(*b*) Paul may be using baptism as a metaphor for death to
vividly depict a believer's death with Christ. This type of usage was
well attested in the classical and New Testament period (LSJM,
305-6, MM, 102). In other places Christ associated the baptism-
metaphor with death (Matt 20:22; Mark 10:38; Luke 12:50). This
would then mean: All that were *put to death* (baptized) into Christ
Jesus were *participants by death* (baptized) into His death (cf. 2 Cor
5:14-15; Dunn, *Romans 1–8*, 312-13). Paul uses baptism as a
metaphor for death that severed believers from sin's power. While
this is true, this view does not explain both aorist passive verbs
ebaptisthēmen (baptized) in v 3 implying believers received the
action performed by another. Perhaps one may understand that
believers undergo a death baptism (metaphorically) caused by sin,
directly answering why the passive verbs occur. However the context does not allow the interpretation of a metaphorical baptism
symbolizing spiritual death, but a real judicial event that at the

moment of faith in Jesus believers die to sin and are raised in *new-ness of life* with Christ. Hence the Spirit must be the baptizing agent in this event (cf. John 3:1-8).

(c) Thus, Spirit baptism fits best. First, the context suggests not a mere ritual of water baptism or metaphorical death for believers, but a judicial participation when all **were buried with Him through** (*dia*) **baptism into death** (cf. Gal 2:20). Second, the instrumental use of *dia* (=through) makes Spirit *baptism* the vehicle by which believers participate in Christ's death. Further, *baptized into Christ* finds a close parallel in 1 Cor 12:13 that speaks of being baptized by the Spirit into Christ's body, both of which are done by the Spirit simultaneously at the point of faith in Christ (cf. Col 2:11-12). The Spirit appears in the larger context (chap 8) furnishing the practical solution acquired by a believer's positional status at regeneration (8:9). Furthermore, Paul consistently uses the phrase *baptism in the name* when he speaks of water baptism (1 Cor 1:13-15; cf. Matt 28:19; Acts 2:38; 8:16; 10:48; 19:5), but when speaking of the Spirit's baptism he uses the phrase *baptism into Christ* (1 Cor 12:13; Gal 3:27).

Believers did not only die to the old realm like and with Christ, but God's purpose is **that** (*hina*, begins a purpose clause) **just as Christ was raised from the dead** (cf. 4:24; 8:11) **by the glory** (used synonymously here for God's power, cf. Exod 15:6; 1 Chr 16:28; Ps 145:11; Eph 1:19; Col 1:11; 2:12; 1 Pet 4:11; Rev 1:6; 4:11; 5:12; 7:12; 19:1) **of the Father even so** (=*houtōs kai*) **we also should walk in newness** (from *kainotēs*) **of life** (cf. Gal 2:20; 5:16ff.). The believers became united with Christ by Spirit baptism in two ways: The *with* (=*syn*; cf. "we died with,"=*apethanomen syn Christō* in v 8) compound showed they were buried with Him, and the comparison connector *houtōs kai* shows the believers' link to Christ's resurrection life (cf. "we shall live with"= *syzēsomenin*, v

8*b*) which they also share. This life, according to the Greek term *kainotē* (=newness; cf. 6:4), has "the implication of superiority" in quality (Louw & Nida, *Lexical Semantics*, 58:70). Until now Paul has spoken about *freedom from* sin not *freedom to* sin. Thus the penalty of sin was broken in our participation in death with Christ; but the power of sin is crushed when believers live in new resurrection-life since they are also raised with Him. Christians need not, and should not, live in the old realm (cf. Gal 2:20; 5:24; 6:14). Paul will unfold this wonderful truth in the next six verses.

6:5. The structure of vv 5-7 and vv 8-10 present a similar syntax and concept. Verses 5 and 8 both begin with conditional statements (*ei*= if) presenting a fact that believers died and rose with Christ (cf. vv 5, 8). Verses 6 and 9 then explain the significance of death by using at the beginning of the sentence the participle "knowing" (*ginōskontes* and *eidotes*). Then in vv 7 and 10 each begin with an explanatory conjunction "for" (*gar*) to further clarify. Thus, the English words *if . . . knowing . . .* and *for* illustrate the parallel syntax and concept each sentence presents (cf. Congdon, "New Real" in *Abiding to be Bold*).

For (*gar*) is conjunction used to explain the *new resurrection life* that believers possess mentioned at the end of v 4. Paul reiterates the truth of v 4 by using stronger terms: Since (not **if**) **we have been united together in the likeness of His death,** this statement assumes the reality of the union believers participated in at Christ's death. Logically, since Christ also rose this guarantees the following reality believers experience with Christ: **we also shall be** (*esometha*) **in the likeness** of (="united with Him," NIV) ***His* resurrection.** The future verb tense *esometha* should not be understood as a strict-future but a logical-future (cf. 5:9-10). Paul does not refer to the eschatological resurrection of believers at Christ's second coming. That is foreign to the context. His idea is this:

Since believers, by faith in Christ, share in Christ's *death*, so they also, by faith, share logically in *His resurrection*. This refers to the power believers presently possess in order to overcome the power of sin in their lives (vv 6, 11, 13).

6:6. As a result of the truth of v 4, **knowing this** serves to further Paul's argument: The **old man was crucified with** Christ (as vv 4*a* and 5*a*) for the purpose (**that**=*hina*, begins a purpose clause) of overcoming the lordship of sin.

The *old man* refers to the person Christians were prior to becoming believers. Considerable confusion exists about the use of the expressions "old man" or "new man" (cf. Col 3:9-10; Eph 4:22-24). These are but appropriate figures of speech to portray the change that occurs at regeneration. The expression "old man" connotes the unredeemed life in Adam with its inherent corrupt disposition, and the expression "new man" represents the redeemed life in Christ with its inherent upright disposition (Showers, "*The New Nature*," [Th. D. diss, Grace Theological Seminary, 1975], 40). *New man* may also be understood as "the church" composed of Jews and Gentiles (Eph 2:15; perhaps the following passages should be interpreted likewise in Eph 4:24; Col 3:10-11, 15). Unfortunately these expressions are often thought to refer to the essence that make up a person's nature, and thus equate person and nature. Crucial to understanding Paul's argument here and in chapters 7:13-25; 8:10-11 one must distinguish between *person* and *nature*. Often the term "nature" is thought of as a *kind of substance* or *essence*. This is incorrect. Human nature refers generally *to a complex of attributes* (Buswell, *Theology*, 1:251; II:52) and narrowly *to an inherent inclination* or *disposition* that affects the conduct and character of a person (Showers, "*New Nature*," 6-8, 23-26). Thus at regeneration a person was judicially acquitted and received two things: (1) a new supernaturally endowed disposition (to comply with God's mandates) similar to the endowment of spiritual gifts which are not part of any metaphysical substance, and (2) the Holy Spirit to aid believers through the newly endowed disposition to obey; but the regenerate man remains no less the same metaphysical person with the entire complex of attributes of fallen humanity in Adam (Showers, *New Nature*, 19, 23, 26). Hence it is wrong to understand a person's nature as altered at the spiritual level, but not at the fleshly level (i.e., the body). This understanding results in a dualism (see the critic by Howe, a review of *Birthright*, by David C. Needham *Bsac* 141 [January 1984]: 69-78). Two things may be said against this approach: If the new *you* (=the new spiritual nature) becomes a new ontological entity and the body remains sinful, when the "I" sins, who sins (cf. 7:15-16, 18-21)? Furthermore, the believer's whole person is described in 1 Corinthians 6:19-20 as being redeemed by Christ (see how the *you* pronouns refer to the complete personal entity, not just the spirit as set above unredeemed flesh). A correct view understands that believers receive the gift of the indwelling Spirit, who works wonderfully in conjunction with prayer and God's Word to produce fruits. At the point of regeneration, a new complex of attributes are added to the believer that differ radically from the ones inherited in Adam. Thus at regeneration man was *judicially* acquitted, received a *new disposition* (not a spirit or person but a *new inclination* that is not made up of any essence but a supernatural ability empowered by the Holy Spirit to comply with God's mandate) and simultaneously the *Spirit indwelled* him. Hence this effected a *real* change in order to release man from sin's grip.

God's purpose for crucifying the *old man . . . with Him* is for man to control the old disposition inherent in fallen humanity (cf. Pentecost, *Designed to Be Like Him*, 91-92, 99-100), thus doing away with **the body of sin**. The expression *body of sin* may be understood in various ways: (1) The phrase *body of sin* may be a figurative reference. That is, the mass of sin as a body having many members. This may be too subtle. (2) The physical material body controlled by *sin*. This is too narrow a view based on how Paul uses *body* in other places as the whole person (see above; cf. 7:24; 8:10). (3) Hence Paul's meaning is the whole man where *sin* resides seen manifested through the *body*. Paul uses the expression *body* as a synecdoche (a part [body] stands for the whole [body + spirit = man], cf. Gen 6:12; Prov 1:16; John 12:19) for *man*, because that is where sin visibly manifests itself. Thus since the *old man was crucified* that *the body of sin* **be done away** (from *katargeō*, aorist passive, to render ineffective or powerless by an agent), one **should no longer be slaves of sin.** That is, the passive voice of the verb *katargeō*, translated *destroyed* by the RSV, may indicate the Spirit is the agent that rendered *the body of sin* (="body of death" in 7:24) powerless at regeneration. The *hina* conjunction *that* indicates the purpose the *body of sin* (i.e., the whole man controlled by the Adamic disposition) was disannulled not eradicated (cf. Pentecost, *Designed to Be Like Him*, 99-100); this occurred in order that sin *would no longer dominate us* (NET). All believers are removed from sin's domain of power. Since sin has been dethroned, only when one heeds sin's call can it exercise dominion over man's realm.

6:7. For (*gar*) serves to explain Paul's clinching argument: **he who has died has been freed** (*dedikaiōtai* from *dikaioō*) **from sin.** The perfect tense Greek word *dedikaiōtai* literally means, "has been justified or declared righteous." Paul's choice of tense and word here suggests that the believer's liberation from sin was completed by justification in the past with ongoing results. Thus, sin's claim on believers legally ended when they believed in Christ.

6:8. Paul reiterates in vv 8-10 what he mentioned in vv 5-7 (cf. v 5), but introduces a new concept: Since (not **if**) **we** are *now* dead

with Christ, we believe (*pisteuomen*) **that we shall** (*syzēsomen*) **also** *now* **live with Him** (*autō*) as well. Paul's new concept here refers to the Christian's cognitive state that should affect behavior. Christians must not only know the facts just previously stated that they have died to sin's enslavement, but they must also *believe* (or be confident) they possess power to live now since they *live with Him* (i.e., in the realm of the resurrection-power). The present tense *pisteuomen* may imply "to keep on *believing*" in order to affect behavior and not cease when one fails to live in a Christ-like manner. Even if the verb *syzēsomen* (*we shall...live*) appears as a future tense, the context clearly refers to the Christian life that one *now* has *with Him* (cf. v 5; 5:9). The expression *with Him* could be classified as dative of reference, i.e., "we shall live *with reference to Him*," or dative of means, i.e., "we shall live *by means of Him*." Both are valid options here. Christians live with reference to their union with Christ and by means of the resurrection power they have *with Him* (Carballosa, *Romanos*, 127).

6:9-10. As a result of the truth of v 8, **knowing that** serves to affirm believers of their power over sin and death. The basis of Paul's logic refers to how **Christ, having been raised from the dead, dies no more.** Hence if *death* **no longer has dominion** (*kyrieuei*, reign as lord) **over Him**, it should not rule over Christians. **For** (*gar*) explains why that is so: ***the death* that He died, He died to sin** (i.e., in reference to sin's realm; cf. v 2 and below) **once for all.** In Christ's earthly life death in a sense had dominion over Him, because He (though sinless) died for our sins (e.g., 3:24-26; 4:25; 5:6-8; 8:3; 1 Cor 15:3; 2 Cor 5:21; Gal 3:13). Yet contextually Paul does not desire to stress Christ's substitutionary atonement, but the event that took "place once and to the exclusion of any further occurrence" (BDAG, 417, cf. Heb 7:27; 9:12, 28; 10:10, contra Roman Catholicism that teaches Christ's perpetual sacrificial death). Hence Christ's death was not a triumph for sin; instead, death released Him from the power of sin to hurt Him anymore (Robinson, *The Body*, 42). In contrast (seen through the contrastive sequential marker **but**), *the life* **that He lives, He lives** (*zē*, the present tense indicates ongoing action) **to God** (*tō theō*). The expression *to God* may be understood as a dative of reference: "He lives continually in resurrection power *with reference to God*." That is, while on earth, Christ always lived for God, but not in the same sense as after the resurrection. Now Christ's resurrection-power allows Him to fulfill God's purpose *with reference* to the new and powerful realm of existence (cf. 1:4); and so it is for the believer who possesses resurrection power that Paul develops in the following section.

6:11. Shifting from the indicative to the imperative mood, Paul supersedes positional instruction with practical exhortation: **Likewise** (*houtōs*) **you also, reckon** (lit. means "to calculate or consider") **yourselves to be dead indeed to sin** (i.e., with reference to sin; cf. vv 2, 10). The term *houtōs* points back to the correspondent reality between Christ's experience of dying to sin and living "to God" (v 10) and the attitude believers must adopt by reckoning themselves *dead to sin*, **but alive to God in Christ Jesus our Lord**. Paul does not only mean to draw an inference from v 10, but to the entire set of truths mentioned from vv 1-10. Christians are commanded to continually "calculate" (=*logizesthe*, present middle imperative; cf. 4:3) the reality of being dead to sin (similarly to how *pisteuomen* in v 8 functions) since they are positionally *in Christ Jesus*, and *alive with reference* to God's new and powerful realm of existence similar to Christ's (v 10).

6:12. Having established in v 11 that Christians undergo a death to life transference upon believing, Paul exhorts believers in vv 12-14 to live resurrection-lives by working. Verses 12-14 form a chiastic structure *a-b-c-b-a*. The imperative phrase of v 12 (*a*) "do not let sin reign" matches the indicative phrase of v 14 (*a*) "sin shall not have dominion." Also the imperative phrase in v 13 (*b*) "do not present your members as instruments of unrighteousness to sin," is balanced by the implied imperatival phrase of v 13 (*b*) "[present] your members as instruments of righteousness to God." But Paul's central thought is developed by the imperatival phrase in v 13 (*c*) "present yourselves to God as being alive from the dead" (cf. Congdon, "New Real" in *Abiding to be Bold*).

Therefore draws a conclusion that logically commands Christians to live according to their duty **to not let sin reign** (*basileuetō*) **in your mortal bodies.** The present imperatival term *basileuetō* may imply a continuous action that could be rendered: "Stop allowing sin to continuously rule." Obviously, since Paul commands this prohibition, it implies Christians may allow sin to rule **in** their **mortal** (*thnētos*, lit., "liable to death," Louw & Nida, *Lexical Semantics*, 23:124) **body** (a person's life; cf. v 6; 7:24) if effort is not put forth to stop obeying sin **in its lusts** (i.e., strong desire). The dying *body* is the vehicle where sin manifests itself visibly, since the metaphysical aspect of man is invisible (cf. v 6). Hence Paul uses the term *body* instead of life. Christians may have strong desires arising from the old disposition still resident in them. But one should neither listen to those desires nor carry them out.

6:13. Paul carries the previous thought of the whole man further to discuss the individual parts of a person's involvement in sin. **And do not** (*mēde*) is a term used elsewhere (cf. 1 John 2:15) that juxtaposes a similar whole-parts correlation. Paul's imperatival prohibition becomes more specific: *And do not* **present** (lit., do not go-on presenting; vv 16, 19) **your members as instruments** (lit., Gk "tools" or "weapon") **of unrighteousness to sin.** Concretely speaking, the body has extensions (e.g., feet, hands, tongue, ears, mouth and eyes; cf. 3:13-18) that are either used as "tools" to build God's kingdom or "weapon" to tear it down.

But all human tools can be brought under control by heeding Paul's command: **present** (*parastēsate*) **yourselves to God as being alive from the dead.** Paul's central thought concerns (cf. 6:12) how the Christian overcomes the strong desires spoken of in v 12. Paul used the Greek term *parastēsate*, used frequently in the LXX of a person placing himself at a king's disposal to serve him (cf. 2 Chr 9:7; Prov 22:29). Thus, *parastēsate* should not be understood as having a passive nuance of "surrender," but the active sense "to place oneself at the disposal" "to serve" (Bertram, *TDNT*, 5:837-38). Hence before believers can *present* (the last clause does not have the Gk word *paristēmi* but it is supplied from 13*a*) their individual **members *as* instruments of** ethical **righteousness** (*dikaiosynēs*, unlike 4:5; cf. 6:19; 8:10) **to God**, the whole person needs to place himself at God's disposal so that his tools will follow. Mustering enough power to overcome sin's dominion is not the meaning here. Instead, by Christians placing themselves continually (implied by the pres imp use of *"paristanete"* in 13*a*) at God's disposal (i.e., attending church, reading the Word, praying, having fellowship, and exercing gifts) by the power of the Spirit they will miraculously begin to *do righteous acts* (cf. 8:4).

6:14. For (*gar*) is marker explaining the result of the previous verse. By heeding the command to "present your members" and "present yourselves to God," logically **sin shall not have dominion** (*kyrieusei*, future tense) **over you.** The future tense here does not function as a promise or a command but as a logical-future stating what is naturally expected. Logically, Christians that obey Paul's command of v 13 will experience the truth contained in v 14: sin will not master the them. Paul further explains (**for**=*gar*) this is possible for believers because they **are not under law but**

under grace. That is, one of the purposes of the Mosaic Law was to expose and condemn sin in the heart. It was never intended to to control it (3:20); in fact, the Law heightened sin (5:20-21; 7:8-12). On the other hand Christians are under the system of *grace* that reigns in power (5:2, 17, 21; 6:23; 7:1-6). Believers died to sin as 6:1-13 showed, and presently stand under a system of grace that supplies the Spirit (5:2, 5; 8:9). Hence, logically, *sin shall* **not have dominion over** Christians because God supplies the necessary means to overcome it under the new system of *grace* (cf. 7:1-6).

6:15. Before discussing Christian liberty fully (7:1-6), Paul opposes the notion that it leads to license. **What then?** This rhetorical question recalls the faulty conclusion of v 1 (stemming from 5:20) that to continue in sin will heighten grace. Here the inference drawn from v 14 raises the question: **Shall we sin because we are not under law but under grace?** The implication is sin does not matter since believers are *under grace*, not *law*. Paul answers with the strongest negative in the Greek: **Certainly not!** Freedom from the Law does not give one license to sin. For Christians have simply exchanged masters, they have not expelled morality.

6:16. Thus Christians are still slaves but now have a choice: to serve their new master in righteousness or return to the old taskmaster of sin and experience death as 6:16-23 will develop. **Do you not know** (cf. 6:3; 7:1; 11:2) is one of many other rhetorical phrases Paul uses to further his argument (cf. 3:1-3). Paul's argument is simple. The master **to whom** Christians **present** (i.e., "to place oneself at the disposal of service"; cf. 6:13) themselves to serve will determine who controls them and what consequence they reap: **obey .. sin** *leading* **to death or obedience** *leading* **to righteousness** (*dikaiosynēn*)? The contrasting terms *death* and *righteousness* may seem odd. For one may expect Paul to contrast "death" with "life." However, Paul uses the term *righteousness* because he wants to convey "moral behavior," which is what will issue from believers if they choose to obey. This contrast does not emphasize one's positional status, i.e., eternal death vs. eternal life (=*righteousness*). Rather the immediate context refers to the potential experience of the Christian. Believers can experience the present separation (*death*) of fellowship from God by living in sin (cf. 6:21; 8:11-13). In contrast, *dikaiosynēn* in this section refers to "moral righteousness" (Moo, *Romans*, 400) not final justification since Paul uses it in like manner in vv 13, 19-20. Paul may be understood in light of Moses' statement in Deuteronomy 30:15: "See, I have set before you today life and good, death and evil." As Moses set forth two choices for the Israelites to make, Paul sets forth two choices for Christians to make: *Obey sin and experience broken fellowship from God* or *obey God and experience the moral righteousness that allows a Christian to experience life* (cf. 1:17; 5:18; 6:22-23, 8:13).

6:17. In recognition that God makes overcoming sin possible by His grace (v 14), Paul says, **God be thanked.** He explains why: **though you were** (*ēte*) **slaves of sin, yet you obeyed from the heart that form** (*typos*) **of doctrine to which you were delivered** (*paredothēte*). The imperfect verb *ēte* conveys a past continuous action. That is, prior to becoming Christians people were *continuously* in bondage to sin. However, this is not the believers' present position. They *obeyed* at a point in time (hence the aorist verb *hypēkousate*) *that form of doctrine* which may be understood as believing in Christ; but this act should not be confined to exclude Christian doctrine that is to "mold" (hence *typos* is used; cf. Goppelt, *TDNT*, 8:250; Moo, *Romans*, 402) the lives of believers (cf. 1:5; 10:16; 16:26). The only other mention of the term *doctrine* in Romans occurs in 16:17. Paul uses *doctrine*, being the object of what believers *obeyed* here, in a similar way to remind believers of the "doctrine" they "learned" in 16:17 in order to mold them to serve the Lord (v 18) (Cranfield, *Romans*, 1:324). Hence believers were delivered (*paredothēte*). The passive form of the verb suggests something done to believers. Usually Paul refers to "delivered" as tradition or teaching "handed over" to the church (cf. 1 Cor 11:2, 23; 15:3). Yet, here, it is not the doctrine that is delivered to Christians but Christians that are delivered to doctrine. Though unusual, Paul wants to convey two points: That deliverance from sin's mastery begins by faith in Christ (by dying with Him in baptism), and continues by obedience to this doctrine, as a resurrection-outgrowth of God's "handing us over" to this doctrine at the moment of faith (Moo, *Romans*, 401). Roman readers could have remembered *paradidōmi* from chapter 1 to which unbelievers were given over to sin's slavery (1:24, 26, 28), but now as Christians they are handed over by God to a new realm of power to serve as slaves of righteousness (6:16; cf. Goppelt, *TDNT*, 8:250).

6:18. To confirm the new status and realm where believers reside **having been set free** (*eleutherōthentes*) **from sin**, Paul uses "freedom" language for the first time. The passive voice of the verb *eleutherōthentes* indicates God was the One that set Christians free from the lordship of sin. Also, the passive voice of the verb *edoulōthēte* (=**you became slaves**) indicates God placed Christians under a new mastery and realm **of righteousness** by which they can serve. Thus, as a result, all believers are legal slaves of God set free to resist sin and to live as slaves *of righteousness* (i.e., moral righteousness).

6:19. Paul moves from the believers' position of legal righteousness of v 18 to exhorting believers to live righteously, but not before adding a disclaimer: **I speak in human *terms*.** Paul understood the imagery of "slavery" to be contrary to the believer's loving and personal relationship to God. However, he uses this language **because of the weakness of your flesh**. The phrase *weakness of your flesh* refers to a lack of ability to make sound moral judgments (BDAG, 142; cf. 8:26). That is, because the flesh (=fallen humanity, cf. 7:5; 8:4) desires to live independently of God, Paul uses slavery language to convey the Christian's moral duty (Käsemann, *Romans*, 182) as he did for himself in 1:1.

By using the language of comparison (**just as**; cf. v 13) Paul explains that Christians ought to have the same zeal for living righteously that they had for living sinfully. Paul employed a double imperative in v 13 to contrast what believers should and should not do. Now he employs an aorist indicative verb **presented** (*parestēsate*) to characterize pre-conversion behavior, contrasted to an aorist imperative verb **present** (*parastēsate*), to indicate what believers must do post-conversion. Paul may be recalling the pre-conversion experience of 1:18-32 since the only other use of *uncleanness* (*akatharsia*) occurs in 1:24 where, as a result of being "handed over," the zeal to sin consumed the unbeliever. Likewise, with that same zeal, Paul commands believers: **present your members** (cf. v 13) *as* **slaves *of* righteousness for holiness**. The contrasting imagery is startling: As service of *uncleanness* results in an increase of *lawlessness* so doing righteousness results in being set-apart in progressive sanctification to serve God (cf. v 22)

6:20-23. The structure at the end of this chapter is as follows: (1) The consequences of the pre-conversion life are noted in vv 20-21, (2) this is contrasted to the post-conversion life in v 22, and (3) both contrasting aspects of life's principles are finally summarized in v 23.

For (*gar*) is an explanatory marker pointing to Paul's second reason (begun in v 19*b*) why believers should not continue in sin but *must* present themselves as "slaves to righteousness," or else be enslaved like unbelievers. Thus human independence that people pride themselves over is **free in regard to** *not practicing moral* **righteousness** that really enslaves. God's power does *not* have an inner affect on the unbeliever in reference *to righteousness* (dative of reference). As unbelievers are not *free* (i.e., not bound) to live righteously because they are enslaved by sin, believers are totally free *only* when they live righteously (cf. John 8:32).

Unbelievers as a result of living this way reap the fruit of their labor, death. Various commentators (cf. Moo, *Romans*, 407; Dunn, *Romans 1–8*, 348; Cranfield, *Romans*, 1:328) indicate that one should punctuate with a question mark *then* (*tote*) in v 21*a*: **What fruit did you have then** [?]. That is, the only *fruit* believers had prior to conversion shamed them. Reading it as such brings out the clear antithetical parallelism in vv 20-21 and 22:

	Position	Product	End Result
"then" (*tote*):	free from righteousness	fruit resulting in shame	Death
"now" (*nyni*):	slaves of God, free from sin	fruit resulting in sanctification	Eternal Life

Then contrary to most versions (ASV, NASB, NIV, KJV, NKJV, NET) the punctuation in the original Greek occurs right after "then" (*tote*). Thus, Paul teaches that unbelievers bear *fruit* (cf. 7:5). In fact, the context indicates this type of fruit shames and enslaves, which leads to uncleanness and lawlessness (vv 19-21). The **end of those things** *is* **death**. While *death* for non-Christians is eternal, it also includes a present experience of death that sin always brings that Paul believes Christians (though eternally secure; cf. 8:28-39) can experience if they do not obey his commands (vv 12-13, 19; 8:12-13).

While disobedient Christians can live experiencing death, this is always an unnatural Christian experience, which is Paul's very point contextually. Hence he contrasts the previous verse: **But now having been set free from sin, and having become slaves of God, you have your fruit to holiness, and the end, everlasting life.** Paul reiterates the positional truth of Christian freedom from sin (6:7, 18) since they have died to sin's lordship (6:1-2, 6, 10-11) and *become* God's slave. Christians live in the realm of righteousness. Therefore, if believers "present" themselves voluntarily to God in obedience, they will experience the *fruit* (i.e., "benefit") resulting in progressive sanctification, which "goal" (=*telos*) is to experience the fullness of eternal life (cf. John 10:10: 17:3; Rom 5:21; Gal 6:8; 1 Tim 6:12, 19).

In v 23, Paul summarizes both contrasting aspects of life principles of vv 20-22, and also crystallizes the entire chapter's subject matter in one pithy sentence. **For** (*gar*) is an explanatory particle linking vv 20-22 by clarifying the contrasting ends of both ways of life, **the wages** (*opsōnia*) **of sin** *is* **death, but the gift** (lit. Gk "grace") **of God** *is* **eternal life in Christ Jesus our Lord.** By using the phrase *the wages of sin* (*ta opsōnia tēs hamartias*), Paul personifies sin as a master paying wages (subjective genitive) to slaves. If the sense of "weapons" in v 13 could be read here, then Paul may be using the term *opsōnia* as an imagery of a military commander paying a soldier for services rendered (Cranfield, *Romans*, 1:329). Wages serve to provide the sustenance of life that in this case ends in death. By contrasting *death* and the concept of *wages*, Paul conveys a vivid imagery: The subsistence sin pays ends in death. Sin deceived: While promising life it yields death (7:10-11). Wages is not a single but a continuous payment. Hence *death* should not only be viewed as the final penalty of the unsaved, "but is also the active shadow which this death projects on life" (Heiland, *TDNT*, 5:592) which believers can experience if they enlist.

In contrast, God provides through "grace" (unmerited favor) the means by which believers attain *eternal life* finally and experientially. This is nothing less than the resurrection-life experience that Paul developed in 6:1-23 (5:20-21).

Eternal life at glorification (the last stage of Christian salvation) will transpire in the future (Matt 25:46; Mark 10:30) but it is also a present possession of Christians (John 3:16; 5:24; 6:47). Hence believers may experience the effects of eternal life now since they exist in the realm of resurrection-power (cf. Rom 6:1-14; John 10:10). Thus, though all Christians have eternal life now and can experience it now, the full revelation of this life will not be manifested until the resurrection (1 Cor 15:35-58). While the *death* and *life* motif here is a general principle applicable to everyone, the primary thrust of Paul's point is for believers to overcome the deadly effects of sin and experience life; which in the fullest sense may be called *eternal life* (cf. 5:21). Thus, Paul concludes by stating how Christian victory, as described in chapter 6, is possible: First by being *in . . . Christ* and second by adhering to Him as *Lord* (cf. 5:21).

7
PROBLEMS WITH THE LAW

4. Justified believers have changed regimes: from the Law to the Spirit (7:1-6)

Chapter 7:1-6 returns to the issue raised in 6:14 about the Law's termination. In 6:15-23, Paul digressed to correct a misconception suggesting that freedom from the Law means freedom to be lawless. In vv 1-6, Paul informs believers how they are not under any obligation to keep the Mosaic Law because of their union with Christ. The Law can be viewed as a regime that governed Old Testament people in the way of life. This regime is no longer in power. The new regime of grace through union with Christ governs believers in the way of life by the power of the Spirit that aids believers to obey God.

7:1-3. The apostle spoke to the Roman readers as **to those who know the law**. Since the article *the* before the term *law* is absent in the Greek text, this may refer to "law in general" or "Roman law." However, in Romans Paul never uses the term *law* in a "secular sense" (Moo, *Romans*, 411). The word *law* does not appear with the article in 6:14-15 and most of chapter 7 where the reference is clearly the Mosaic Law. The term *law* appearing without the article commonly refers to the Mosaic Law (cf. 2:12, 17, 25, 27; 3:31; 4:13-14; 10:4, et al., cf. Thayer, *Greek-English Lexicon*, 428). Hence the referent here of the term *law* that Jews and Gentiles (having probably studied in synagogues) had general knowledge of is the Mosaic Law (cf. BDAG, 677).

Paul settled the issue, from 6:15-23, that freedom from the Law does not give license to sin. Now he returns to the concept of 6:14; but he furthers the argument to convey that freedom from **the law** is the solution to sin's **dominion** over the believer (notice how "dominion" is used in 6:9, 14) since the Law intensifies sin in Christians (7:8-11).

The concept of the Law's *dominion* only applying **over a man as long as he lives** leads Paul to use a marriage metaphor to illustrate this principle. A married **woman . . . is bound by law to** *her* **husband.** Only *he*r husband's death can legitimately free her from the bonds of marriage (v 3) according to Old Testament Law (cf. Deut 25:5) since this Law only allowed a husband the right to divorce her (Deut 24:1). Otherwise, if she remarries, **she will be called** (i.e., to be identified publicly) **an adulteress.** Conversely, upon the husband's death, she can marry **another man.** Although considerable debate exists on whether or not the New Testament permits divorce, this issue is not germane to Paul's point. By using the marriage analogy Paul proves that while the Law was operative people were bound to obey it as the women is bound to her husband while he still lives. Now the Law is inoperative. Hence no one is obligated to keep it. In vv 1-3, the two husbands metaphor indicates two types of systems that govern believers. The first husband who dies becomes analogous to the Law. Please note: Paul did not imply believers were *only* released from the ceremonial part of the Law but the entire Mosaic system (cf. Ryrie, *The End of the Law*, 240-41; Moo, "'*Law*,' '*Works of the Law*,'" 73-100). The Jews understood the Mosaic Law as a unified code (Thayer, *Greek-English Lexicon*, 428). It contained the general precepts of the moral law (ten commandments) and the elements of the ceremonial and civil law which detailed how the commandments were to be carried out in everyday life (Exod 20–Num 10; cf. Ryrie, "The End of the Law," 239-47). God terminated the entire code (10:4; 14:17; 2 Cor 3:6-11; Heb 7:12; 9:10; Gal 3:24; 4:9-11; 5:1); which is analogous to the whole man dying. While the husband lived, people were bound to that system understood as the Law (v 2). However, when the husband died, people became free from that system. This allows the remarriage to the second husband; which becomes analogous to the system of grace (known as the "law of Christ," in Gal 6:2; cf. 5:20-21; 6:14). By this Paul means: Husband 1=the Law and husband 2=Christ (v 4). Paul became fond of using the marriage analogy to describe the intimate relationship between Christ and the believer (1 Cor 6:17; 2 Cor 11:2; Eph 5:25-33) as the prophets did with Israel and God (cf. Isa 54:5-6; 62:4-5; Jer 2:2; Ezek 16:7-8; Hos 1:2; 2:19; Dunn, *Romans 1–8*, 362).

7:4-6. Therefore (*hōste*) is a marker of result used to transition by drawing a conclusion from a previous point (cf. vv 6, 12). While vv 1-3 focused only on illustrating how one system became inoperative and the other operative, vv 4-6 switch the focus of the analogy to the believer's relationship to the system. Now believers are the ones who **become dead to the law** (the old system) **through** (*dia* indicates the means) **the body of Christ**. The *body of Christ* refers to the literal body of Christ that died on the cross freeing Him (and us) from the system and penalty of the Law forever (cf. Col 1:22; Heb 10:5, 10; 1 Pet 2:24). Baptism into Christ's death then became the means that severed believers from the Law and allowed marriage **to Him who was raised from the dead**. As His death became our death, His life becomes our life (6:1-10). The purpose of this marriage is to **bear fruit to God** (6:22). Intimacy in marriage issues in the fruit of children, so intimacy with the

Lord will issue in the fruit of good-works (cf. John 15:1-6; Gal 5:23–6:10).

For (*gar*) is an explanatory marker, introducing vv 5-6 parenthetically, to explain v 4. Paul says: **when we were in the flesh.** Though *in the flesh* can refer to an external part of the body (2:28), to the Christian life as being part of this world (2 Cor 10:3; Gal 2:20; Phil 1:22), or to a believer's fallen nature (7:17-18), the phrase here clearly refers to the pre-conversion experience as in 8:8-9. That is, before regeneration people belonged to a sphere where **the sinful passions** (*pathēma*, lit. means "to experience strong physical desire, particularly of a sexual nature; cf. 1:26; Gal 5:24; 1 Thess 4:5) **which were aroused by the law were at work in our members** (i.e., *members* is a synecdoche that stands for the whole person [typically appearing in the OT by naming a body part for the person, cf. Bullinger, *Figures of Speech*, 640-56] that here it emphasizes one's Adamic nature resident in all believers; cf. 6:6; 7:14, 18, 25). As the union with Christ results in good fruit to life (v 4; 6:22), life *in the flesh* prompted by the law produced **fruit to death** (6:21). This was the only option available to the unregenerate. The prohibitions in the law arouse the "fallen nature" to sin, whether unregenerate or regenerate (who still possesses the Adamic nature; cf. 7:7-25), which leads to *death* finally (for unbelievers only) or experientially (for both) (cf. 5:15, 17, 21; 6:16, 21, 23; 7:10-11, 13; 8:2, 6, 10, 13). However, for believers another option exists that is not available to unbelievers.

Paul concludes in v 6 by summarizing vv 1-5: **But now we have been delivered** (*katergēthēmen*) **from the law, having died to what we were held by.** This refers to the Christian's new condition that "rendered powerless or idled" (lit. meaning of *katargeō*) the rule of *the law*. As *the law* "rendered powerless" (*katargeō* as in 6:2) the woman's marital bond at her husband's death, so *the law* was "rendered idle" to condemn Christians as a governing system of life. By Christians dying and being raised with Christ (6:1-10; 7:4), God leveled the playing field. Now Christians have a new disposition (6:6) and Spirit-power **to serve in the newness** (*kainotēs*, lit. "new or different being relatively recent") **of the Spirit and not** *in* **the oldness of the letter.** Paul made this earlier contrast of Spirit/letter in 2:29. Though one may understand the contrast here to refer to spirit of the law, the Holy Spirit seems more probable (cf. 2:29 for comments). The new (cf. *kainotēs* in 6:4) epoch introduced by Christ marks the era of the Spirit (cf. 2:29; 5:5; 8:9) that is lived in terms of the Spirit (8:12-13; Dunn, *Romans 1–8*, 366). Thus contextually Paul is contrasting two spheres of existence for believers by emphasizing that the new era of the Spirit is where their power resides issuing into life (2 Cor 3:6; Rom 8:13).

5. The Law's inability to sanctify believers (7:7-25)

If believers persist on following the Law, Paul warns by penning 7:7-25 that it will result in a defeated Christian experience. Normally people view the Law as a means of sanctification. However, the Law is like a mirror. It can show only what is wrong. It cannot correct it. Since Paul already proved that the Law was worthless in justification (3:20), he now broaches the Law's relationship to progressive sanctification.

7:7-8. Paul has emphatically stated how believers are not under the old system of Law but under the new system of grace (5:20; 6:14; 7:1-6). One might logically conclude that the Law was the problem. Hence Paul rhetorically says: **What shall we say then?** *Is the law sin?* (cf. 3:1; 6:1, 15). To which he retorts: **Certainly not!** Since the Law reveals God's character, it indirectly implies God's character is under attack (cf. 3:4 for comments). **On the contrary, Paul (I) would not have known sin except through the law.** So far

Paul has employed third, second and first person plural pronouns. For the remainder of the chapter, the personal pronoun *I* may be used to indicate Paul's early Christian experience, and the bout he had with sin and *the law*. Or *I* may be used for the sake of vividness in a universal way of speaking of "all of us" (Wallace, *Greek Grammar*, 391-92) believers who, illustrated in 7:7-25, will attempt to use the Law as a means of sanctification (BDAG, 425). The Law reveals sin to the unsaved (3:19-20) as light reveals a dirty stain on a shirt. The light is not the problem; it reveals the problem. **For** (*gar*) Paul, by using an explanatory marker, clarifies the role of *the law* by using one of the Ten Commandments to reveal the problem: **I would not have known covetousness unless the law had said, "You shall not covet."** This last commandment stood for the whole Law by synecdoche (i.e., one part stands for the whole; cf. 6:6; 7:5). By using the tenth commandment, Paul intended to convey that the whole Mosaic Law was terminated (7:2). However, this does not imply Christians may live immorally (6:1-23; 8:1, 4, 13). Believers received a new code called "the law of Christ" (Gal 6:2; 1 Cor 9:20-21) with numerous new mandates mentioned by the Apostles in the epistles. This code repeats some commandments that illustrate how to fulfill the supreme command of the new code to "love": "*You shall love your neighbor as yourself*" (cf. Rom 13:8-10; Gal 5:13-14). Yet, even if some of the commandments are repeated it does not mean the whole Old Testament system carries over. Only the strands reiterated by the Apostles are now worked into the new system that believers must obey with the aid of the Spirit (cf. chap 8; Gal 5:22-25; Eph 4:1–5:18).

Nevertheless, regardless of how good the commandment is, it cannot help the believer overcome sin. **But** instead of the commandment helping one, it produced a strong desire to **sin**. Paul was not using *sin* from 7:7-12 so much as an act, but as *sin* being a compelling force igniting the fallen nature within believers to rebel when confronted with a commandment. Hence Paul says: **For apart from the law sin *was* dead.** Paul does not mean *sin* did not exist *apart* from *the law*, because he already said it does (5:13; cf. 4:15). Instead, apart from the law *sin was dormant* and *inactive*. Sin is like the inactive HIV virus that can lead to AIDS. A person might not know he has it, but all it takes is for it to be activated for the person to know and be consumed by AIDS. The Law becomes that which activates sin within believers allowing them to know and be consumed by sin. The Law precipitates rebellion, not because it is sinful, but because man is. Psychologically when a person focuses on a negative (as the "shall not" of the Law dictates) the pressure heightens making the violation extremely desirable.

7:9-12. The Apostle may now be describing how he experienced the truth of v 8 in Christian infancy: **I was alive (*ezōn*) once without the law.** One may interpret the latter sentence in three possible ways: (1) This may mean *when no law existed*; Paul refers to his existence in Adam in the garden before the command came and Adam sinned (Genesis 2:16ff.; 3:3). (2) It refers to the period of Paul's life prior to his conversion when he was not conscious of the existence and significance of the Law. (3) Yet, in "view of Paul's climactic affirmation in Ro 7:25, Paul probably illustrates in the first person the perils of a Christian who succumbs to the illusion that moral action is connected with Law rather than with the 'spirit of life in Christ'" (BDAG, 425; cf. Rom 8:2). It is highly improbable that Paul uses the verb *ezōn* to describe his pre-conversion experience when he was "dead in trespasses and sins" (cf. Wallace, *Greek Grammar*, 392) since the phrase in v 22 "I delight in the law of God according to the inward man" seems to express the results of a justified man. How can Paul describe his unregenerate experience as *being alive* and being able to *delight in the law*? What does this mean if he is talking about his unregenerate state? How can anyone be *alive without the law* while being in an unregenerate state? However, if Paul refers to the experience of the life of God in believers, then he means: "I was living unhindered as a Christian, until I was confronted by a commandment that focused me upon my sin. As a result, sin robbed me of this vital experience, because it focused me on a negative." Early in Paul's conversion he *was alive* in fellowship with God *without the law* (6:8, 11, 13). Then as soon as Paul tried to incorporate the Law into his Christian life **sin revived and** he **died**. That is, he *died* experientially when his fallen nature aroused sin to a greater degree severing his fellowship with God. As a result, the **commandment** Paul thought would ***bring*** a **life** experience (as originally stated in Lev 18:5) brought **death**. Not because the Law was bad, but because **sin** that was dormant **deceived** (7:8) Paul into thinking he could obtain life focusing on a negative command. Thus, *sin* by using the commandment as a weapon figuratively speaking **killed** Paul's spiritual fellowship with God.

Satan here can be seen as personifying sin in the garden and the commandment as the tree of the knowledge of good and evil. As Satan caused Eve in the Garden to focus on the negative command to avoid eating from the tree of the knowledge of good and evil, she lost sight of God's positive command to eat of the tree of life (Gen 2:16; 3:2). Though initially Eve did not have sin, Satan acting as sin deceived her, causing her to concentrate on God's prohibition (cf. Gen 3:1, 3). From this point on all people are born sinners (3:23; 5:12). Thus, Satan's original handywork of deception in the garden is at work in man through sin (cf. commentary in 6:23). By luring man to concentrate on the negative command, sin causes him to lose focus on "the law of Christ" (Gal 6:2) or the perfect "law of liberty" (Jas 1:25; 2:12.). Consequently, the continual focus on prohibitions does not lead to holiness but to more sin (by arousing desires; cf., 7:8) that results in a death experience (cf., 7:9; Jas 1:14-16).

Therefore Paul concludes the argument begun in v 7: **the law is holy . . . just and good.** Man's problem is not *the law*, but his fallen humanity that is unable to respond adequately to it (vv 8, 11, 13-25).

7:13. The astute Apostle knowing that someone might logically misconstrue (v 7; 6:1, 15) the relationship between Law and sin concludes by asking a rhetorical question that he answers: **Has then what is good become death to me?** The expression *what is good* refers to the Law in v 12 to which the imaginary objector (cf. 2:1) may rhetorically ask: Is the Law to blame for our death experience? To which Paul emphatically replies with the strongest negative in the Greek: **Certainly not** (cf. 3:4 for comments)! The problem is **sin** not the Law. All that the Law (**through the commandment**) did was allow *sin* to surface in order to expose it for what it is **exceedingly sinful.** That is, since *sin* may at times be dormant (7:8), it allows people to think (because it is not apparently visible) they are sinless. Hence people shift blame to another, but in reality the *sinful human nature* in people is what causes *death.* The commandment just happens to be the agent that allows *sin* to be shown for what it is: *sinful in the extreme* (BDAG, 1032).

7:14. Having clarified in v 13 that sin, not the Law, is the real problem the argument is further strengthened: **For we know that the law is spiritual.** Many passages affirm the spiritual origin of the Law that connects the Holy Spirit's work with Scripture (Matt 22:43; Mark 12:36; Acts 1:16; 4:25; 28:25; 2 Pet 1:21). By implication then the Law's origin is from God (Deut 30:10) who is Spirit (John 4:24) holy and pure.

Conversely, Paul said of himself (representative of all believers): **but I am carnal, sold** (*pepramenos*) **under sin**. That is, though the Law is spiritual in its essence and origins, the origin of man (indicative of the personal pronoun *I*) as "unspiritual" (NIV; lit., "fleshly") still belongs to the fallen human nature (=disposition, cf. 6:6) inherited from Adam. The expression *pepramenos* (*=sold*) *under sin* appears in the perfect tense implying a completed action with ongoing results (i.e., having been sold to sin one continues in that same state). This is the state of the unregenerate in 3:9, "under sin," but having been regenerated does not mean sin loses its appeal for believers. Though Christians need not be enslaved to sin's dominion (6:1-14), vv 6:15-23 showed that Christians could still have strong attractions to sin (hence the imperative of v 19). While chapter 6 spoke of the person from the standpoint of his new nature in Christ, chapter 7 speaks of the person from the standpoint of his fallen nature (termed in many passages as *flesh* or *carnal*; cf. 7:5, 18, 25; 8:1, 3-5, 7, 12-13; 13:14; 1 Cor 3:1, 3; 2 Cor 10:2-3; cf. v 18) that he may still try to control incorrectly through the Law.

Whereas Paul previously used the aorist and imperfect tenses, from vv 14-25, Paul will consistently use the present tense to indicate vividly the struggle the infant Christian has with sin in light of using the Law for sanctification. One should *not* understand this section as the normal Christian experience, but the experience of a struggling Christian who tries to control sin by inappropriate use of the Law (cf. Fung, "The Impotence of the Law: Toward a Fresh Understanding of Romans 7:14-25," in *Scripture, Tradition and Interpretation*, 42).

7:15-17. For (*gar*) explains the phrase "sold under sin" of v 14*b* with its full implications appearing from vv 15-25. Knowing full well that at regeneration the believer acquires a new nature (=disposition) to help him grow, yet Paul says: **what I am doing**

(*katergazomai*, present tense implies he continuously tries), **I do not understand**. No doubt Paul described a past event since he shares the component to overcoming this problem in chapter 8. However, Paul uses the present tense from 7:14-25 to vividly portray his, or by extension every Christian's struggles, in using the Law for sanctification. Consequently, he confesses how the *old* Adamic disposition continues to hinder growth and battle the *new* Christ-like disposition (cf. 6:6 for comments): **For what I** (*the new*) **will to do, that I** (*the old*) **do not practice; but what I** (*the new*) **hate, that I** (*the old*) **do** (cf. Pentecost, *Designed to Be Like Him*, 80-81). As a result of using the Law for sanctification the old capacity within Paul revives. Though influenced by the new capacity he desires to do the right thing, he concludes by doing *what* he *hates*. This results in spiritual schizophrenia (since he possesses two opposing dispositions/inclinations) like Dr. Jekyll and Mr. Hyde. The personal pronoun "*I*" should be viewed as the whole person. Yet within the person there are two competing dispositions (i.e., the *flesh* against the *Spirit*; Gal 5:16-17; cf. v 14) warring to gain mastery over the Christian. Therefore, if Paul does **what** he wishes **not to do**, then he knows **the law** must be **good**. Because Paul cannot keep the Law, he does not conclude that it is not a good moral guide. **But** he knows **sin that dwells in** him is the problem, i.e., his fallen human nature. The personal pronoun "*I*" does not refer to the body as opposed to a new spirit. Instead, the "*I*" here refers to the whole person functioning either under the new disposition or under the fallen human disposition "*I*" of vv 15-16 (cf. vv 19-20).

7:18-20. For (*gar*) functions as an explanatory particle clarifying Paul's inability to overcome sin in v 17, because it is deeply rooted within him (i.e., *sin that dwells in me*, vv 20, 23). Paul having possibly struggled for years to live Christianity (perhaps while in Arabia as Gal 1:17 indicates and the contrasting Law and grace principle in 4:25; cf. Intro *A Biographical Sketch*) by his own power to fulfill the Law, at one point became cognizant of the real problem: **I know that in me (that is, in my flesh,** [from, *sarx*]) **nothing good dwells**. The expression *in me* clarified as *in my flesh* refers to the fallen Adamic nature (cf. vv 14-16) within Paul that all men continue to possess. The term *sarx* does not refer to man's body as opposed to his new spirit but to the whole being functioning under the aspect of the *flesh*:

> Hence it frequently stands, as in the Old Testament, simply for 'man'. 'I conferred not with flesh and blood' (Gal 1:16) means 'with no other human beings'. 'No flesh', in the regular Old Testament phrase, means 'nobody' (Rom 3:20; Gal 2.16; 1 Cor 1:29. . . . So, very often, the word 'flesh' is interchangeable with the personal pronoun—for instance, in Eph 5:28: 'He that loveth his own wife loveth himself: for no man ever hated his own flesh'. In 2 Cor 7:5, 'Our flesh had no relief' is simply a periphrasis for 'I' (it is indistinguishable from 'I had no relief in my spirit' in 2 Cor 2.13), and the explanatory words 'without were fighting, within were fears' make it clear that the flesh does not here refer simply to the external body. So, in Col 1:24, to 'fill up . . . that which is lacking of the afflictions of Christ in my flesh' means 'in my person'. Similarly, 'in our mortal flesh' (Rom 6:19)= 'seeing you are weak people'. Finally, in Rom. 7.18, 'in me, that is in my flesh, dwelleth no good thing' is equivalent to saying that for me, [i.e., *sarx*] . . . (Robinson, *The Body*, 18-19).

Paul explains (**for**=*gar*), as in v 15, that even a desire to do **what is good** is not enough to "carry it out" (NIV). The *good* here refers to keeping the Law (cf. vv 12, 16), which cannot be fully obeyed. Rather, when one sets out to do **the good** he desires, it results in **the evil** he had no intention to **practice**. Thus, one's Christian experience of trying to live by the Law results in a constant battle (vv 16-17). Paul summarizes these paradoxical attributes waging war within as follows: **Now if I** (the fallen nature) **do what I** (the resurrection nature) **will not to do, it is no longer I** (the person's desire) **who do it, but sin** (i.e., sin principle dominant in the fallen nature) **that dwells in me** (i.e., *in me* refers to the whole person; cf. v 18; 6:6 for comments and Pentecost, *Designed to Be Like Him*, 80, 91-92, 99,107).

7:21-23. Paul experientially discovered (**I find**, Cranfield, *Romans*, 1:362), by using the marker **then** (*ara*) draws an inference made on the basis of what preceded (BDAG, 127, i.e., "in me"), that **a** specific **law** (lit. in the Gk "the law," cf. v 22) was deeply rooted in his very being. Paul emphasizes this experience in the Greek by placing the phrase *the one who wills to do good* before describing **that evil** within him dwarfs it. As the Law of God exposes His holy incorruptible nature, the *law* principle within Paul (representative of fallen humanity) shows *that evil* **is present with** him, thus exposing his corrupt nature and reason why he (and humanity) fails in carrying out the Law's mandates.

Having said this Paul quickly explains (v 21) his inner desire for God's Law: **For I delight in the law of God according to the inward man**, even if he cannot carry it out. Delighting in God's Law was repeatedly the psalmist's reaction (Pss 19:8; 119:14, 16, 24, 35, 47, 70, 77, 92). The phrase *of God* modifying *the law* was added for clarity since v 21 also mentions literally "the law" referring to the law principle of sin (as v 23 also explains; Cranfield, *Romans*, 1:363). The phrase *inward man* also appears in two other places in the Greek New Testament (2 Cor 4:16 and Eph 3:16). In both places the *inward man* is something within believers that can be "renewed" daily and "strengthened" by the Holy Spirit. In v 23 Paul clarifies this phrase as being practically synonymous with **the law of the mind** (*noos*), which in 12:2 he commands believers to transform. The phrase *another law in* Paul's *members* is also a virtual synonym of the phrase **law of sin which is in my members** (the fallen nature; cf. v 5). This *law* waged war *against the law of* his *mind* (i.e., "the inward man") and won since it was stronger.

7:24-25. Thus, in a time of frustration he replied: **O wretched man that I am! Who will deliver me from this body of death** (="body of sin," cf. 6:6)? Paul knew that an inner desire could not overcome humanity's natural bent to do evil. Christians feel *wretched* when sin overtakes them. Believers experience defeat, as did Paul, when by their own power, apart from the Spirit, they try to live by the Law. In Romans 6:6, Paul used the phrase "body of sin" equivalent to the phrase *body of death*. The whole man where sin resides, manifested through the *body*, is Paul's meaning (cf. 6:6 for comments). One's body becomes the visible vehicle where "sin" displays itself (6:6, 12-13, 19; 7:5) that brings "death" (6:16, 21, 23; 7:10-11, 13; 8:10-11, 13). Therefore, the *body*, representative here of fallen humanity, needs supernatural aid from an external source to help overcome this internal struggle. Nevertheless, vv 7-24 recorded, up to now, Paul's past Christian experience before presently understanding and thanking **God** for supplying **through** (*dia*, implying instrumental use "through") **Jesus Christ our Lord** the means to "deliver" believers from this struggle (cf. 5:9-10; 6:1-10). **So then**, Paul closes the entire section from vv 7-25 by drawing an inference: Man's fallen nature is the problem, not God's Law. Verse 25 ends with a summary of the struggle: Paul **with the mind** (a synecdoche of the new disposition; cf. 6:6; 7:5, 7) **served** God's law, **but with the flesh** (old disposition) **the law of sin** (vv 22-23). Paul does not disclaim responsibility or make excuses. He simply acknowledges the inward pull towards sin that is very much a part of him. Paul cannot overcome it in his own strength through the Law. Until one reaches chapter 8 the solution to the present dilemma will not be resolved. That is, how can believers overcome sin in order to experience resurrection-life instead of the death experience mentioned in 7:7-25?

THE KEY TO SPIRITUAL POWER

6. The Spirit's ability to sanctify believers (8:1-17)

Since believers operate under a new system named the "law of Christ" (Gal 6:2; also known as the "law of liberty," Jas 1:25; 2:12), they need not obey the old system of the Old Testament Law (7:1-6). Nor can they. Those who persist on living by the Law's standard will encounter frustration and defeat (7:7-25), because the Law cannot aid Christians in overcoming sin (but reveals it; cf. 3:20). To overcome sin believers need the help of the Holy Spirit (8:1-17). He not only helps believers obey God but also gives special aid to those who suffer for Christ (8:18-30). However, since suffering may cause believers to doubt God's favor, Paul ends the chapter by affirming those who suffer for Christ that God will never abandon them (8:31-39).

8:1. After having shown the impossibility of overcoming the Adamic nature (termed *flesh*; cf. 7:18-20) by obeying the Law (7:7-25), Paul develops now the *only* solution available for the Christian to stymie the effects of sin and live victoriously. Hence the phrase **therefore now** (*ara nyn*) draws a strong conclusion from what preceded, but emphasizes what will presently be said (cf. 5:18; 7:3, 25; 8:12; 9:16, 18; 14:12, 19 where *ara nyn* is used this way).

There is *therefore now* **no condemnation** (*katakrima*) **to those who are in Christ Jesus.** Numerous interpretations are put forth to understand Paul's meaning: (1) Some interpret *no katakrima* to refer to one's deliverance from sin's penalty of eternal judgment, since the judicial phrase *in Christ Jesus* (3:24; 6:11, 23) is connected to the term *condemnation* (Moo, *Romans*, 472-73). This would imply eternal security for all believers, since they are *not* in the unregenerate state Paul described in 3:20 or perhaps 7:7-25. Thus Romans 8:1 ending in v 34 may form an *inclusio* (cf. 1:5 for definition) teaching eternal security to strengthen believers. (2) Since the first view does not completely account for the issue of sanctification of chapters 7 and 8, one may opt to take a synergistic view of justification and sanctification. That is, although works are not the primary cause of one's justification, they play a secondary cause effecting a believer's final judgment (Lowe, "'*There is No Condemnation*' [Romans 8:1]: But Why Not?," 231-50). Logically, this not only reduces grace theology to works (whether stemming from primary or secondary causes), but it totally confuses the Pauline doctrine of justification by faith taught in 3:21–4:25 apart from any secondary cause of works. (3) Hence *katakrima* refers to sin's effect that enslaves believers to its power causing one to sin more and experience frustration. Believers are not obliged to experience the effects of sins, because they are *in Christ Jesus* (cf. 6:11-12; cf. 8:2). That is, *katakrima* refers not only to the judicial (unregenerate) state Christians have overcome by believing *in Christ*, but contextually it refers to the effects resulting from the sentence itself (BDAG, 518; MM, 327-28; Murray, *Romans*, 1:274-75; Harrison, *Romans*, in *EBC*, 86; Bruce, *Romans*, 151). Hence believers do not have to experience the effects of sin's slavery described in 7:13-25 that Paul calls here *katakrima*. They now have the power to overcome sin's mastery through the help of the Holy Spirit resident in them. Furthermore, the sanctification context from vv 1-17 also argues for understanding *katakrima* as referring to the enslavement of sin's dominion that believers are free from, *if* Christians **do not**

walk according to the flesh, but according to the Spirit.
Although the latter phrases do not appear in the two earliest Greek
manuscripts of the fifth century (Aleph and B), it does appear in
another two early manuscripts of the sixth century (A and D),
along with the majority of New Testament manuscripts.
Contextually the inclusion of the phrases is also supported (8:4).

The term *walk* (*peripateō*) is a New Testament word "decided-
ly Pauline" that refers "to conduct one's life, *comport oneself, behave,
live*" (BDAG, 803; cf. 4:12; 6:4; 8:4; 13:13). The preposition
according (*kata*) implies a similar characteristic that could be translated *like* (Abbott-Smith, *Greek Lexicon*, 232). Thus Paul means
that only those who do not live *according to the flesh* (*kata sarka*,
like unbelievers) but *according to the Spirit* (*kata pneuma*, like
believers) are the ones who will not experience sin's power as in 8:4
(cf. 8:13). Hence, from vv 1-13, Paul puts forth the possibility that
believers can behave *like* (*kata*) *mere men* (1 Cor 3:3). These are
two real possibilities Christians can experience. Thus, what Paul
means in v 1 is that believers do not have to serve *sin* (as in 7:13-
25) and be enslaved to it. Instead if they live through *the Spirit's*
enabling (developed in chapter 8) they will serve God and experience what they are in their position: free from sin's slavery.

8:2. For (*gar*) connects to the previous verse explaining why
believers can indeed overcome the power of sin in their daily lives.
First, there is another principle at work in believers called **the law
of the Spirit of life in Christ Jesus.** The *law of the Spirit* refers to
a principle power brought by the Holy Spirit that resides only in
those who were baptized into Christ and are *in Christ Jesus* (6:1-11;
8:1, 9-11; cf. Cranfield, *Romans*, 1:373-78).

Second, in Romans 5:5 *the Spirit* was not mentioned, but
chapter 8 will mention Him 21 times. This is appropriate since *the
Spirit* brings *life* (a dynamic reality) setting one **free** to overcome

the principle power **from the law** (not the Mosaic Law) **of sin** (resident in the Adamic nature; cf. 7:18-23) that results in a **death** experience (mentioned in 5:15, 17, 21; 6:16, 21, 23; 7:5, 10-11, 13; 8:6, 10, 13).

8:3-4. For (*gar*) is an explanatory conjunction that further clarifies why **the** (Mosaic) **law** (not the law as a principle power of v 2; cf. 7:21-23) could not bring a life experience. Not because *the law* was bad (7:7, 12), but **it was** "powerless" (NIV) and not **weak** in itself as numerous versions imply. That is, *the law* could not curtail sin because of the Adamic nature in all believers called **the flesh** (7:18-23; 8:1). Hence, *the law* was not the problem, but humanity's fallen disposition (referred to as *the flesh* 10 out the 12 times in chap 8) that is powerless to obey its demands.

Yet, what *the law* could not accomplish **God *did* by sending His own Son in the likeness of sinful flesh, on account of sin: He condemned sin in the flesh.** Christ came as a human in all aspects, except sin, as the word *likeness* (instead of the term *same*) suggests. He was sinless (1 Pet 2:22) and did not inherit Adam's falleness since He was protected by Mary directly conceiving Him through the Holy Spirit (Matt 1:18, 23). Hence the Greek phrase *peri hamartias* is best understood as representing Jesus as the perfect "offering for sin" (BDAG, 798; 2 Cor 5:21) as rendered by the NASB, instead of the ambiguous phrase *on account of sin* translated by the NKJV. As a result, Christ *condemned* (*katakrinō*) *sin in the flesh*. Thus, "God deprived sin (which is the ground of the *katakrima* [of v 1]) of its power in human nature" by breaking its deadly sway (Thayer, *Greek-English Lexicon*, 332).

Therefore, *sin in the flesh* refers to *sin* in Christ's flesh (Bruce, *Romans*, 152). Sin at the cross was dethroned (as a controlling power hindering the believer's obedience; cf. 5:17-21; 6:6-12; 7:4-6) in order **that** (*hina*, indicating purpose) **the righteous requirement** (*dikaiōma*) **of the law might be fulfilled in us**. The term *dikaiōma* refers to the *righteous* acts, not a judicial acquittal (BDAG, 249; cf. 5:16), of *the law* that can now come to fruition *in believers*, because Christ deprived sin of its power (as seen above by the terms *katakrima* or *katakrinō* in 8:1, 4). However, *only if* believers **do not walk according to the flesh** (i.e., directed by the Adamic nature and value system of the world) **but according to the Spirit** (cf. 6:13; 8:1; directed by the new disposition aided by the Spirit and value system of the Word) can the holy standards of the Law be lived out. Thus, the Christian, through the life of Christ (5:9-10, 17-21; 6:1-23; 8:37) lived *in us* by means of *the Spirit* (8:1-17; Gal 5:16), can behave according to the standard of the Law known as *love* (cf. 13:8-10).

8:5-7. For (*gar*) connects to the previous verse by using an explanatory conjunction that clarifies what will influence Christian behavior. As chapters 7–8 show, the Christian life cannot be lived by observing the Law but by the power of the Spirit. The other side of this secret to living the Christian life is found by understanding *how* this change can take place. If Christians **live according to the flesh** (*kata sarka*) it is only because they **set their minds** (*phroneō*) **on the things of the flesh, but those *who live* according to the Spirit** (*kata pneuma*)**, the things of the Spirit.** Both Greek phrases *kata sarka* and *kata pneuma* do not literally contain the term *live.* Yet it is appropriate to translate it as such since *living* is what is meant by similar phrases in v 4 (cf. Acts 11:1 where the lit. Gk "those who are according to Judea" means "those who live in Judea). Furthermore, some may see the term *Spirit* here to refer to the regenerate human "spirit," but this is highly improbable since the chapter began (v 2) and continues to refer to the Holy Spirit.

The key to understanding why believers often behave like unbelievers is defined by the term *phroneō*. Though one may define *set their minds* as "changing one's thought pattern" (cf. 12:2-3), in order to produce godly behavior, it involves much more than that. The term *phroneō* involves man's intellect, emotion and will through careful thinking, a change of attitude and compelling behavior to pursue the things of God (Thayer, *Greek-English Lexicon*, 658; cf. Phil 2:5-8; Col 3:2). Not that one should fall into the same trap of chapter 7 by obeying a set of rules. Instead, Christians should actively seek to place themselves in a position to be influenced and changed by *the Spirit* through daily prayer, constant reading of God's Word and attending church. Though doing these things do not transform believers, these are mere avenues that place them in a position to be transformed by *the Spirit*. Consequently, believers will begin to think and thus *live according to the Spirit* (cf. 6:13).

A Christian's choice called for in v 5 will determine the outcome explained in v 6. Thus **to be carnally** (Gk lit. *the flesh*) **minded** (*phronēma* from *phroneō* above which means a strong focus and strive, BDAG, 1066) *is* **death, but to be spiritually minded** *is* **life and peace**. These contrasting outcomes mentioned here do not refer to eternal *death* versus eternal *life*. Contextually, Paul's exhortation is to believers. Hence *death* refers to a death experience (6:16, 21, 23; 7:10-13, 24; 8:13; Gal 5:16-17, 19-21), a result of heeding one's fallen disposition (known as *the flesh*; 7:18-21; 8:1) that is still a part of all believers (cf. 6:6). Conversely, the meaning of *life* refers to that experience available to all believers who orient themselves to the things of *the Spirit* (cf. v 5; Gal 5:22-25; 8:13). If so, a believer will experience the *peace* of God (14:17, 19; 15:13, 33; 16:20) available *only* to the obedient. That is altogether different than peace *with* God available to all believers (cf. 5:1).

Hence it follows that **the carnal mind**, which entails the fallen nature in all, *is* **enmity against God.** The reason fallen man can never obey **the law of God** is not only because of his wicked inclination, but also because he is powerless to do so (cf. 7:24-25).

8:8-9. Then it logically follows that **those who are in the flesh cannot please God.** To be *in the flesh* is different than living *according to the flesh* (cf. 8:1, 4-5) that can only apply to believers. As indicated in 7:5 and the following v 9, being *in the flesh* refers to the unregenerate state. Therefore the unregenerate will never be able to carry out the *righteous requirement of the Law* of v 4 to *please God* since they lack the Spirit.

But although this is true of unbelievers, Paul's readers **are not in the flesh but** (*alla,* a strong contrast) **in** (*en*) **the Spirit.** That is, *in the Spirit* refers to a Christian's *position* as the preposition *en* indicates, not *practice,* as the other preposition *kata* (cf. 8:1, 4-5) dictates.

The second half of v 9 may be interpreted in two ways: (1) *if* (*eiper*) may be understood as true for the sake of argument that may be translated "since" (Wallace, *Greek Grammar,* 690, 694; cf. Rom 3:30; 2 Thess 1:6). Paul does this so that believers can acknowledge the power resident in them to live godly. (2) Yet **if** (*eiper*) **indeed** may be understood as leaving the question open (cf. Rom 8:17; 1 Cor 8:5; 15:15) to whether this condition of having **the Spirit** is fulfilled. Though Paul implies contingency in this verse of whether one has the Spirit, his main thrust is positive. This means he uses the conjunction *if* to draw a positive response from his readers while leaving the question open for them to respond: *Of course the Spirit dwells in us* (cf. Wallace, *Greek Grammar,* 694). A person is an unbeliever **if** he **does not have the Spirit of Christ.** This affirms that unless the Spirit dwells in the person, unlike the Old Testament and early dispensation of the church, **he is not His** (lit., he is not of Him).

8:10-11. A further intimacy of the relationship that exists between Christ and the Holy Spirit, united to the believer, may be seen through the phrase **if** (best understood as *since*) **Christ is in you.** The variation of the phrases "the Spirit of God," "the Spirit of Christ" and *Christ in you* above all have similar affects. Noticing the latter Murray correctly warns: "This does not mean, however, that here is any blurring of the distinction between Christ and the Holy Spirit. Neither does it eliminate the distinctive modes of indwelling or the distinctive operations of the respective persons of the Godhead. But it does underline the intimacy of the relationship that exists between Christ and the Holy Spirit in that union by which the believer becomes the habitation of both" (*Romans*, 1:288-89). What this means is that, "Christ and the Spirit are so closely related in communicating to believers the benefits of salvation that Paul can move from one to the other almost unconsciously" (cf. 8:9-11; Moo, *Romans*, 491).

Since *Christ is in* the believers, **the body is dead because of sin.** Various views exist to explain the latter clause. (1) The clause *the body is dead because of sin* may refer to the physical death of the body that all believers must endure as a result of their Adamic nature (5:12; 6:23; cf. Cranfield, *Romans*, 1:389; Byrne, *Romans*, 96; Dunn, *Romans 1–8*, 431). Yet, since *Christ is in* believers, **the Spirit is life because of righteousness.** All believers at the point of *righteousness* (i.e., the justification of 3:21–4:25) are guaranteed by the Spirit's power future resurrection *life*. Though some may interpret *the spirit* as human here, use of the noun "life" (*zōē*) instead of the verb "alive" (*zaō*) makes this interpretation unrealistic. Or else, what did Paul mean in saying that the human spirit is *life*? The following v 11 may further substantiate the future resurrection view by the word *life*, for it refers to Christ's resurrection as well as the believers'. Yet, the immediate context does not strictly refer to any future resurrection but to the inherent problem of sin in the present life of the believer. (2) The *body is dead because of sin* may be understood in terms of the Romans 6 principle where Christians, at the point of Spirit baptism into Christ, died to the power of sin's dominion (c.f., 6:1-11; Käsemann, *Romans*, 224; Barrett, *Romans*, 149; Ziesler, *Romans*, 211; Bultmann, *TDNT*, 4:894). Though some have argued this is not death *to sin* as in 6:2, 11 but death *because of sin* (Schreiner, *Romans*, 414), this may be too refined an argument since similar terms and concepts pervade both contexts in 6:1-12 and 8:10-11. Hence Paul seems to mean in v 10 that the believer's *body is dead* (i.e., death of the whole person with reference to sin's dominion stemming from the Adamic nature; cf. 5:17; 6:6; 7:24), by virtue of dying with Christ, at baptism caused by *sin*. As sin caused Christ to die and the believer in Christ, *the Spirit* gives *life because of* the *righteousness* accomplished by Christ (i.e., at justification; 5:17-21; 6:7-8). Nevertheless, it still remains true that baptismal death must be constantly realized as 6:11 commands (Barrett, *Romans*, 149). (3) Certainly the phrase *body is dead* may be understood in terms of Christian baptism of Romans 6, but only if the preposition *dia* means "for the sake of" *sin*. That is, when Christians undergo Spirit baptism, they (*the body* representative of the whole person's Adamic nature; cf. 6:6; 7:24) die for the sake of (or "with reference to," Käsemann, *Romans*, 224) not sinning (as the basic point of chaps 6 and 8). Yet the Spirit gives *life* for the sake of acting righteously (cf. 6:13, 16). The Spirit effects this life of *righteousness* described in 6:14-23. Hence contextually *righteousness* cannot refer to the justification sentence. Instead, it refers to "walking by the Spirit in bodily service in a way which is pleasing to God" (Käsemann, *Romans*, 224). That makes more sense in lieu of the context of sanctification. In v 10 Paul basically means: Since Christ is in believers by virtue of undergoing Spirit baptism, the visible vehicle, the body, that manifests the Adamic nature was dethroned (died) for the sake of not sinning; but by virtue of the Spirit's indwelling, God gave believers a new disposition (cf. 6:6), called life, for the sake of behaving obediently.

Thus, **if** (is better understood as *since*) **the Spirit** . . . **who raised Jesus from the dead dwells** in believers, **He** . . . **will also give life** (*zōopoiēsei*) **to** empower the **mortal** (*thnēta*) **bodies** of all believers. Now Paul takes the argument a step further: From an internal power that reigns over the believer's Adamic inclinations (v 10) to an external empowerment to effect change in the weak vehicle (physical body) in order to obey. Clearly, this verse argues strongly for the physical resurrection of all believers. However, in keeping with the context, the future verb *zōopiēsei* refers to an event that takes place in the present, since *the Spirit* is able to empower the immediate body called *thnēta*, meaning "humanity" in all of its weakness (6:12). If Paul meant a future resurrection body, one would expect him to use the term "dead" to imply complete cessation of either one's old nature positionally (as in v 10) or one's body physically (as in 1 Cor 15:12-19, 42-54). Rather he uses the term *mortal* to describe the *body* that belongs to believers in this life (Murray, *Romans*, 1:291). Hence, Paul does not refer to a future resurrection body (which occurs in a moment), but to an empowerment of life through the Spirit that can gradually mortify the flesh since He **dwells in** believers (Calvin, *Romans*, 293). Though this verse may imply the final act of physical resurrection for all believers, Paul means to say that one can actualized this resurrection-life *now* when one lives by the power of the Holy Spirit.

8:12-14. Therefore (*ara nyn*; cf. 8:1) draws a strong conclusion in lieu of vv 1-11 but emphasizes what will presently be said to the **brethren,** an intimate term for Christians (cf. 7:1, 4; 10:1;

11:25; 12:1; 14:10, 13, 15, 21; 15:14, 30; 16:14, 17, 23). Up to this point Paul showed how believers are not **debtors** (or obligated) **to the flesh** that enslaves one to sin's power known as "condemnation" in 8:1. Believers do not have to **live according to the flesh** (i.e., live like unbelievers; 8:1, 4-5), because, as vv 10-11 show, they have resurrection-power to overcome the deadly power of sin. Thus believers ought not to follow after their Adamic inclinations.

For (*gar*) is a conjunction that explains two possible outcomes believers will experience (similar to 6:9-10, 16; 8:2, 6) depending on their choice: **if you live according to the flesh you will die; but if by the Spirit you put to death the deeds of the body, you will live.** Three possible views exist to explain the two contrasting obligations and outcomes: (1) The Reformed Calvinist views one who *lives according to flesh* as unregenerate. While believers may commit fleshly acts, they will not be governed by a lifestyle of sin (Moo, *Romans*, 494). This only proves such a person was never saved; thus he will *die*, which contrasted to the phrase *will live* expresses eternal realities.

(2) The Arminians view it as follows: To *live according to the flesh* expresses a real warning to believers to live holily by "putting" *to death* the desires and inclinations of the Adamic nature. If not, a believer will forfeit sonship and *die*. This parallel to the phrase *will live* is understood as having eternal verities (Shank, *Life in the Son*, 112, 144). Uniformly, in the Arminian as in the Reformed Calvinist view, works play an ultimate and synergistic role in one's eternal destiny (Osborne, *Romans*, 203; Moo, *Romans*, 494-95). Obviously, both of these views are antithetical to Paul's doctrine of justification by faith alone in Christ alone found in 3:21–4:25.

(3) Numerous arguments clearly militate against both of the former views. First, both views jump the contextual ship that

continues to express the believer's victory over sin by the resident power of *the Spirit*. Second, Paul's plural pronoun *you*, prefixed to the verb *live* (*zēte*), refers to the antecedent noun *brethren* in v 12, who are believers according to the use of the term in the epistle (except 9:3; cf. v 12). Third, chapters 7:7-24 and 8:1-12 demonstrate the possibility of a regenerate person living after the flesh. Not once does Paul imply that the one who lives according to the flesh will forfeit eternal life. Fourth, the present tense verb *thanatoute*, translated "putting to death"(NASB), involves an ongoing work to mortify *the deeds of the body* (i.e., the sinful inclinations manifested through the visible vehicle; cf. 6:6). Elsewhere Paul understood how believers ought to continuously "present" (present imperative tense; 6:12, 16) themselves as those who have been set free from bondage to overcome evil inclinations (cf. 6:11, 13; 12:1; 13:14). Logically, since these acts involve works, Paul cannot contradict himself (cf. 3:21–4:25; Eph 2:8-9) or Scripture (John's Gospel; Acts 16:31) that teach justification and eternal life result from faith alone in Christ alone. Fifth, hence Paul's use of the terms *die* and *live* convey temporal, not eternal, realities. This is a common use of both of these terms that result from either sin or obedience. For example, sin produces various forms of death. Physical death occurs to believers due to sin (1 Cor 11:30; 1 John 5:16; Jas 5:19-20). Psychological death caused by sin brought mental distress and guilt to Saul and David (1 Sam 15–16; Ps 51:2-9), or social death caused by sin brings a loss of fellowship with others (1 Cor 5:1–6:12) and Christ (1 John 1:5-10). Conversely, obedient acts of honesty and fidelity can fulfill the "law of love" and produce a life experience that results in various blessings: Physical longevity (Ps 119:144; Prov 4:4; 7:2; 15:27; Eph 6:3; Jas 1:21), psychological wellness (Ps 69:32) and quality of a life of fellowship (John 10:10; 15:11) that is also called "eternal life" (cf. Gal 6:8). To really live, however, one must put the old self to death over and over again. Thus Paul warns Christians to seek the best of both of these outcomes: Obey through the power of a Spirit-led-life and experience life in its fullest sense filled with meaning and significance.

8:14. **For** (*gar*) functions as an explanatory particle describing the nature of those believers who stop obeying their evil disposition (v 13). Only those mature Christians (implied by the term **as many as**) that **are led** (*agontai*, present passive) **by the Spirit** can rightly be called **sons** (i.e. *huios*) **of God,** not just "children" (cf. 17).

First, the Greek verb *agontai* appears in the present tense referring to a continuous leading, and the passive voice refers to someone else acting on the Christians. The passive voice emphasizes the power supplied by *the Spirit* to overcome sin instead of the spiritual infancy believers were in when they were under the Law (Gal 4; 5:18). However, this is not to be viewed as a subjective mystical power or guide compelling believers apart from their own initiative (as v 13 suggest). Instead, Christians *led by the Spirit* implies a *willingness* to "*allow oneself to be led*" (BDAG, 16), which involves *following*. This leading involves obeying God's objective revealed will in Scripture.

Second, to become *sons of God* occurs by virtue of "faith in Christ" (Gal 3:26). Yet, receiving the privileges and experiences of full sonship occurs by virtue of faith and obedience by yielding to the leading of *the Spirit*. These are two different aspects of sonship (cf. v 19). Paul refers to the latter here. When a son exemplifies a specific characteristic of his father, that father may claim: "That is my boy!" By this the father does not state a biological relationship but a characteristic relationship (similar to Matt 5:9, 45; Rev 21:7). When obedient Christians exemplify similar characteristics to their heavenly Father (1 John 3:10) or Christ, they may be called "sons indeed" (Dillow, *Reign of the Servant Kings*, 369-71) or "disciples indeed" (John 8:31).

8:15-17. For (*gar*) again is used to explain the contrasting characteristic to the previous verse. That is, believers have nothing to **fear**, because they **received the Spirit of** sonship (as the NIV renders lit. *huiothesias* instead of **adoption** suggest; cf vv 18-23). The phrase *spirit of bondage* should not be taken as actually existing, "but means only that the Holy Spirit whom they have received is not a spirit of bondage but the Spirit of adoption" (Cranfield, *Romans*, 1:396).

The idea of sonship (cf. vv 14-15, 17-22) seems to refer to the Old Testament Jewish view of the adoption rights (i.e., benefits) of the firstborn that now belong to all believers. Paul's use of the *filial* (Jewish) not the *legal* (Roman) (cf. Cranfield, *Romans*, 1:397) concept seems strengthened by the Aramaic expression **Abba, Father**, who believers have as a benefit to call upon in times of need. Paul uses *huiothesias* in 9:4 in a similar way to refer to the benefits or advantages that belonged to the Jews. Thus believers have nothing to *fear* because they *received a Spirit of* sonship that comes with all of the benefits that pertain to it (Gal 4:5). In a sense this double portion belong to all believers at birth, but it must be valued by living up to the honor of that right in order not to lose it as Esau did (Gen 25:34; Heb 12:16-17; cf. Dillow, *Reign of the Servant Kings*, 370).

It is at this point that the **Spirit Himself** aids believers in crying out to God. Many people misread the verb *symmartyreō* as **bears witness** *to* (instead of **with**) **our spirit that we are children of God**. As a result, many view this verse as the Spirit's internal witness *to* assure believers of their eternal-salvation. Actually the Greek compound verb *symmartyreō* conveys the meaning of "bear witness with," not *to* (BDAG, 957; 2:15; 9:1). Contextually, in vv 16-29 *syn* compound words occur nine times and in all cases (except v 29) it clearly means "with, jointly or together with." Hence the Greek preposition *syn* prefixed to the verb *witness* clearly means *with* or *accompaniment besides with* (BADG, 961-62). This speaks of two witnesses (the Holy Spirit and human spirit) in keeping with the Old Testament principles that all matters must be verified by a minimum of two witnesses (Deut 19:15; Matt 18:16).

Paul means that the Spirit bears witness, *along with* (but unde-tectable to) our spirit, in prayer (as v 26 clearly suggests) to God affirming our relationship as His children. Thus, this verse serves to assure believers of our sense of privilege having received the Spirit of sonship that helps us in prayer (as part of the Spirit's lead-ing of v 14) by reminding God in a time of need of our status as children. This is not an innovative concept. In the Old Testament, prayer directed at God in a time of need occurs by reminding God that the people of Israel are His people (1 Kings 8:51-52; Exod 33:13; Deut 9:26, 29). This is analogous to reminding God in a time of need that we are His children. Not that God needs remind-ing, but in times of need it serves to solidify the believer's petition by virtue of the relational status they share with God.

In times of suffering, the relational status further strengthens believers to endure suffering by confirming that: **if** (or better understood as *since*) we are **children** (*teknon*), **then heirs—heirs of God.** All Christians are *heirs of God* simply by faith alone. However to be **joint heirs with** (*sygklēronomoi*) **Christ,** occurs only **if indeed** (*eiper*) believers **suffer with** *Him* (cf. Dillow, *Reign of the Servant Kings*, 374-81).

The term *teknon* (=children, vv 16-17, 21) has a more distinct nuance than the terms *huios* (=son, vv 14, 19) and *huiothesia* (=sonship, vv 15, 23) used by Paul. The term *teknon* is used in many ways, but here it simply means "believers" (BDAG, 995).

Out of the ninety-nine times the word *teknon* occurs in the New Testament it is used only once with Jesus (Luke 2:48), when Mary wrongly rebukes Jesus for staying behind. Paul, or other writers, never refer to Jesus by *teknon* but by *huios* (cf. Dunn, *Romans 1–8*, 454). This is significant. In the English language as in Greek, one can use the term *son* when speaking of a mature person or of a genetic relationship (cf. Gal 4:5-7). The word *son* can carry both ideas (e.g., My son is 45 years old) but child does not (e.g., My child is 45 years old). Thus, the term *huios* carries a broader meaning in various contexts that can express "follower," or in "a special sense the devout, . . . people of special status and privilege" (BDAG, 1024-25).

Contextually it is the mature sons of God who live righteously as they are led by the Spirit (vv 13-15) that possess co-heirship *with Christ*. Four things clearly indicate that co-heirship with Christ (cf. 2 Tim 2:11-13) is conditioned upon suffering with Him. **(1)** There are two different Greek terms used to distinguish mere heirship (=*klēronomoi*) occurring upon believing in Christ, from co-heirship (=*sygklēronomoi*) occurring upon suffering for Christ. This distinction is further seen by *syn* compound verbs *suffer with* (*sympaschomen*) **that we may also be gloried together** (*syndoxasthōmen*, lit. we may also be glorified with; cf. v 18 to define the meaning of glory). **(2)** The first particle *if* (*ei*, that should be translated *since*) is different than the second conditional particle *if indeed* (*eiper*), which necessitates Christian suffering as an indispensable condition of future glory (Michaelis, *TDNT*, 5:926). The shift of particles then indicates a shift in thought, from an established fact to a condition that follows. **(3)** Two other important particles in the Greek appear between *heirs of God* and *joint heirs with Christ* (*men . de*) that indicate two contrasting heirships are in view. Not seen in the English translations, the contrastive sense may be rendered as follows: "On the one hand (*men*) *heirs of God*, but on the other hand (*de*) *joint heirs with Christ*. Paul uses this same structure throughout Romans (2:7-8, 25; 5:16; 6:11; 7:25; 8:10, 17; 9:21; 11:22, 28; 14:2, 5; 16:19) always to indicate contrastive never conjunctive construction (cf. Dillow, *Reign of the Servant Kings*, 376). **(4)** Scripture clearly supports this view in other places by showing that rewards are conditioned upon works or suffering (Acts 20:32; 1 Cor 9:27; 2 Cor 5:10; 1 Pet 1:4; Col 3:24; 2 Tim 2:11-13; Jas 2:5; 1 John 2:28; Rev 2–3). Thus, Paul teaches here that all believers upon regeneration become *heirs of God*, but only those who *suffer* will "be glorified with Him" (NASB).

7. Justification guarantees glorification but suffering enhances a greater kind of glorification (8:18-39)

In overcoming sin believers need the help of the Holy Spirit as shown above (8:1-17), but He not only helps believers obey God but also helps those who suffer for Christ (8:18-30). Therefore, Christians who suffer for Christ can rest assured that God would never abandon them (8:31-39).

8:18-22. For (*gar*) is an explanatory conjunction that expands the meaning of **suffering of this present time** (expressed in v 17). Hence believers ought to *consider* (cf. 4:3 for the meaning of the Gk term *logizomai*) it beneficial to undergo struggles now, because the future rewards for the faithful (cf. 2 Cor 4:17) in the Messianic age far outweighs present *suffering*. Sharing in Christ's suffering is a precursor to being *glorified*.

One should distinguish between two kinds of glory expressed in chapter 8. Glorification corresponds to the third stage of Christian salvation that occurs at resurrection as a result of solely believing in Christ (5:2; 8:21, 30; cf. 1 John 3:2). Yet, **glory** here

revealed in the mature **sons of God** (cf. v 17) refers to faithful believers who will share in the *honor, prestige* and *reward* of co-reigning with Christ over **creation** (Heb 1:8-9; 2 Tim 2:12; Rev 2:26-28). When a king was crowned (for his faithfulness to the kingdom for which he served; cf. Heb 1:5-9), he was glorified. So believers will be crowned (1 Cor 9:25; Phil 4:1; 1 Thess 2:19; 2 Tim 4:8; Jas 1:12; 1 Pet 5:4; Rev 2:10; 3:11) and glorified (for their faithfulness; cf. Rom 8:18-27) with many rewards. But especially in this context, this glorification refers to the rewards of exercising dominion over creation with Christ (8:18-23; cf. Rev 2:26-27). Presently creation **was subjected to futility** (lit. a state of being without use or value, *emptiness, purposelessness* or *transitoriness*, BDAG, 621) since the curse of the fall (Gen 3:17-19).

However, the *creation* **will be delivered** from the curse (described as *futility* in v 20) **into the glorious liberty of the children of God.** Noticed how Paul carefully distinguishes the meaning of the latter phrase *liberty of the children of God* from the *earnest expectation* to be revealed by the *sons of God* (v 19). Both phrases have distinct meanings. The *earnest expectation* that awaits creation refers to the ones committed to Christ (vv 13-19) revealed as the future ruling *sons of God*. That is creation waits to be under the control of these future rulers. Conversely, Paul does not state that creation awaits the *liberty* of the *sons of God*. That would elevate creation to the place belonging to its future rulers. All *children of God* equally inherit the earth liberated from the curse of the fall. However, only the *sons of God* as committed believers who suffer for Christ will receive a double portion (vv 13-15, 17-19) as first-born sons to rule creation.

Finally v 22 concludes the preceding theme by summarizing the current state of the earth. By stating that **we know**, Paul implies a common knowledge obvious to all by merely looking at

creation. It **groans** (*systenazei*) **and labors with** (*synōdinei*) **birth pangs**. The latter phrase expresses the imagery of a pregnant woman giving birth (cf. BDAG, 977) appropriately since the imagery of *birth pangs* refers elsewhere in Scripture as a sign immediately preceding the arrival of the new child, the Messianic era (Isa 13:8; 26:17-19; 66:7; Jer 30:7, 8; Mic 4:9-10; Matt 24:8; Mark 13:8; 1 Thess 5:3; cf. Bruce, *Romans*, 164).

Many commentators correctly interpret groaning here to refer solely to creation as opposed to including believers (Schreiner, *Romans*, 437). The terms *systenaze* and *synōdinei* literally mean *groan with* and *labors with*. Paul personifies creation as an animate thing to be able to compare it to believers (in v 23) who also *groan with* it **until now**. Such imagery stimulates one to have *hope* (vv 20, 24-25). That is, as creation is personified as a woman in labor that brings forth a new world born out of suffering, believers who suffer can ultimately expect a double portion born out of their suffering. This encourages believers to endure suffering.

8:23-25. Not only *that* is a transitional phrase (cf. 5:3) Paul includes to add believers alongside creation's groaning. Paul stresses the believer's groaning by the emphatic phrases **ourselves** and **within ourselves** (Cranfield, *Romans*, 1:417; Schreiner, *Romans*, 437).

The concept of suffering was not mentioned since v 18, yet now Paul returns to it (indicated by the term **groan**) in order to further engender hope in those believers who endure suffering (seen in vv 24-25). Paul points to the believer's present possession of *the firstfruits of the Spirit*. The concept of *firstfruits* of the Law refers to bringing the first part of the harvest to the temple as an offering to God (Lev 23:10-11). However, this carries the idea (by the word "first") that more of that harvest will come at a later date. Hence, contextually, Paul refers to the harvest of the possession of the Spirit that aids believers' present and final experience of suffering. The *firstfruits* refer to more than just possessing *the Spirit*. It means the *firstfruits* of what believers experience now by controlling the body (i.e., the Adamic inclination; cf. 8:13-18) through the Spirit. That is believers presently experience in part the **adoption** (=*huiothesia*; lit. "sonship" as in v 15) privileges and life that will be fully realized in the future when **the redemption of our body** occurs. Hence, believers groan even more having tasted now a portion of what that experience of *adoption* will be fully in the future.

For (*gar*) is an explanatory particle that Paul uses to clarify the experience mentioned in v 23. Those who tasted the liberating power and life of *the firstfruits of the Spirit* anticipate future resurrection having been **saved** (*esōthēmen*) **in this hope** (*elpidi*). The Greek aorist tense of the term *esōthēmen* refers contextually to the deliverance experience occurring at a point in time (vv 11-13) indicated by the previous phrase *have the firstfruits of the Spirit* (v 23). That is, the point in time that believers are *saved* refers to their experience when they first tasted these *firstfruits* of the Spirit's quickening power that gave life to this mortal body (v 11); which does not merely mean justifying but also the sanctifying affects of being delivered from sin's power. Believers *hope* for this experience to become permanent in the future.

Thus, the term *elpidi* may be classified as dative of association expressing the idea that believers are saved *with hope* (Moo, *Romans*, 522). That is *we were saved* in association *with hope* (or in anticipation) of a better future to come when believers no longer feel the sinful effects of the body (i.e., Adamic inclinations).

Obviously this **hope** that awaits a full salvation-sanctification experience from sin remains in the future and cannot presently be **seen** (cf. 2 Cor 4:18; Heb 11). Paul began in 5:2-5 with *hope* and ended in 5:5 with *hope* through the Spirit's link properly expressed as a now-and-not-yet experience. Yet Paul's *hope* from the viewpoint of this salvation experience of having tasted the "firstfruits of the Spirit" is to groan **for it with perseverance**. Paul means to say that upon experiencing this salvation-sanctification aspect (to be fully realized in the future) from sin (as a "firstfruits" product developed from vv 11-18) believers ought to endure suffering by *perseverance* through tribulations, which will ultimately produce hope (cf. 5:3-5). That is, the more one perseveres the more one tastes the "firstfruits" of the Spirit, which in turn produces more hope.

8:26-27. As hope aids the believers in suffering (5:3-5; 8:24-25), **the Spirit also helps** (*synantilambanetai*, the present tense means "keeps helping") **in our weaknesses** (*astheneia*). The term *astheneia* refers to the believer's "lack of spiritual insight" (BDAG, 142; cf. 6:19) in knowing **what we should pray**. Thus since believers lack sound judgment in how to present their case before God, **the Spirit Himself makes intercession** (*hyperentygchanei*, the present tense means "keeps interceding") **for us**. Though Scripture records the proper content, method (Matt 6:9-15) and principle of praying in harmony with God's will (John 14:13; 15:16; 16:123-24; 1 John 5:13-14), believers still struggle in the midst of suffering with how to ascertain God's will and in what way to pray more effectively. Therefore, as creation (vv 20-21) and believers groan (vv 22-23), now *the Spirit* intercedes by praying *for us with* compassion (i.e., **groanings**; cf. Eph 6:18). This groaning done by *the Spirit*, not believers, should not be interpreted as speaking in tongues for two reasons: All believers experiences this help, not only those who have the gift of tongues, and Scripture never connects intercessory prayer with speaking in tongues.

Therefore, even if believers cannot ascertain God's will in hard times, God the Father (implied by **He** who knows **the hearts** of men; cf. 1 Sam 16:7; 1 Kings 8:39; Heb 4:13) **knows what** is in **the mind of the Spirit** as **He makes intercession for the saints according to** *the will of* **God**. Two astonishing things should not be overlooked. Though believers or the Spirit may not utter a word of help, the believer's need is known by God's omniscience. Furthermore, in times of suffering when things look cloudy, believers need not worry to ascertain God's will correctly because the Spirit knows and appeals on that basis for us. Knowing this can bring peace to those who need it in times of suffering.

8:28-30. Based on the Spirit's intercession (vv 26-27), Paul comforts those who suffer by stating **we know** (cf. 2:3; 3:19; 6:6; 7:14; 8:22) as "common knowledge of a key truth" (Osborne, *Romans*, 219): **all things work together for good to those who love God.** Two possible interpretations exist that explain the latter statement: (1) Since all Christians are in view in vv 26-27 and 29-30, the *all things* that *work together for good* refers to all believers, whether faithful or not. Thus the phrase *those who love God* is equivalent of all who by faith in Christ have become believers, regardless of their sanctification since this is an efficacious call (seen from vv 28*b*-30) involving only justification and glorification. (2) On the other hand, the phrase *those who love God* refers only to faithful believers as opposed to all Christians (cf. John 14:15, 23-24). That is, in a sense all Christians cannot avoid human suffering, but in the larger context Paul keeps speaking to those who are Spirit led (cf. vv 13-18). Part of this experience includes suffering. Although the truth mentioned in vv 26-27 and 28*b*-30 by default applies to all believers, those believers who are suffering with Christ (vv 17-18) are the referent. Hence the phrase *all things work together for good* refers to the benefits that committed believers ought to look for in the midst of suffering. Therefore *all things*, qualified by the phrase *those who love God* (Cranfield, *Romans*, 1:428), must be viewed as applicable only to obedient believers. Thus *all things that work together for good* cannot be understood as including a believer's sinful behavior (although God allows it), because this would imply even rebellion works for the good of believers, which concept contradicts Scripture (13:4-5; 1 Cor 1:10–6:12; 2 Cor 5:10-11). Then one must conclude: Bad things happen to obedient believers for their good, whether it makes sense or not (Gen 50:20).

As those that *love God* suffer, Paul reveals that it is part of God's plan to be **called** ("invitation to experience a special privilege," BDAG, 549) to suffer because it is **according to *His* purpose**. The *called* here refers to more than an obedient response to the Spirit's leading that is obviously God's *purpose* for all Christians (Rom 5:5; 8:11-18; Eph 4:25-32; 5:18; 1 Thes 5:19; 1 John 4:19-20). It is an efficacious call guaranteeing the justification-salvation and eternal security of believers (Matt 22:14; Rom 1:1, 6-7; 11:29) as v 30 suggested by directly connecting *justification* with *glorification* and excluding *sanctification*.

To strengthen those who suffer Paul further validates this view by the term **foreknew**, which not only means *know beforehand* but *chose beforehand* (BDAG, 866; cf. MM, 538; Thayer, *Greek-English Lexicon*, 538). Hence one may argue by the following evidence that a predetermined choice made by God to elect (which in context refers to suffering believers) expresses Paul's view contextually: (1) The word *foreknew* used elsewhere by Paul in 11:2, clearly means *chose beforehand* (cf. 1 Pet 1:2, 20). This foreknowledge is not merely an acquaintance of the facts, but an active choice on God's part to have an intimate relationship with an individual (cf. Jer 1:4-5; Amos 3:2; Eph 1:4; cf. Luke 1:15; cf. Gal 1:15). (2) Furthermore the term *foreknew* appearing together with the term **predestined**, which means to *decide beforehand* as in making a choice (BDAG, 873), indicates God took the initiative in electing beforehand these suffering believers. While *foreknew* implies a gracious election, *predestined* refers to a gracious decision to carry it out (cf. Cranfield, *Romans*, 1:432). Both of which are God's sovereign doing.

God's purpose in foreknowledge and predestination is that suffering believers may share with Christ (i.e., **He**) in **firstborn** privileges (cf. cf. vv 14-15, 17-22). Hence these **many brethren**, contextually, are those who (although part of the new human race; cf. 1 John 3:2; 1 Cor 15:42-49) will have a special status as *firstborn* (=*prōtotokos*, BDAG, 894) who will reign with Christ since they also suffered with Him (v 17; 2 Tim 2:12; Heb 1:9; 3:14; Rev 2:26). As Adam needed a companion to rule the earth, Christ will have companions to rule the earth.

To further comfort suffering believers, Paul stresses God's unbroken purpose of the **called** (*ekalesen*) who are the **justified** (*edikaiōsen*) and **glorified** (*edoxasen*). That all three verbs in the Greek appear in the aorist "past" tense is significant. One's call occurs in eternity past (i.e., in human terms since God is eternal and outside of time) as v 28 showed, and the *justified* refers to those who believed. Yet the future of these believers is so certain that Paul uses the aorist past tense to describe glorification (since it is guaranteed at justification) as "an event that is not yet past as though it were already completed" (Wallace, *Greek Grammar*, 563-64). The glorification with Christ determined by suffering in vv 17-18 differs from this glorification since the *syn* prefix is not attached to the verb and is something dependent on Christ's sacrificial death (vv 31-34).

8:31-36. What then (*Ti oun*; cf. 3:1)**?** This phrase appears as a transition to affirm the certainty of God's unbroken plan called **these things** mentioned in vv 28-30. Consequently, Paul gives the utmost security and comfort to these suffering believers (which is also true of all Christians) by bringing to a climax, from vv 31-39, God's unbroken promises that by default apply to all believers.

Paul begins by stating seven rhetorical questions from vv 31-36. (1) *What then* (?) reaffirms the truth of vv 28-30. (2) **If** (i.e., since) **God *is* for us, who *can be* against us?** This points forward and means: If God's omnipotence works on our behalf, no lesser power can defeat His purpose. (3) Since God did the greatest thing of all by not sparing **His own Son** to die on the cross **for us all** to pay for sin, will He not do the lesser thing and **also freely give us all things?** The phrase *all things* is a functional equivalent of *the universe* (cf. Rev 4:11; 21:5). Therefore since the *Son* happens to be greater than the universe (cf. Col 1:13-18; Heb 1:2-3) this makes the lesser gift completely credible (cf. 5:9-10 for a greater to lesser argument, and the reverse in 4:8). (4) Paul's legal language in v 32 continues here in vv 33-34: **Who** charges **God's elect?** No power lesser than God can, since He **justifies** and is greater than all. (5) **Who** then **condemns?** No one. Christ died (v 32) and rose (v 34) from the dead making condemnation of anyone who believes impossible (5:17; cf. 4:25; 10:9). Furthermore, as the Spirit continuously helps those who suffer (cf. v 26), Christ also continuously **makes intercession** (*entygchanei*, the present tense "keeps interceding"). (6) Hence since God made the legal payment to demonstrate His love for believers (John 3:16; Rom 5:8), Paul rhetorically asks again: **Who** then can **separate** believers from Christ's **love?** (7) Absolutely nothing can separate Christians from this *love*: **Shall tribulation, or distress, or persecution, or famine, or nakedness, or peril, or sword?** Paul having undergone these very things remained faithful (2 Cor 11:26-27; 12:10). In fact, the common experience of suffering usually follows believers that love God (cf. 1 Pet 4:12-13; Rom 8:17-18). Hence Paul quotes Psalm 44:22

referring to those who face daily persecution for their conviction.

8:37-39. **Yet** (*alla*) is the strongest contrasting conjunction in the Greek used by Paul to negate the thought (stemming from vv 35-36) that suffering and death implies defeat. It is not unusual for Christians suffering through trials to doubt their eternal place in God's plan. Therefore, Paul assures the suffering believers **in all these things** (*these things* refer to all the hindrances of vv 35-36) **we are more than conquerors** (*hypernikōmen*, lit. "hyperconquerors," present tense implies "keeps on overcoming"). Obviously, Christian victory becomes possible only **through Him** (Christ) **who loved us** (cf. v 35; 2 Cor 2:14), unlike the self-sufficient attitude found in 7:14-25 (Osborne, *Romans*, 229).

Just in case the reader wonders if anything else can sever the believer's relationship with Christ or God, Paul explains (seen by the use of *gar*) the immensity of this *love* by including a list of ten things that are in contrasting pairs, except for *powers* and *other created things*. The earthly realm: (1) Beginning the list **death** picks up Paul's thought from vv 35-36. Death cannot defeat Christians as v 37 showed. (2) The word **life** may imply that while believers are still alive they can lose their eternal-salvation. Believers in death or life exist in God's presence (2 Cor 5:8-9). Consequently, eternal life cannot be lost. The spiritual realm: (3) God's **angels** would not cause believers to lose their eternal status, and neither can they. (4) The **principalities** and (5) **powers** refer to demons and the hierarchy of fallen angels that are the *powers* trying to control the present world (Eph 1:21; 3:10; 6:12). Yet, these were creatures that were not only made by Christ (Col 1:16) but were also overthrown by Him at the cross (2:15). Because these principalities were defeated they are powerless over the believer's eternal destiny. The temporal realm: (6) Neither the **present** perils mentioned above (7) **nor things to come** can sever this relationship since a believer's future is secure due to Christ's payment of sin on his behalf (vv 32-34).

The spatial realm: (8) Some scholars think **height** and (9) **depth** refer to realms where spiritual beings dwell, thus personifying them (Fitzmyer, *Romans*, 535; Käsemann, *Romans*, 251). Nowhere in the New Testament are these terms used this way (Moo, *Romans*, 546). Furthermore, Paul already covered the spiritual domain by the use of the terms *angels*, *principalities* and *powers* earlier. Hence the meaning here probably refers to the extremity of two points: heaven and hell. That is, these terms as used elsewhere in Ephesians 3:18-19 expresses the immensity of God's love. (10) In case something has evaded Paul, he says: **nor any other created thing** can absolutely **separate us from the love of God** found **in Christ Jesus our Lord**. Paul (as John 10:28-29) links Christ and God (Rom 8:35, 37) as the guarantors that keep believers eternally secure. Since God's love is unconditional, this *love* can cover any sin imaginable that might cause believers to fear being separated from Him eternally.

The phrase *Christ Jesus our Lord* occurs at the end of the justification, sanctification and glorification section. This may imply Christ's Lordship-power is involved in accomplishing all three aspects of a believer's salvation (4:24; 5:1, 21; 6:23; 7:25).

Thus the thrust of Romans 8:18-39 is to motivate committed believers to endure suffering, knowing that victory is already accomplished through Christ.

ELECTED BY GOD'S MERCY

D. The Promise of the Gospel Stands: God is Vindicated through His Sovereign Choice, in Rejecting Israel, by Extending Mercy to all and by His Wisdom (9:1–11:36)

One might expect Paul having expounded God's gracious love and promises to believers in 8:31-39 to exhort them to continue their suffering for Christ with numerous applications that usually conclude his letters. Yet, this does not occur until chapter 12 (Moo, *Romans*, 547). Instead, from chapters 9–11, Paul deals with a question that may have arisen in the minds of his Christian Jewish and Gentile readers after reading 8:31-39: *If God loves the elect and His promises cannot be dwarfed, how can He forget His chosen people and promises made to them from the Old Testament?* In other words, have the promises of Israel been transferred to the Church and if so, how can one be sure God's promises to New Testament believers will be fulfilled (cf. Schreiner, *Romans*, 471)?

Though some scholars hold that chapters 9–11 disrupts the flow of thought (Dodd, *Romans*, 148-50; Sanday and Headlam, *Romans,* 225), many today see them as an indispensable part of the letter (Schreiner, *Romans*, 469; Moo, *Romans*, 547). Since Paul also writes to ease Jewish-Gentile controversy in relation to curbing legalism in the Church (see Intro.), one must not divorce chapters 9–11 from the main thrust of the letter. Thus Paul defends the integrity of the gospel, in regard to the unfulfilled promises to Israel, by quoting extensively from the Old Testament; in Romans 9–11, specifically Isaiah, to corroborate "the gospel by showing that it provides fully for God's promises to Israel, when those promises are rightly understood" (Moo, *Romans*, 550-51; cf. 1:2; 3:21).

Thus, Paul's purpose of writing chapters 9–11 is two-fold: To vindicate God for temporarily excluding national Israel from His present plan in light of His promises in 8:28-39 to the church, and to curb Gentile arrogance having received mercy, since Israel in the future will again be grafted into God's plan. Paul's answer covers God's dealing with Israel's past (chap 9:1-29), present (chap 9:30–10:21) and future (chap 11) (MacDonald, "Romans," in *BBC*, 1714).

1. God's sovereign choice vindicates Him (9:1-29)

One should not understand the central issue in these chapters to be about predestination or even Israel's justification-salvation (Schreiner, *Romans*, 472), but about vindicating God's sovereign choice of mercy found in the Word that has not failed (9:6*a*). Although many Jews became believers, the majority did not (vv 1-5). This, however, did not nullify God's promises to the nation (v 6*a*). Paul then explains 9:6*b*-29 why God's Word did not fail. One may detect (as Schreiner, *Romans*, 472 noticed) a chiastic structure in Paul's presentation:

A. God's choice of Israel as the seed (9:6-9)
   B. God's love for His chosen (9:10-13)
      C. God's mercy, will and power to choose (9:14-18)
      C.' God's mercy, will and power to choose (9:19-24)
   B.' God's love for His chosen (9:25-26)
A.' God's choice of Israel as the seed (9:27-29)

The main theme of this chiastic structure centers on God's freedom to choose apart from any human works or knowledge involved in the choice. Yet, if these suffering believers Paul addressed in 8:13-30 ought to understand God's love mentioned in vv 31-39, they must see it against the backdrop of God's love and plan for Israel. Then the sacrifices these believers are exhorted to make in 12:1-2 will be understood as a privilege of grace and be motivated to live by God's electing grace, found in chapters 9–11.

9:1-2. Paul now addresses the subject of God's promises and plan with Israel as a way to motivate Christian obedience (cf. 12:1-2). Paul's entire treatise of chapters 9–11 is couched in a personal and legal testimony. His personal testimony appears in a positive and negative statement: **I tell the truth** and **I am not lying**. When Paul is under attack or giving an important doctrinal truth these expressions have appeared (2 Cor 11:31; Gal 1:20; 1 Tim 2:7). His premise is also legally influenced in keeping with the Old Testament Law that all matters must be verified by a minimum of two witnesses (cf. 8:16; Num 35:30; Deut 17:6; 19:15; Matt 18:16). Paul's **conscience** (as it were a separate entity) bears **witness** (*symmartyrousēs*) along with him (Schreiner, *Romans*, 479). The *syn* prefix added to the verb *witness* should be understood as bearing witness *with* not *to* (cf. 2:15; 8:16; Cranfield, *Romans*, 2:452).

Both, *Christ* and **the Holy Spirit**, bear witness to the truthfulness of Paul's concern with Israel's present predicament: **that** (*hoti*, specifies the content of that concern) **I have great sorrow and continual grief in my heart**. In keeping with the lamentations of the Old Testament prophets over sinful Israel (Jer 4:19; 14:17; Lam; Dan 9:3), Paul expresses *sorrow* and *grief* (sighing) that may directly allude to Isaiah 35:10 and 51:11 (Fitzmyer, *Romans*, 544). Paul goes through the trouble to personally and legally validate his concern because an anti-Jewish reputation preceded him (cf. Acts 21:20-26).

9:3-4. For (*gar*) explains the content and reason for Paul's *sorrow* and *grief* of v 2. If Paul **could wish** (i.e., pray, cf. Cranfield, *Romans*, 2:454-57; 10:1), hypothetically speaking, he would be **accursed** (*separated* if it were possible; cf. Gal 1:8-9) **from Christ for** (*hyper*, i.e., "on behalf of") **my brethren** (i.e., **countrymen** as ethnic **Israelites**; cf. 16:7, 11, 21). Of course, he cannot be *accursed* since nothing can *separate us from the love of God* (cf. 8:31-39). Moses spoke a similar self-sacrificing wish on behalf of Israel's deliverance (Exod 32:30-35). Paul's love, manifested by using the same preposition *hyper* above (8:31-32 indicated by Christ's atonement for men), echoes Christ's love (5:8) duplicated here as the greatest love one can have for anyone (John 15:13). Even if Israel's rejection of Christ is not clearly stated here, the context, use of the term *hyper* and vv 30-33 reveal Paul's concern of Israel's eternally unsaved status.

Even if v 3 reveals Paul's agony over Israel's unsaved state, vv 4-5 states their special privileges as recipients of God's affection in a series of six statements (composed of two sets of three) that contribute to Paul's argument vindicating God (Schreiner, *Romans*, 482-83; cf. v 6): (1) **the adoption** (cf. 8:15, 23; Exod 4:22; Jer 31:9; Hos 11:1; Jub 1:24) = *the law* (Deut 5:1-22), (2) **the glory** (refers to God's guidance and presence, Exod 16:10; 24:17; 40:34; 1 Kgs 8:11) = the service (*latreia*, to serve in temple worship; Exod 12:25-26; 13:5; Josh 22:27; 1 Chr 28:13; 1 Macc 2:22) *of God* and (3) **the covenants** (Gen 15:18; 2 Sam 7:12-16) = *the promises* (similar to that of the *covenants* [Eph 2:12] including all other promises given to Israel [2 Sam 7:12, 16, 28; Isa 9:6; Jer 31:31; Ezek 34:23], but especially the Abrahamic promises [Gen 12:1-3, 7; 13:14-17; 15; 17:1-8; 22:16-18; Rom 4:13-14, 16, 20; 9:8-9] as the term **fathers** [patriarchs, NIV] also indicates Isaac [9:10], Jacob

[Jon 4:12] and David [Acts 2:29]).

If that is not enough, God allowed the Savior of all men, **Christ**, to come from Israel. That is amazing, for He is not only a man but also **the eternally blessed God**. Elsewhere Paul and other apostles also called Jesus *God* (John 1:1; 8:58; 12:37-41; Titus 2:13; 2 Pet 1:2) providing ample proof that New Testament writers affirmed Jesus' deity.

9.6-7. These promises contextually refer to **the word of God**. They are not passed on to the Church but belong to ethnic Israel (Schreiner, *Romans*, 485). Hence the details of vv 4-5 bolster Paul's argument to vindicate God, since the failure of these promises to be realized (indicated by the phrase **taken no effect**) calls into question God's faithfulness (Schreiner, *Romans*, 482). Thus Paul explains that **not all Israel are** truly **Israel, nor *are they* all children because they are the seed** (ethnically) **of Abraham** (11:1). That is, Paul defends God's promises as being presently (through the acceptance of Christ) and eschatologically fulfilled (11:1-7, 24-29) to those who belong to spiritual not only ethnic Israel (cf. 2:28-29). Spiritual Israel is *never* called the Church, although they now belong to the Church (Acts 15:4; Eph 2:15; Gal 6:16). Instead Spiritual Israel, illustrated through the calling of *Isaac* (Gen 21:12), refers to ethnic descendants of Abraham who place their faith in Christ (cf. Acts 15:7-18; Gal 6:15-16).

There are *universal* covenants of promise (Eph 2:12) that also pertain to the New Testament Church (like partaking in Christ and the New Covenant that brings the indwelling Spirit which refers to the unconditional soteriological [i.e., justification-salvation] and sanctification [separation] elements of the covenants [cf. Gen 3:15; 12:3; Luke 22:20; Acts 10:44-45; 11:17; 2 Cor 3:6; Heb 8:13; 9:15]). Other promises pertain solely to Spiritual Israel (Rom 9:5; cf., Jer 31:31-34) and can only be attained through faith alone by accepting Jesus as the Messiah (3:21–4: 25) and by turning from sins in order to establish God's earthly kingdom (cf. Mark 1:15; Acts 3:19; see commentary in 11:26). The former concept conditioned by faith alone guarantees a person a position in the kingdom, while the latter concept conditioned by faith and obedience guarantees the establishment of the kingdom on earth.

9:8-9. To strengthen the point that physical ancestry alone (indicated by the phrase **children of the flesh**) does not guarantee a place in God's family, Paul illustrates this first through *Isaac* and then through *Jacob*. By using a strong contrast **but** (*alla*) Paul clarifies that only **children of the promise are counted as the seed**. To further elucidate that this is by God's sovereign choice, Genesis 18:10, 14 is quoted to show that *Sarah,* while being barren (Gen 11:30), bore *a son*. God rejected Ishmael because he was born through the will of man (Gen 16:15; 17:18; Gal 4:22-25), but Isaac (in order to establish God's calling according to election) was born supernaturally through the sole will of God. Hence true Israel is supernaturally born of God.

9.10-13. To further validate God's sovereign choice apart from man's actions, Paul adds another illustration from Isaac's sons, since God's covenant was not only established with *Isaac,* but also *with his descendants after him* (Gen 17:19). Thus by stating that **Rebecca also had conceived**, Paul may be thinking of her barrenness since she also *conceived* supernaturally (Gen 25:21).

In case someone might object that God's sovereign choice to bless Isaac is not unusual since he was Abraham's firstborn from Sarah, the example of Jacob and Esau's birth should dispel that argument since both children came from the same mother and father. Furthermore, before *the children* were even **born**, or had **done any good or evil** God chose. Thus **the purpose according to election** refers to God's determination to distribute blessings apart from man's **works** (disallowing foreseen faith as a basis for God's election) **but of Him who calls** (i.e., an efficacious call apart from works, cf. 8:28, 30; 9:7). God makes this clear by going against the cultural norm of the day when the younger served the older, to show His sovereign choice in the matter: *"The older shall serve the younger"* (Gen 25:23; i.e., the Edomite descendants of Esau served Jacob, 1 Sam 14:47; 2 Sam 8:14; 1 Kgs 11:15-16; 22:47). Through God's choice Jacob receives the blessing. Although men are free to choose or reject God, since they are sinners they reject Him (Rom 3:10-12, 23). Yet for those who God elects, He rigorously pursues (by grace) them to secure their eternal destiny.

Though God secures the elects' eternal destiny, the main point here is a sovereign choice for service that includes salvation. Hence Paul switches now from individual to national election by quoting Malachi 1:2-3: *"Jacob I have loved, but Esau I have hated."* The term *hated* here is an idiom understood as loving less (Gen 29:30-31; Matt 6:24; Luke 14:26; John 12:25). The two concepts of *love* and *hate* here are not to be viewed as feelings but a decision God took to bestow His mercy on Jacob and not Esau's descendants (Moo, *Romans*, 587). Paul's point is to show that God remained true to His electing purpose in passing judgment on Esau's descendants, the Edomites, who rightly deserved it; instead, He had mercy on Jacob's descendants, the Israelites, who also rightly deserved judgment but received grace (unmerited favor). Hence since God's electing purposes cannot fail neither can His promises (9:6*b*).

9:14-18. What shall we say then? This typical Pauline transition raises a question (through an imaginary objector) from something previously taught to advance his argument (cf. 3:1). As a result of God choosing Isaac over Ishmael (vv 7-9) and Jacob over Esau (vv 10-13), the question of God's fairness naturally arises: *Is* *there* **unrighteousness with God?** To which Paul strongly replies: **Certainly not!** (cf. 3:4). The issue here is not God's justice but His sovereign choice to have mercy on whomever He wills as He indicated **to Moses** (Exod 33:19). Therefore, it really does not depend on man's conduct (i.e., **not of him who wills, nor of him who runs**), but is solely based on **God who shows mercy**. Hence, one should not view God's choice as being unfair to those who do not receive mercy; instead, one should wonder why God is being merciful to anyone.

Furthermore, these passages refer to earthly privileges and promised blessings that include eternal life. God bypassing Ishmael and Esau does not mean they could not be eternally saved. However, those that form part of spiritual Israel, who inherit the promises of God (cf. 9:5), are the elect that also place their faith in Christ.

Some argue that chapters 9–11 refer to the historical destiny of different nations and not individual salvation (Morris, *Romans*, 356; Cranfield, *Romans*, 2:479). While that is true, chapters 9–11 cannot be viewed as excluding individual salvation for the following reasons Schreiner documents ("Does Romans 9 Teach Individual Election Unto Salvation?" 25-34): (1) Contextually, in chapters 9–11 Paul agonized over Israel because the majority of them were not eternally saved as vv 1-5, 30-33, 10:3-4, 11:1-7 and 26-32 indicates (cf. 9:3-4). (2) The whole premise of chapters 9–11 is to support Paul's thesis in 9:6*a*. That *God's word has not failed* must be linked to Paul's agonizing statements of vv 1-5 about Israel's separation from Christ. The rest of the chapters attest that God's Word has not failed even if a great portion of Israel did not believe in Christ. (3) The phrases *children of God* and *children of the promise* in 9:8 are always used by Paul for believers (cf. 8:16, 21; Phil 2:15; Gal 4:28). (4) The terms *works* and *calls* in v 11 used by Paul here and elsewhere refer to justification. Thus the *works of the* *law* or any kind of *works* justify no one (3:20, 27-28; 4:2; 9:32; 11:6; Gal 2:16; 3:2, 5, 10; Eph 2:9; 2 Tim 1:9; Titus 3:5). Paul's use of the term *call* (by God), in the preceding and proceeding context (8:28, 30; 9:24-26; 11:29 and similar terminology in 2 Timothy 1:9) validates the individual salvation view here. That also holds true most of the time when Paul uses the term *call* elsewhere (1 Cor 1:9; Gal 1:6, 15; 5:8; Eph 4:1, 4; 1 Thess 2:12; 4:7; 5:24; 2 Thess 2:14; 1 Tim 6:12). (5) In Romans 9:21-23 Paul mentions two key parallel terms *destruction* and *glory* with eternal verities, since *glory* in Romans and elsewhere most of the time comes with eternal implications (2:7, 10; 5:2; 8:21, 28-30; 1 Cor 2:7; 15:41; Eph 1:18; Phil 3:21; Col 1:27; 3:4; 1 Thess 2:12; 2 Thess 2:14). (6) Finally, the remnant of God's sovereign choice in 11:1-7 confirms that the entire context of chapters 9–11 involves Israel's eternal salvation. Otherwise, Israel left alone would never believe in Christ and turn to God to be delivered from wrath (11:26-32), which will result in their King and kingdom's arrival on earth (Isa 66; Matt 23:37–25:26; Mark 1:15; Acts 3:19).

At this point one might wonder about man's free will. Thus, the question arises: *Does God accomplish His purpose in election by letting human freedom take its course?* Yes, but one should not presuppose that human freedom takes precedence over God's electing choice. Rather an omniscient God aware of all possible scenarios and their outcomes, elects first (using an undisclosed criterion), but then accomplishes His purpose through human freedom. That God uses human freedom to accomplish, as well as enforce, His choice may be illustrated through **the Scripture** account of **Pharaoh** (Exod 9:16). Only after Pharaoh initially rebels (5:2) and hardens his *own* heart (7:13, 14, 22; 8:15, 19, 32; 9:7) does God harden his heart (3:19-20; 4:21; 9:12). God, knowing beforehand Pharaoh's response (cf. Exod 4:21-23), uses him to demonstrate

His *power* and declare His *name* throughout **the earth**. Therefore, if God chooses to withhold **mercy** and **harden** a heart, He still reserves the right to deal with sinful man as He wishes.

9:19. Paul again anticipates an objection (**"Why does He still find fault? For who has resisted** [=*anthestēken* perfect tense, and *continues to resist*] **His will?"**) from his readers from what he has just argued: Mercy is neither a human right nor a divine obligation. Rather God extends mercy to undeserving men as He wills. Hence the objector thinks, *if all rebellious men like Pharaoh serve God's purpose why should God blame them? Could they have acted otherwise?* Thus one may conclude: Is God's will not the basis of human behavior instead of judgment?

9:20-21. Paul's answer here concerns itself with how men, being the object of judgment, sit in judgment of God their Judge. It is as if man blames God for being **formed** or **made** a sinner. Yet, man has no right since it is by man's (not God's) choice that (beginning with Adam; cf. Gen 3:6-7) all sin (Rom 3:10-12, 23). Hence Paul quotes the parody of Isaiah 29:16; 45:9 to affirm this point. The creature talking back to the Creator is like a child taking back to his parents; punishment will ensue (Osborne, *Romans*, 252). Paul, of course, would argue that God's hardening was not a capricious act, but God makes permanent what originates in man's sinfulness from birth (cf. Rom 3:23; 5:12). Furthermore, Paul's original intent is to communicate divine prerogatives based on godly wisdom unknown in Scripture. If not he would have also pointed to Pharaoh's initial hardening that preceded divine hardening (cf. v 18).

Thus God, the Creator (as **the potter**), has **power** (i.e., divine right) over man, the creature (**the clay**). Hence out of one **lump** of clay, two vessels are formed: **one vessel for honor and another for dishonor** (a common metaphor used in Judaism and Scripture; Job

10:9; 38:14; Ps 2:9; Is 29:16; 41:25; 45:9; 64:7; Jer 18:1-6; Sir 27:5; 33:13; Wis 15:7; *T. Naph.* 2:2, 4; 1QS 11:22; 2 Tim 2:20). Rebecca's twins (analogous to the *lump*) may also be in Paul's mind (cf. vv 11-13) along with the Gentiles and Israel (Isa 29:16; Jer 18:6) who are now the vessels of God's wrath (cf. vv 22-26). As one man serves God as an honorable utensil, another serves Him as a dishonorable utensil. All kitchens require different kinds of utensils: nice dinnerware to eat and metal pans to catch the grease. Both are useful, but Paul insists God reserves the right to make both serve His end.

9:22-24. Immediately Paul moves to defend God's sovereign right as *the potter* over *the clay* from the illustration to the following application (Cranfield, *Romans*, 2:493). **What if** (lit. Gk, *ei de*=But if) begins a conditional sentence without completing it (e.g., it has no apodosis). Though various solutions exist (Moo, *Romans*, 604) one of the solutions interprets the conditional sentence as describing a hypothetical situation. Such a construction that supplies an expression concluding a thought (known as an apodosis) of a conditional clause is common in Classical Greek (LSJM, 481) and elsewhere in the New Testament (Luke 19:42; John 6:62; Acts 23:9 [NU text]). This means Paul expects the readers to complete the thought *What if God* by contextually supplying the apodosis: "and He has the right" (v 21), which Paul believes to be true, not hypothetical.

God is revealed in both kinds of vessels (by showing His wrath and mercy to both Gentiles and Jews) developed in 1:16–4:25 and 9:22-26. He wants **to show *His* wrath** (*tēn orgēn*) **and to make His power known.** Both terms *show* and *power* also used of Pharaoh in v 17 suggest Paul is still thinking of him as the primary example of God's wrath. Thus God **endured** Pharaoh a prototype of **the vessels of wrath prepared for destruction** so that He could demonstrate His power through the ten plagues of Egypt.

Two theological issues arise in vv 22-23. Is the *wrath* spoken of here eternal and do vv 22-23 teach double predestination? First, numerous reasons argue for understanding *wrath* to be a time-bound manifestation of God's displeasure and display against sin. (1) The Greek *tēn orgēn* having the article of previous reference refers to God's wrath in 1:18 (cf. 1:18; 2:5, 8; 3:5; 5:9; 13:4-5). (2) Logic dictates that the phrase *vessels of wrath* refers to a present event, because the parallel phrase *vessels of mercy* (the **called…Jews** and **Gentiles**) must be a present occurrence that God is now making *known* to *show* (vv 17, 22) *the riches of His glory*. (3) Even if the parallel expressions *destruction* and *glory* in context encompass a temporal and eternal scope (cf. v 16), it does not logically prove that wrath is eternal, since *destruction* is the result of *wrath*. This *destruction* is not equal to *wrath*, but is the final outcome of it. That is, wrath is what draws God's time-bound judgment, while destruction is the outcome of final judgment. To interpret the cause (wrath) as equal to the final effect (destruction) results in merging two related but distinct concepts (cf. Lopez, *Wrath of God*, 45-66).

Second, though one may misinterpret this verse as teaching double predestination, enough details exist to prove otherwise. (1) The first occurrence of the word *prepared* (*katērtismena*, perfect passive) appears in a different grammatical construction than the second word *prepared beforehand* (*proētoimasen*, aorist active). Since the passive and middle voices are similar in form in the Greek, perhaps *katērtismena* may be understood as a middle that emphasizes: "they prepared themselves," implying also that people may have the ability to change their course if they so choose (Cranfield, *Romans*, 2:495-96; cf. Murray, *Romans*, 2:36). The view that interprets *katērtismena* as meaning: "they prepared themselves," originated with Chrysostom and was later reiterated by Pelagius. Attractive as this view may seem, by shifting the act of preparation to the vessel instead of God, it is debatable on a purely grammatical basis (cf. Wallace, *Greek Grammar*, 417-18) since the thirteen occurrences of this word in the New Testament appear in both voices. While it is true that the perfect passive implies a divine predetermined action, Paul may have just wanted to point simply to the vessels' *readiness* for destruction that began beforehand and continues to the present. Thus, even if one understood *katērtismena* as a perfect passive here, it does not mean God prepared them for destruction or even that the vessels prepared themselves (cf. Cranfield, *Romans*, 2:495-96). (2) Furthermore, the second verb *proētoimasen* includes an active verb with a *pro* prefix implying divine preparation in advance, meaning: "He prepared in advance." (3) Since the first verb is a first person plural participle and the second verb is in the third person singular, this implies two different entities are doing the preparation. Therefore, to assume the verb *katērtismena* appears in the passive voice is highly questionable based on this piece of evidence since the plural form indicates people other than God were involved in the preparation in v 22. Thus God cannot be the One doing the preparation in v 22. (4) Even if one interprets two different entities doing the preparing, the contextual sense showing God's sovereignty is not lost because He still reserves the right (as argued in vv 16-18) to withhold or extend mercy to whom He wishes. (5) To interpret the first occurrence of *prepared* in the passive voice, as God doing it, still does not imply double predestination, because this verse does not show what criterion God used for preparation. This is seen through how God dealt with Pharaoh. For example, Pharaoh hardens his heart prior to God preparing him to show His glory (see commentary in 9:14-18, 20-21). God placing Pharaoh in a state of hardening does not imply He was unfair since Pharaoh hardens his heart initially and was the primary cause of his own demise. God only prolonged what was Pharaoh's initial choice in order to manifest

His glory. Scripture always implicates sinful-man as the criterion used of God to condemn him (Gen 3:1-19; Rom 1:18–3:20, 23; 5:12; 9:17-18). Conversely, Scripture shows the *vessels of mercy* (Jews and Gentiles), that God *called* by preparing them before time began (cf. Rom 8:28-31; 9:7-13, 15-18; cf. Eph 1:4), as the objects of His grace. This is not unfair since having unmerited favor towards sinners is never a matter of justice. Justice demands that all of humanity be summoned to eternal punishment. By what criterion God bypasses some people to their own demise and actively chooses others to be the *vessels of mercy* is an undisclosed and divine mystery of Scripture.

9:25-29. God's calling of both Jews and Gentiles, who made up the church in Rome (cf. Intro.), is verified as something planned beforehand. Hence Paul quotes, from vv 25-29, a number of Old Testament passages to support his point (Hos 2:23; 1:10; Isa 10:22-23; 1:9; 13:19).

Paul's two quotes from **Hosea** (2:23; 1:10) in the original context refers to the sinful Northern Kingdom of Israel who God forsook to the Assyrian invasion and exile (1:2-9). Hence God directs Hosea to name his children *Lo-ammi* (***not My people***) and *Lo-ruhamah* (***not beloved***) to symbolize God's abandonment. However, God promised to again restore them as His *people to be called sons of the living God*. Yet, Paul applies it here to the Gentiles. Three things may be said. (1) Paul could have changed the original meaning. This is highly unlikely since elsewhere when Paul uses Scripture he never subverts the original context. (2) God could have meant, whether Hosea knew it or not, to include Gentiles under a fuller meaning that progressive revelation later reveals. (3) Paul makes simply an analogical application here to Gentiles similar to the use of Hosea 2:23 in 1 Peter 2:10. This latter option seems to be the case.

Nevertheless, Israel is still the prime example of God's wrath in chapters 9–11 (causing many to think God's promises to Israel failed). Paul by quoting verses from **Isaiah** (10:22-23; 1:9; 13:19) refers to God's wrath coming through the Assyrian invasion in 722 B.C. that demolished Israel's (northern tribes) national existence. The context in Isaiah 10:6 also mentions wrath, "...the people of My wrath" which refers to Israel. Yet, God, by His mercy, intervenes and says through Isaiah that a *remnant will* return (10:22). Isaiah's passage does not use the Hebrew word *saved* (*yāŝa*) but "return" (*šûb*). Paul uses the term *saved* (*sōzō*) quoted from the LXX because it exhibits the same range of meaning as the Hebrew term *šûb* that one could translate here *delivered* (cf. Lopez, *Old Testament Salvation–From What?* 49-64). Thereby implying *the remnant will be delivered.* That is, those delivered are the Jewish believers (implied by the term *remnant*; cf. Rom 11:5) that return to dwell in the land. Thus, the common meaning of *deliverance from wrath* (cf. 5:9) used throughout Romans also appears here, as Israel will ultimately be *delivered* (return) to their land from God's wrath revealed in the exile (11:26-32). Hence, unlike the quote from Hosea applied to Gentiles, Paul's quotations from Isaiah indicate a common feature in Jewish thought: God's covenant people were to be spiritually redeemed, but also expected to dwell in their promised land (e.g., Gen 12:1-3; 15:7-21; Deut 28–30) where Messiah would reign over them (2 Sam 7:10-16; Ps 89). Therefore, to exclude these features as part of Paul's main emphasis seen in these quotes misses the point he is defending about God's unfulfilled promises (cf. 9:6).

2. God is vindicated by Israel's rejection (9:30–10:21)

From chapters 9:30–10:21, Paul switches subject matter from God's sovereign vindication of Israel's past election, to His vindication of abandoning Israel presently, due to their rejection of His righteousness. Hence the term *righteousness* occurs eleven times in this section (9:30 [3x], 31; 10:3 [3x], 4-6, 10). Accepting this *righteousness* resulting in justification is only a means, but the end is for Israel to be delivered from God's wrath and that comes only through obedience (10:9-21). In turn, Israel will enjoy the earthly privileges and promises expected (cf. 9:4-5, 27-29).

9.30-33. Paul, anticipating an objection from the previous point, asks a rhetorical question: **What shall we say then?** (cf. 3:1; 4:1; 6:1; 8:31; 9:14). This leads to a comparison of **Gentiles** and Jews as if they are two runners (understood by the term **pursue** *diōkō*, lit. "to follow in haste, *run after*," BDAG, 254). The pursuing-prize is **righteousness**. This *righteousness* is what all men need in order to be acquitted before God (3:21–4:25). The Gentiles, not running to win (1:18-32), found this **righteousness** because they went about it the right way, on the basis **of faith** (cf. 1:17; 3:30); **but Israel**, running harder to win (2:1–3:20), in **pursuing** the same *righteousness* went about it the wrong way, through **the law of righteousness** (i.e., the *law* as the road to achieving *righteousness* before God). Obedience is not the point here; the point is being rightly related to God. Thus since the Jews did not **seek** God **by faith** (see intro. to section 3:21–4:25) but instead **by the works of the law** (i.e., the Mosaic Law; cf. 2:12) **they stumbled** over **the stone** by rejecting the righteousness offered by faith in Christ (11:11; 1 Pet 2:4-8). Israel missed the principle law of faith (cf. 3:27-28) and established the law of works as a means to be rightly related to God. Therefore, when Christ arrived offering a righteousness by faith alone, the Jews were offended. To show that God was not surprised and anticipated the rejection of the *stone* (i.e., Jesus Christ and His righteousness) as part of His overall plan, Paul combines citations from Isaiah 8:14 and 28:18.

10 DELIVERANCE FROM THE SIN PROBLEM

10:1-4. Having explained why Israel stumbled, Paul echoes a similar concern to that of 9:1-6 before elaborating further. Paul's **desire and prayer to God** is that **Israel ...be saved** (Gk *sōtērian*, lit. the noun *salvation*).

The *salvation* in 10:1 echoes the *salvation from wrath* of 1:16-18 that began the argument of the book. Israel rejected God's righteousness by not believing in Messiah (9:3, 30-33; 10:2-4), a doctrine established in the Old Testament (cf. comments 4:3). That Israel is under God's wrath (2:1–3:20; 9:22, 26-29) is evident in the immediate context. Therefore, this *salvation* must contextually be understood as *saved* (=deliverance) from the type of *wrath* found in 9:27. Upon closer examination of 9:27-29, one finds Paul's concern for corporate Israel illustrated through the *remnant* that will be delivered from God's wrath by returning from exile to inhabit the Promised Land. Paul's quote, in 10:13 from Joel 2:32 "day of the Lord" (=day of wrath) along with 11:26 "all Israel will be saved," also proves he has Israel's national deliverance in mind as the primary meaning of the word *salvation*. This *salvation* experience finds its basis in justification (3:21–4:25; 9:30-33; 10:2-4), but includes a broader scope that entails national deliverance from their enemies (9:27-29; 10:9–11:1-7, 26); that includes the world, the flesh and the devil (Dillow, *Reign of the Servant Kings*, 123).

For (*gar*) is an explanatory conjunction occurring four times linking vv 2-5. Paul uses it each time to further elaborate the pre-vious point. Verse 2 gives further reason for Paul's longing to see Israel delivered (v 1), but revisits the same theme of 9:30-33, since their deliverance will never occur until they first accept God's righteousness.

This time Paul personally testifies of Israel's **zeal** (*zēlos*, "an intense interest ...marked by a sense of dedication," BDAG, 427) **for God, but not according to knowledge** (*epignōsis*, implies a "*precise and correct knowledge*," Thayer, *Greek-English Lexicon*, 237; cf. MM, 237). Lacking an accurate understanding (implied also by the word **ignorant**) **of God's righteousness** they **established** (*histēmi*) **their own righteousness.** The term *histēmi* refers to "put into force" in a legal way similar to its use, in Acts 7:60 and Hebrews 10:9, of the sacrificial system (BDAG, 482). Since the Jews resorted to the legal system to attain righteousness by works (9:32; 3:20, 27-28; 4:2, 6; 9:11), they obviously misunderstood and therefore rejected **the righteousness of God** that establishes a relationship solely on the basis of faith in Christ (9:32; 3:21-30). This is not some new doctrine but is well established in the Old Testament (cf. 1:2; 3:21; 4:1-5).

Thus, Paul's readers should not be surprised with his explana-tion of the original intent of the Law. Verse 4a, **Christ is the end** (*telos*) **of the law for righteousness**, may be understood in various ways since the Greek term *telos* refers to either *termination* (by put-ting an end to something) or *goal* (the purpose toward which some-thing is directed) (BDAG, 998).

(1) By Christ fulfilling the Mosaic Law He terminated it (7:1-6; Gal 3:19, 23; 4:9-11; 5:1; Mark 7:18-19; Luke 16:16; John 1:17; 2 Cor 3:6-11; Heb 7:12; 9:10). Paul has contrasted in 9:31-32 and 10:2-3 that righteousness comes by faith in Christ not the Law. He fulfilled the Law (Matt 5:17-18). Hence the Law no

longer has use in pointing one to Christ since the reality to which it pointed has now arrived. Almost all Bible translations render the word *telos* as *end*. Almost all advocates of this view understand that the Law was never intended to be the means of justification (Murray, *Romans*, 2:50-51). This view along with view three has strong contextual support.

(2) Christ's arrival is the end of the Law for righteousness that one obtained through obeying the Mosaic Law. This contradicts Paul's argument that righteousness is attained by faith alone (3:21–4:25; 9:30-33).

(3) Faith in Christ to obtain righteousness is the goal the Law intended (Gal 3:24ff.). God gave Israel the Mosaic Law primarily with the purpose to reveal His character and standards of holiness. Accordingly, man would realize his inability to be good enough to earn a righteous standing before God (3:20; 7:7-13). Hence man had to look elsewhere to obtain the righteousness the Law provided by having faith in the Seed to come (cf. 4:3), known today as Jesus. Therefore, anyone who believes in Christ fulfills the Law's aim.

(4) Some have joined views one and three and argue for a combination with a slight nuance. That is, the *goal* of the Law was to point one to faith in Christ, but using the Law as an operating principle that leads one to Christ has now *ended* (cf. Gal 3:24ff; BDAG, 998; Barrett, *Romans*, 184). One may understand v 4 in both ways. Even if the subject of terminating the Law is contextually not broached until now, the issue of works-salvation related to Law (9:31-32; 10:2-3) allows the subject to surface. To understand *goal* and *end* contextually also aids in interpreting the racing terminology of 9:30-33. That is, *Christ is the goal* of the race to righteousness which the Jews *rejected* but the Gentiles *accepted* by faith; in addition Christ is also the *end* of the race since the *goal* to which

it pointed has arrived. Thus, the combination view fits the context best; the correct *goal* of the Law was to lead one to Christ, but Jews turned it into a works-based-salvation; and the Law reached the *end* of its use as an operating principle that points to Christ since He has now arrived and furnishes the righteousness **to everyone who believes** (cf. 1:16). The Greek word *telos* and English words *goal* and *end* convey perfectly both of these meanings (cf. BDAG, 998-99).

10:5-8. Having explained the *end* and correct *goal* of the Law to obtain a righteous standing before God, Paul now clarifies (**For**), by quoting Leviticus 18:5, the correct way to obtain a sanctifying **righteousness** by keeping **the law**. Numerous views exist to explain Paul's use of this Old Testament verse.

(1) This verse explains (e.g., *for*) v 4 by showing how Christ was able to provide the righteousness men needed by keeping *the law* perfectly. Paul quotes Leviticus 18:5 to express Christ's victory in keeping the Law (Cranfield, *Romans*, 2:521-22). However, the context and verse preclude a direct reference to Christ, since man is the specific referent here (***The man who does;*** cf. Schreiner, *Romans*, 551).

(2) The Old Testament taught that man can obtain a justify-ing-righteousness by works of the Law. Yet, this view contradicts the Old Testament and Paul's teaching in Romans (cf. 1:2; 3:20; 4:3).

(3) Perhaps Paul speaks hypothetically referring (by quoting Lev 18:5) to how man could obtain a righteous standing before God if he kept the Law flawlessly (cf. 2:7-8, 13). While Paul may entertain a hypothetical argument here, three reasons militate against this view as the following and final position explains.

(4) First, the Jews were zealous in keeping the Mosaic Law to obtain a justifying-righteousness. Hence the use of Leviticus 18:5

clarifies (*For*) v 4 by depicting the correct way to understand the Law. As Romans 4 clearly teaches, Israel received the Law after understanding that justifying-righteousness came by faith alone (Gen 15:6; Gal 3:17-18), but to obtain a sanctifying **righteousness** one kept **the law** that stems from faith (cf. Kaiser, "Leviticus 18:5 and Paul: Do this and You Shall Live [Eternally?]," 24). The obedience indicated by Leviticus 18:5 was not viewed as a way of earning justification-salvation, but refers to living obediently to the Law in contrast to other nations (Lev 18:3-4). Consequently, an obedient lifestyle to the Law produces a quality of life (v 5). Second, Romans 10:5 cannot stand in contrast in the overall context of vv 6-8, for Paul would be opposing one Old Testament passage (Lev 18.5) with another that teaches the possibility of keeping God's mandate for sanctification (Deut 30:12-14). Consequently this would not sit well with Jews who Paul desires to convince (Schreiner, *Romans*, 552). Hence Paul also does not pit two Old Testament passages against each other in Galatians 3:11-12, but corrects the misuse of the Law as a means of justification. The Law was meant as a means for sanctification; however, New Testament believers are not under the Law. Thus, anyone not obeying the Law totally (like the Galatian believers who advocated keeping part of it) would come under a curse, but Christ lifted that curse and placed Christians under a new system for sanctification (Gal 3:10-13). Third, Leviticus 18:5 points to works (i.e., *does*) stemming from faith similar to the Old Testament passage of Deuteronomy 30:12-14 cited in the context of vv 6-8 developed below.

Connecting v 5 to vv 6-8 is vital in understanding Paul's thrust of the remaining section that concludes with v 21. **But** contrasts one mode of obtaining sanctifying-righteousness (the righteousness of the Law in v 5) with another. That is, since the Law is no longer the mode by which one obtains a sanctifying-righteousness, Paul switches to the new mode of this dispensation undergirded by **the righteousness of faith** (i.e., justification by faith; cf. 1:17; 3:26, 30; 4:16; 5:1; 9:30, 32). This refers to a justifying-faith as the prerequisite to produce sanctifying-righteousness before anyone can obey and call on God for aid seen in Deuteronomy 30:12-14 and Romans 10:9-10, 13.

Though the *modes* of how to obtain sanctification have changed with the coming of Christ (cf. 7:1-6; Gal 3:19, 24-25), the same *means* continues: in both eras sanctification (seen here through confession and calling on the Lord) follows a righteousness that stems from *faith* (vv 6, 8-10). To prove this point, Paul quotes the major parts of Deuteronomy 30:12-14, to show how Israel should have sought divine help stemming from faith (Hart, *Why Confess Christ?* 28-29). Paul's initial phrase in v 6: **Do not say in your heart** comes from Deuteronomy 9:4. Contextually this refers to a warning against a heart of self-sufficiency and self-righteousness derived from a lack of justifying-faith. Hence Deuteronomy 30:12-14 must be seen in light of possessing justification prior to obedience taking place. In addition, Paul probably thought of the immediate context in 30:1-10 that spoke of God's exile-judgment and return of Israel (at Christ's second coming; cf. Rom 11:26-32) occurring on the basis of faith when God would circumcise their hearts (i.e., the New Covenant of Jer 31:31-34). Then, Paul's quote (Deut 30:12-14) finds the basis of obeying the commandments stemming from faith (Deut 9:4).

The phrases, *'Who will ascend into heaven?'* and *'Who will descend into the abyss?'* (i.e., "sea," but *abyss* applies since "abyss" and "sea" were closely linked in Jewish thought; cf. Ps 107:26; Jonah 2:3-10) in vv 6-7 refer in the original context of going to great extremes in order to decipher God's will (Deut 30:11). Yet, His will was revealed by the *commandment* (which is the antecedent of both phrases) indicative of the entire Law mentioned in Deuteronomy that Israel was urged to *obey* (Deut 30:10-11). Therefore, any excuse for not obeying was out of the question, because it was not as if Israel had to go up to heaven to bring the Law down or below to bring it up. God delivered the Law to them and they knew it and needed to *do it* (vv 12-14). Though Paul does not include the phrase *do it,* found at the end of each verse of Deuteronomy 30:12-14, it must surely be in his thoughts. Otherwise Paul is guilty of misusing the original context that referred to obeying the Law. The partial citing of a passage followed by an explanation that encompasses the entire concept of the passage was common in Jewish interpretation (cf. the DSS; Philo, *Posterity of Cain,* 24 §§ 84-85 [pp 140]; Baruch 3:29-30; Dunn, *Romans 9–16*: 604-5).

Now Paul applies the same truth of *having* and *obeying* the Word to the person of Christ who is now God's final revelation (Heb 1:2). Since Christ has come in the flesh (John 1:14; Phil 2:5-8) through the incarnation, no one needs to *ascend into heaven to bring Christ down from above.* Nor does anyone need **to bring Christ up from the dead**, since He has already risen from the dead (Matt 27:53; Acts 1:22; 2:31; 4:33; Rom 6:5; 10:9; 1 Cor 15:4-6). Therefore, as the Old Testament revelation was given to the Jews to be believed and obeyed by faith (cf. v 5), Christ is God's New Testament revelation given to Jews and Gentiles to be believed and obeyed by faith (John 1:1, 17; Matt 17:5; Luke 6:46; cf. Moo, *Romans,* 653). Similar to that of Israel (cf. Rom 10:5-8), sanctifying-righteousness for Christians that produces the ability to obey stems from justifying-faith. This is developed below by the expressions *heart* (where belief takes place) and *mouth* (where obedience takes place). Thus believers need not view God's mandates as too hard to obey, if only they would ask for divine assistance. Hence, the term **word** (Gk *rhēma*, what is said or spoken; cf. BDAG, 905) is something verbally pronounced that *is near* to the recipient, since it is done with the **mouth** as the vehicle used to ask for help. The term **heart** is the center or intellect where man believes. Thus, the spoken **word of faith** refers to what must first be believed by the *heart* (i.e., mind or center where thoughts occur; BDAG, 508) before believers can ask with the *mouth* for divine assistance to obey God (cf. Deut 30:14). That is, when a listener believes in Christ, that belief occurs in the *heart* (i.e., mind). Having believed, Christ also comes *near* to deliver the Christian but only when public confession occurs, as an expression of the *mouth* (cf. Deut 4:7). The nearness of the spoken *word* verbalized through the *mouth* that was already believed in the *heart* expresses two different aspects of the believer's response to *the word of faith* (cf. 1: 5) that Paul develops in vv 9-13.

10:9-13. Paul explains the content (i.e., *hoti*=**that** instead of *because*) of *the word of faith* that functions as a synonym for the gospel message found in Romans 10:9-10: **if you confess with your mouth the Lord Jesus and believe in your heart that God has raised Him from the dead, you will be saved. For with the heart one believes unto righteousness, and with the mouth confession is made unto salvation.** Perhaps no other verses have been as widely misunderstood as these. Hence numerous interpretations appear in the commentary tradition.

(1) *Lordship salvation view*: Confessing *the Lord Jesus* refers to a personal conviction that includes trusting, repenting from sins and submission to His lordship (MacArthur, *Student Bible*, 1522). A passage like Matthew 16:25-26 seems to suggest the same. However, none of these conditions appear here, and the term *Lord* refers to Jesus' deity (cf. view 5) not His mastery over the believer. John's gospel, which is primarily evangelistic in purpose (20:31),

never mentions Jesus' lordship as a condition for eternal life. Though Jesus' call for allegiance in Matthew demands obedience, His offer of salvation refers to a host of blessings now and in eternity (cf. Glasscock, *Matthew*, 350) but not eternal life. Hence one must ask, "*Does salvation here refer to justification?*"

(2) *Two condition view*: Some interpret these verses as referring to justification-salvation conditioned upon two separate prerequisites, *confess* and *believe* (Boice, *Romans 9–11*, 3:1209; Hodge, *Romans*, 341, 343). Clearly Paul states at the end of both verses that salvation rests upon two conditions. Yet, this view lacks any parallel support in the New Testament that conditions justification-salvation upon confession (cf. 1 Tim 6:12). Hence Paul does not mention confession as a condition for obtaining justification in section 3:21–4:25.

(3) *Synonymous view*: Others also view vv 9-10 as referring to justification-salvation, but the apparent conditions of confession and faith are relegated as mere synonyms (Nygren, *Romans*, 383; Moo, *Romans*, 657). In this view, confession and faith can be interpreted as Old Testament parallel statements, since both terms appear in vv 9-10 (Bultmann, *TDNT*, 6:209). Three things argue against this view: If confession and faith are synonyms, why are two conditions set forth before obtaining salvation? Furthermore, vv 9-10 really develop a chiastic not a parallel structure (Edwards, *Romans*, 254). Also, it is not wise to blur the distinction between *mouth* and *heart* since out of forty-two occurrences where both of these terms appear in the same verse, they are almost always distinguished.

(4) *Genuine evidence view*: One may see confession of the mouth as the external evidence of the genuineness of internal faith (Murray, *Romans*, 2:56). Matthew 15:18 supports the idea that verbal confession expresses external evidence of an internal reality. Yet, there is nothing in the context to suggest that confession is an evidence of

true faith. That is totally imported into the passage. In other places where people believe in Christ, automatic confession does not result (cf. John 12:42).

(5) *The deity of Christ view*: Yet, others understand confession to be a creedal statement (e.g., Deut 6:4) based on faith that Jesus is God. This would imply that believing in Jesus' deity is a condition for justification-salvation (Harrison, *Romans*, in *EBC*, 112; Ryrie, *So Great Salvation*, 70-73). While confessing Jesus as Lord does refer to His deity (as vv 13 and 14:11 supports), the question remains, *"Does confession refer to justification-salvation?"* If confessing Jesus' deity is a prerequisite condition to obtaining justification how were the early disciples in the Old Testament and New Testament justified since they did not grasp His deity (Mark 4:41; John 14:7-9)? One would have to postulate an existing condition for justification *now* that was absent in a previous era. While information about the object of faith (Jesus) increases through new revelation (name, status, place of birth, type of death and resurrection, etc…), the bare minimum of information and sole condition for justification does not change: the object of faith is God's promised Messiah (cf. 4:3) and the only condition for justification is to believe in Him alone (cf. 3:21–4:25).

(6) *Christian deliverance view*: Contextually, vv 9-10 reiterate the truth in Deuteronomy 9:4 and 30:12-14, which is quoted in vv 5-8: namely that obeying and calling for divine help (conceptually understood as "salvation") is available to all who are justified (v 6; Hart, *Why Confess Christ?* 29, 31). No doubt Paul thinks of Christ's coming "from above" and rising "from the dead" (vv 6-8) to correspond with the truth of vv 9-10. Hence one should link the theme of salvation-deliverance to live in vv 1, 5 and 9-13 as providing abundant life only to those who *believe* and *confess*. Although Paul begins v 9 by mentioning confession before belief, the conjunction

for in 10:10 explains the correct logical sequence of occurrence, as v 14 explains the correct sequence that leads to a proper interpretation of the kind of salvation in view.

Therefore, one must first, *believe in your heart* (v 9)…which is paralleled with and explained in v 10 as, *with the heart one believes unto righteousness.* When faith in the heart (=mind, cf. v 8) occurs, one receives God's imputed righteousness (*dikaiosynē*). Paul normally uses the term *dikaiosynē* in Romans for justification by faith (1:17; 3:21–425; 10:6). Hence the word *saved* cannot mean salvation from hell (which justification provides; cf. 5:9) since faith alone is not the sole requirement for this deliverance. One must *confess* (=call, see below) with the *mouth* here as a condition for salvation (BDAG, 290; cf. vv 14-15). As with the call in vv 12-13, salvation is obtained through the *mouth* but justification comes through the *heart*. Hence these two aspects of how a person responds to the gospel occur sequentially. Though they may occur simultaneously (cf. v 8), causing a bit of confusion, they are not the same event (cf. v 14-15).

Paul consoles those who *believe* and publicly *confess* (or call on divine aid) by quoting part of Isaiah 28:16. This was written in a time when Jerusalem trusted in other gods to deliver them from the Assyrian invasion. Hence Paul's quote encourages believers to rely on God for help: **"Whoever believes on Him will not be put to shame"** because God is the only "basis for spiritual and physical salvation" (Martin, "Romans," in *BKC*, 1078; cf. 1:16). Perhaps analogous to the Assyrian invasion is God's desire to deliver the Jews from the wrath to come at the hand of Rome in A.D. 70. Though chapters 9–11 primarily address Israel (hence the term *saved* must be viewed under its Hebraic rubric; cf. Lopez, *OT Salvation–From What?* 49-64), Paul universalizes the deliverance of vv 9-13 to include **Jew and Greek** alike.

The confession of vv 9-10 is picked up again by the phrase **call upon him** in v 12 and repeated by the phrase in v 13 *"whoever calls on the name of the LORD shall be saved"* quoted from Joel 2:32. In Joel's context calling on God expresses a request of deliverance from temporal wrath. This is the same type of present wrath that continues throughout Romans (1:18; 2:5, 8; 3:5; 5:9; 9:22; 12:19; 13:4-5). Hence those who view the salvation of vv 9-10, 13 as speaking of deliverance from hell have completely ignored the thrust of the book or the context from the passages Paul quotes. To be delivered from God's wrath one must first believe and then obey. Furthermore, the deliverance-from-hell view also ignores that in the Old Testament (believers in Gen 4:26; 26:25; 1 Kgs 18:24-27; Ps 14:4; 18:3; 31:17; 50:15; 53:4; 79:6; 80:18; 116:2; Isa 55:6; 64:7; Jer 29:12) and the New Testament *calling on the name of the Lord* is a Christian practice (cf. Acts 7:59; 1 Cor 1:2; 2 Tim 2:2; 1 Pet 1:17; cf. Fitzmyer, *Romans*, 593). This phrase was a way of identifying Christians who invoked the aid of God and were publicly associated with the risen *Lord* by calling His name (e.g., in Acts 9:14 Paul identifies believers through their public association with Christ). To call on Christ in public praise or prayer acknowledges Him as Lord, because it shows Christian submission by coming to Him who is worthy to receive worship and who responds to one's worries. God never promises to deliver closet Christians; but only those who *confess* or *call on Him* before men will receive aid from heaven (cf. Lev 26:40-42; 1 Kgs 8:33-36; 2 Chr 6:24-26; Matt 10:32; Luke 12:8; Jas 5:16; 1 John 1:9; Rev 3:5).

10:14-15. How then (cf. 4:10) furthers the argument in a form of four rhetorical questions each beginning with the interrogative *how* (vv 14-15). By reiterating each verb that appears at the end of each question at the beginning of the other, Paul creates a distinct and sequential progression that aids in understanding the

type of salvation spoken in 10:9-10, 13. Laying out these five steps
in their proper chronological order reveals the following:

(1) Before they preach, the preacher must be sent
(2) Before they hear, the preacher must preach the message
(3) Before they believe, the message of Christ must be heard
(4) Before they call, the person of Christ must be believed

It is the final step (without the interrogative *how*) in v 13 that
illuminates the passage. (5) Before being "saved," one must call "on
the name of the LORD" (v 13). No one calls on the assistance of a
person in whom one does not believe (as step four illustrates).
Then, contextually, these are Christians who are calling for divine
assistance as the New Testament suggest (see commentary in v 13).
Hence this salvation has a broader concept than simply deliverance-from-hell. It encompasses a whole range of spiritual and
physical deliverance received upon calling on Christ for help
(Hodges, *Absolutely Free!* 196; cf. v 13).

Since carrying this spoken message mentioned above involves
people, Paul quotes Isaiah 52:7. Isaiah, however, writes of the **feet
of** Him (i.e., the Messiah in context) instead of **those.** Paul links
those that follow Jesus' message as the ones preaching the **gospel.**
This *gospel* in the context of Isaiah 52:7 relates to God's power
revealed to the nations by delivering Israel from exile and establishing His rule in Zion (cf. 52:6-10; cf. 9:27-29; 10:1). Paul
intends to include not only the physical aspect of the *gospel* but also
the spiritual as shown below.

10:16-17. The word **they** quoted here from Isaiah 53:1 refers
to Israel in the original context (Delitzsch, *Isaiah*, 7:310). Thus
Paul continues to have Israel in mind as primarily those that have
not **obeyed the gospel.** The Jews rejected this *gospel* that includes

the command to believe in Christ (9:3, 30-33; John 12:37-41), and as seen above encompasses a broader scope of following Christ (cf. vv 1:2, 5, 15-16; 10:8-13). Hence the salvation (included within the term *gospel*) spoken in 10:8-13 and in the original context of Isaiah 52:7–53:12 reflects two ideas: The physical-national deliverance of the nation (Rom 10:15) and the spiritual basis of faith in Messiah (52:13–53:12) that allows God to effect that deliverance for the remnant (Isa 10:20-22; 11:11, 16; Rom 11:1-7, 26; cf. Lopez, *OT Salvation–From What?* 49-64). Thus, this message that embraces both spiritual and physical realities comes by **faith** (cf. Rom 10:6) in **hearing** the **word of God.** Verse 17 further confirms this truth.

10:18-21. Paul quotes Psalm 19:4 to quiet the objections of those who would argue that the Jews have not had ample opportunity to hear. The original context of Psalm 19:1-6 praises God for His revelation evident in nature. However, Paul applies it analogously to those taking the gospel to others, indicated by the following phrases: ***Their sound*** and ***their words*** (Moo, *Romans,* 666-67). People are the present form of creation that now reveal God by witnessing on His behalf. No one can be saved through natural revelation (1:18-32). Hence one has to take the *gospel* **to the ends of the world.** By the *ends of the world* (or *earth*) perhaps Paul means the Roman Empire or simply uses hyperbolic language (cf. 1:8).

In case someone further objects that **Israel** heard but has not understood, Paul confirms they have by quoting Deuteronomy 32:21. By using this passage in a context of Israel's idolatry that provoked God to jealousy, Paul shows how God will likewise ***provoke*** them ***to jealousy*** (11:11) and ***to anger by a foolish nation*** (i.e., the Gentiles). After quoting the Law, Paul also supports his point from the Prophets by quoting Isaiah 65:1 in v 20. As the original context of Hosea 1:10 and 2:23, quoted in Romans 9:25-26, spoke of Israel, this passage also refers to Israel. Paul however applies it analogically to Gentiles. So, what is Paul's point? His purpose is to vindicate God's present rejection of Israel. First, Israel's rejection of her promised Messiah (9:30–10:17) was not due to a lack of hearing or understanding. Of course they heard and understood (vv 18-19). That God would seek the Gentiles was clearly laid out in their Scriptures, validating what was currently occurring. Second, even though the Jews are rebellious, God remains merciful to them by having **stretched out... hands**. Hence God is not the problem but Israel who are *a disobedient and contrary people*. Yet, God continues to wait upon them today, for they will not be blessed until they acknowledge their Messiah by saying: *"Blessed is He who comes in the name of the LORD!"* (Matt 23:39).

11

ISRAEL'S END TIME RESTORATION

3. God's mercy extended to all vindicates Him (11:1-36)

Chapter 9 expressed how God's sovereign choice in the *past* of Israel to proclaim His glory vindicates Him. Election is based on grace not justice. Hence in chapter 10 one should view Israel's rejection of Christ as the grounds by which God is vindicated to reject Israel in the *present*. Yet, chapter 11 shows that even if Gentiles experience God's mercy in the present, this is not to the exclusion of Israel's permanent *future* deliverance. Thus, God's wisdom, by extending mercy to all, vindicates Him.

No doubt, chapter 11 validates Dispensational Theology (i.e., the working of God throughout history distinctively but without merging those periods or people or abandoning His original promises). Perhaps keeping Israel distinct from the church is the *sine qua non* of dispensationalism and the result of literal interpretation. God made numerous *unconditional* promises to Israel that must be kept (Gen 15:7-18; 2 Sam 7:10-29; Jer 31:31-38). Conversely, Covenant Theology teaches that God's promises are fulfilled in the Church, hence blurring these distinctions and promises. Therein lies the importance of chapter 11 (that echoes 9:6): God is vindicated because His original promises of the gospel to Israel (1:2; 10:15-16; 11:28) will be fulfilled *literally* in the future.

a. Gentiles experience present salvation (11:1-25)

11:1-6. Since chapter 10 articulated God's present rejection of Israel, Paul anticipates what the reader may think: **I say then, has God cast away His people** (cf. Ps 94:14)? This rhetorical question in the Greek expects a negative answer: *no* (cf. 10:18-19). If that is not enough, Paul follows with an emphatic: **Certainly not!** (cf. 3:4). Perhaps no other verse (except 11:11, 26) argues more strongly for a future assured for Israel than this one. Paul's proof of this certainty has personal roots. Paul, a Jew as the phrases **seed of Abraham** (9:7) and **Benjamin** (from Saul's tribe; 1 Sam 9:16, 21) indicate (cf. Phil 3:5), persecuted Christians (Acts 9:1-2), but later became a believer.

Hence God's saving of Paul (Acts 9; 22; 26) expresses His compassion by **not** casting **away His people** (i.e., the nation not just the elect) whom **He foreknew** (corporate instead of individuals like 8:29 and 11:4-6). God's purpose to *foreknow* refers to making a choice to have an intimate relationship with Israel composed of elect individuals (Jer 1:5; Amos 3:2). Hence the security of Israel's future lies on God's choice made in eternity past that will not be abandoned (Jer 31:36-37).

Though in the time of **Elijah** the nation appeared to reach its demise (by divine judgment) as 1 Kings 19:10, 14 indicate, God says otherwise. Elijah's self-pitying implicates God's faithfulness. In fact, Elijah's accusation before God could be seen as another example used like Paul's persecution of Christians. That is, since God spares those who persecute and accuse Israel, how will He not spare the nation? Elijah's sole survivor claim demonstrates his lack of faith, but not God's. Though God's answer does not deny Israel's sins, it confirms His covenant loyalty to them by reserving *seven thousand men who have not bowed the knee to Baal* (1 Kgs 19:18). These *seven thousand men* became believers and were preserved by God through sovereign choice. Thus Paul teaches that

God elected corporate Israel but He also elects individuals to justi-fication-salvation (cf. 8:29) to preserve the nation (cf. 9:14-18; 27; Moo, *Romans*, 677-78).

Likewise in Paul's day, **there is a remnant according to the election of grace** of ethnic descendants of Abraham who are believers (cf. 9:7-10). From vv 5-6, Paul transitions by not only expressing God's loyalty in His day but articulates the basis for His loyalty: *grace*. Hence Israelites, as Gentiles, cannot become part of the chosen *remnant* on the basis of **works** but **grace**. This antithe-sis of *works* and *grace* appears in Romans and elsewhere (4:4-5; 9:30–10:4; Eph 2:8-9) to emphasize how a person is justified. Further, by God's sovereign gracious choice, those elected to justi-fication also remained faithful by not committing idolatry in this case (but not always as the many imperatives and warnings to Christians suggest). It follows that God could not elect people on the basis of merit He foresaw in them (cf. 9:14-16). Nevertheless, God's criterion of election remains an undisclosed mystery in Scripture. To be elect is not synonymous with having eternal life. People still have to believe in Christ. Yet, being elect in this context guarantees, by God's sovereign choice based on grace, one day that person will believe. Paul was one of these elect from the womb (Gal 1:15) who experienced God's grace on the road to Damascus (Acts 9; 22; 26).

11:7-10. What then (*Ti oun*) appears as a technical transition-al phrase raising a question of something previously taught to fur-ther develop his argument (cf. Rom 3:1). After explaining the pos-itive privilege of the *elect*, Paul in vv 7-10 explains the negative judgment on the rest of the nation. **Israel** did not obtain favor with God, because **it seeks** God's righteousness by works of the Law (9:31–10:3) instead of Christ's righteousness as the goal of the Law (cf. 10:4; 11:28). However, **the elect have obtained** favor with

God through God's sovereign choice based on grace (vv 4-6; cf. 9:11, 14-16). Yet **the rest** of *Israel* was **blinded** (*epōrōthēsan*, a divine passive tense) by God. Paul validates God's action by quoting from the three-fold division of the Old Testament: the Law (Deut 29:4), the Prophets (Isa 29:10) and the Writings (Ps 69:22-23). The verb *epōrōthēsan* appears in the passive to indicate God's involvement in causing Israel "to have difficulty in understanding" (i.e., *harden*, BDAG, 900). This hardening is not capricious, but results from people rejecting Christ (11:28). Scripture is clear that the hardening of a human heart by God never precedes that person's own hardening by rejecting God's revelation resulting in rebellion (Rom 9:17-18; cf. Isa 6:9-10; Mark 4:12; John 5:40; 12:40; Acts 28:26-27). Though the original context of Deuteronomy 29:4 is a positive account of a supernatural blinding of Israel by God to all He had done for them, its citation in Romans 11:8 is in a negative connotation of how God leaves them to their own *stupor*. Paul also applies Psalm 69:22-23 (a reference to David's enemies) analogously to Israel. Hence God is not unjust in hardening Israel but only seals their own unbelief in judgment. Thus, the cultic Law (Rom 9:4) depicted as a *table* (1 Cor 10:21) that Israel considered a blessing has *become a snare and a trap*. *Table* is used as a metonymy (i.e., a figure of speech in which an attribute or commonly associated feature is used to name or designate something) for the *food* it holds that gives life. The Law, when obeyed, results in temporal life (cf. Rom 10:5; Lev 18:5). Therefore, what was given to provide sanctification (i.e., the cultic Law) was improperly used to provide justification and became a *stumbling block*. Consequently Israel will bear a heavy burden as long as they continue on this path (not *always* [NKJV] or "forever" [NASB], as Rom 11:11, 15, 25-26 indicate; cf. Cranfield, *Romans*, 2:552).

11:11-12. Having described Israel's present state, Paul anticipates the reader's next thought: **I say then, have they stumbled
that they should fall** (*piptō*)? The verb *piptō* means *completely
ruined* (BDAG, 815) and parallels the verb *stumbled* which may
imply: beyond repair. Similar to that of 11:1, this rhetorical question implying Israel's demise expects in the Greek a negative
answer: *no*. To strengthen his answer, Paul adds an emphatic:
Certainly not! (cf. 3:4). Israel is not beyond recovery (11:26).
Instead, in God's masterful plan, Israel's trespass (not **fall** since
paraptōma refers to a *violation*, BDAG, 770) of rejecting the gospel
(11:28) resulted in **salvation** (*hē sōtēria*) coming **to the Gentiles**.
This *salvation,* with the article of previous reference, points to the
"salvation" of 10:1 that is also linked to the salvation in 1:16. Paul
thinks of this *salvation* as having its basis in justification, but justification lacking sanctification does not *provoke* Gentiles *to jealousy*
(cf. 10:19). Hence the broad use of the term *salvation* involves
sanctification. That is confirmed through the use of the plural
"riches" (i.e., enormous blessings that Gentiles possess; cf. Hart,
Why Confess Christ? 21; Osborne, *Romans,* 293) in v 12 that
expresses the same idea of *salvation* (Cranfield, *Romans,* 2:557).

Every time the Jews booted Paul out of synagogues, he turned
to **the world** (i.e., of mankind; cf. v 15) to preach the gospel to the
Gentiles (Acts 13:45-46; 18:6-7; 19:8-10). However, if by Israel's
trespass their numbers have been reduced to a "remnant" (vv 4-5)
now, that resulted in large numbers of Gentiles coming to faith (v
25), **how much more** will **their** numerical **fullness** be upon
Christ's return (vv 26-27)? Paul has consistently used in this context the third personal pronoun "they" or "their" to refer to the
Jews and second personal pronoun "you" to refer to the Gentiles.
Hence the phrase *their fullness* of v 12 refers to all of Israel that will
come to faith before or when Christ returns (cf., 11:25-27).

11:13-15. Paul digresses in vv 13-14 (which are parenthetical), before explaining Israel's (indicated by the plural pronoun, "their"; cf. 12, 17) failure (in vv 12, 15; see "for if"=*ei gar* in v 15 where Paul's main thought continues form v 12), to point out his part in the overall plan of God to reach Israel through his Gentile ministry. Paul speaks **to** the **Gentiles** as an **Apostle to the Gentiles** (Acts 9:15; 22:21; 26:17-18; Gal 1:16; 2:7-8; Eph 3:8), declaring: **I magnify** (*doxazō*, i.e., to extol or flaunt) **my ministry**, to **provoke** the Jews to **jealousy** in order to **save some of them.** Since the term "salvation" in v 11 and here addresses the same subject matter in context, the term *save* involves a broad use encompassing sanctification (cf. 11:11). Thus any Jews won to Christ through Paul's ministry in the church age form part of the elect mentioned earlier (vv 4-5).

Then Paul explains how Israel's rejection of the gospel, which caused God to **cast** them **away**, brought *reconciliation* (NASB) to **the world** (i.e., *the world* of mankind; cf. v 12; John 6:33). The term *reconciliation* does not express a restoration of individuals to fellowship with God, but refers to God's work through Christ that provides the basis for all to be brought to fellowship with God (cf. 5:10-11 for discussion; 2 Cor 5:18-21). Reconciliation does not mean everyone is justified, but *justifiable* by simple faith alone in Christ alone.

Returning to his point, Paul concludes with the vivid analogy of **life from the dead** to express what Israel's return to God will be like. God's *acceptance* of Israel in the future can only be compared to the supernatural event of the resurrection of believers (6:13). Perhaps Paul thinks of the valley of dry bones of Ezekiel 37 that represents Israel who will come to life to be forever with God.

11:16. Paul illustrates Israel's glorious return with two metaphors. The first metaphor comes from Numbers 15:17-21 where upon entering the promised land Israel was to set apart (i.e., *holy*) to the Lord a piece of dough (**firstfruit**) from **the lump**. The second metaphor of trees expresses a similar idea: **the root *is* holy, so *are* the branches**. Seven views exist concerning the referent of both illustrations: (1) Adam, (2) Christ, (3) the remnant Jewish Christians in context, (4) Abraham and the patriarchs, (5) the first metaphor refers to the remnant Jewish Christians in context, but the second refers to the blessings of the patriarchs that Jewish and Gentile Christians partake (Schreiner, *Romans*, 600), (6) the *firstfruit* and *root* represent the patriarchs and the *lump* and *branches* represent Israel or (7) the first metaphor refers to the remnant Jewish Christians in the immediate context, but the second refers to the patriarchs of the Abrahamic covenant of salvation from which only Jewish Christians partake. Though the last two views make the choice difficult, the latter view fits best. The illustration of *firstfruit* that are set apart refer in the immediate context (vv 1-10, 15-24) to the Jewish Christian remnant that are a part of the whole. Paul uses the *firstfruit* concept to refer to new believers elsewhere (Rom 16:15; 1 Cor 16:15; 2 Thess 2:13). Therefore, if the remnant is set apart from the *lump*, how will the rest of the *lump* (the future remnant to come v 26) not also be set apart? Because Paul develops the *root* and *branches* metaphor in vv 17-24 that also sustains Gentile Christians, it does not mean the *lump* or the rest of the *lump* includes Gentile Christians. Until v 17 Paul does not bring Gentiles into the picture. Though one may see a parallel between *firstfruit* and *root* and between *lump* and *branches*, the metaphors do not quite match. The *lump*, from which the *firstfruit* comes, is really set aside first, thus making the *lump* holy; but the *root* comes first, thus making the *branches* that come from it holy. The *root* refers to the patriarchs Abraham, Isaac and Jacob through whom God confirmed and ordained the Abrahamic covenant (cf.

9:5; 11:28; Jub 16:15-28; 1 Enoch 93:4-8; Philo, *the Heir* 56§ 277, 279; Test. Judah 24.5) that Jews as the *branches* partake by being in the place of blessing. The ones who come to *life from the dead* (v 15) refer to Israel (Ezek 37:3-14) who are guaranteed existence illustrated by the *firstfruit* (like the illustration of Christ's resurrection as the firstfruits of those to come; cf. 1 Cor 15:20, 23) and *root-branches* metaphors. Thus both ideas convey one simple thought: Ethnic Israel (*the lump* and *branches*) is guaranteed a future evidenced by the remnant (*firstfruit*) of the present and by the setting apart of the patriarchs (*the root*) in the past (cf. 11:28).

11:17-21. Having explained Israel's guaranteed future, Paul warns Gentiles not to be arrogant, because of the present setting aside of Israel's place of blessing (indicative of the tree metaphor): **branches were broken off**. Hence Paul continues to address Gentiles by using the second personal pronoun **you** in these verses instead of the third personal pronoun "their" used of Israel (cf. vv 12, 15). Gentiles here are referred to as **a wild olive tree** that was **grafted** (i.e., supernaturally added) **in among them** (in the place of blessing by becoming God's people), not *instead* of them since the covenant was originally made with Israel and will be fulfilled with them. Normally a cultivated olive tree was used for grafting, not a *wild olive tree* because it was unproductive. Yet, Paul uses this agricultural analogy to illustrate that nothing in Gentiles warrants God choosing them (Osborne, *Romans*, 298).

Consequently, Gentiles by faith partake **of the root** (the blessings of the patriarchs through whom the Abrahamic Covenant stems; cf. v 16; Gal 3:7) **and fatness** (*piotēs*, means the oil prized product of the olive tree where the root is described as its source, BDAG, 814; this *fatness* is considered the blessing) **of the olive tree** (the place of blessing belonging originally to the people of God Israel; cf. Jer 11:16; Hos 14:6). Though Israel was in the place of blessing as the Old Testament people of God, they are removed from the place of blessing in the present as the people used of God. Even if Israel will always be the chosen people God who possess the promises and covenants (cf. 9:1-6; 11:25-29), they are not the only people of God who partake of His blessings. The Gentiles are now in God's place of blessing by partaking of the *olive tree* (cf. 9:25-26; 2 Cor 6:16; 1 Pet 2:9). All who exercise faith in Christ like Abraham become *sons* of God (Gal 3.7). This should not be confused with becoming *the people* of God who are placed in God's blessing, since participation in this blessing depends on the groups' response to God, which can change (cf. 11:11-12, 15, 19-25). If the phrase "people of God" is synonymous with the phrase the "justified people of God," it implies that justified people can lose their salvation since the branches are broken off. This would contradict Paul's strong stance taken in 8:31-39 on the eternal security of the believer.

Thus, Gentiles do not become part of Israel, but they share with Israel in the blessings that stem from the root. Gentiles now receive numerous blessings (e.g., chapters 6–8; cf. 9:6-7) that originally belonged to Israel (Eph 2:12) which are inherited by faith in the Abrahamic covenant. The *root* refers to the patriarchs and the Abrahamic covenant stemming from them. The *tree* stands for God's place of blessing, and the *branches* stand for the groups (Jew and Gentile) that make up the people of God. Being in the place of blessing does not equate to being a believer which is conditioned on faith in Christ. God has now placed Gentiles, believers and unbelievers, in the place of blessing as His people that form a broader group. Of course, God desires that all individuals within the group become believers (1 Tim 2:4); but as Paul later reveals, this will not occur, and God will again graft Israel back into the *olive tree* (Rom 11:23-32). This tree originally has Jewish roots and "a continuing Jewish element" (Moo, *Romans*, 704).

In v 18, Paul takes a further step and commands Gentiles: **do not boast against** (*katakauchō*, present middle imperative, lit. "do not continue boasting against") **the branches. But** in case Gentiles **boast**, Paul wants them to *remember that* **you do not support the root, but the root supports you.** The source of blessing (cf. v 17, *fatness*) and life of a tree stems from the *root* that is represented by the patriarchs, or Abraham as the father of all believers (Rom 4:11-12, 16:17; Gal 3:7). Hence since Abraham and his covenant as the *root* is the source of life, Gentiles by this connection are indebted to Abraham and the Jews, from whom salvation comes (John 4:22). Thus, how can one *boast against* the one to whom he owes an enormous debt of gratitude?

By now Paul presents an imaginary Gentile objector (cf. 2:1) who seeks to flaunt his superiority over the discarded Jews by concluding: **Branches** (Israel) **were broken off** (vv 12, 15, 17) **that** Gentiles **might be grafted in** the tree symbolizing the place of God's blessings. To which Paul agrees: **Well** *said*. However, he qualifies that because of **unbelief** in rejecting Christ (9:31–10:21; 11:1-12, 20) Israel was **broken off**, but Gentiles are included in God's blessing as the people He presently uses because they **stand** (cf. 5:2) **by** means of **faith** (indicative of the instrumental dative in Greek *tē pistei*; cf. Schreiner, *Romans*, 607; 10:19-20) in Christ. Therefore, Gentiles are in a place of blessing based on faith by accepting God's Messiah, Jesus Christ, who the Jews rejected (cf. 9:30-33). Hence Paul commands the Gentiles: **Do not be haughty** (*phroneō*, present active impertive, i.e., *be proud*, BDAG, 1065), **but fear**.

For (*gar*), Paul explains from v 20 why Gentiles ought to *fear*: because **if God did not spare the natural branches** (Israel) for being proud (cf. *stumbled*, *fall* [v 12], *cast away* [v 15] and *broken* *off* [vv 17, 19-20]), **He** will not **spare** the grafted in branches (Gentiles) **either** who should depend on mercy to gain God's favor. If God judged Israel for acting presumptuously, who are naturally linked to the root, and were originally in the place of blessing, He will surely judge Gentiles who act likewise on the same basis.

11:22-24. Therefore (*oun*) introduces the concluding results from vv 17-21. Paul commands Gentiles to **consider** (*ide*, aorist imperative) **the goodness and severity of God,** because not to **continue in His goodness** will result in being **cut off.** However, **if** Jews **do not continue in unbelief, God** will **graft them in again.**

Two things must be noted from these verses. First, the main reason Israel is not presently involved in God's program is due to *unbelief* in Christ (cf. 9:30–10:3; 11:7, 11, 20, 23, 28). Conversely, Gentiles are participants of God's present program because of their faith in Christ (9:30; 11:20). Hence contextually, this *unbelief* and *belief* refers to *rejecting* or *accepting* Christ, not to perseverance in faith in order to attain eternal life. To *continue in His goodness* refers to Gentiles continuing in the only way acceptable to God: By grace through faith in Christ (cf. 3:21–4:25; 11:5-6, 20) not of works to which the Jews solely sought to gain His favor (cf. 2:1–3:20; 9:30–10:3; 11:7, 11-12). Since those who *fell*, stumbled due to "unbelief" in Christ (v 20), those who remained in *His goodness* (cf. Pss 107:8, 15, 21, 31; Rom 2:4 where this phrase expresses mercy) do so because of their belief in Christ (v 20).

Second, the point here is not individual justification-salvation, but the relative position of Jews and Gentiles in God's place of blessing. Israel, having been the sole recipients of God's blessing in the Old Testament (cf. 9:4-5), is now discarded because the majority rejected Christ. Hence God sovereignly turned to Gentiles who readily believed in Christ (10:19-20). Gentiles find themselves at the center of God's blessing. However, if Gentiles reject the only way to God, which is through Christ alone, God will again turn to the Jews **who *are*** the **natural branches**. Today Christendom is as shallow and as confused as Judaism. People are less inclined to believe in Jesus by faith alone as the only way to God or even mention Jesus in any public forum for fear that it might offend. Hence will God not turn again to the Jews in order to graft them back **into their own olive tree?** Yes! Paul anticipates this in the following verses.

b. Jews experience permanent future salvation (11:25-32)

11:25-27. Everything Paul said up to this point from Romans 9–11 has led to this climactic conclusion: God will fulfill the promises made to Israel when they experience future salvation. **For** (*gar*) explains further the truth of v 24*b* but also works as the concluding explanation of vv 11-24 (Cranfield, *Romans*, 2:573). Every time Paul wants to emphasize something by sharing a truth of particular importance, he uses the formula: **I do not desire, brethren, that you should be ignorant** (cf. 1:13; 1 Cor 10:1; 12:1; 2 Cor 1:8; 1 Thess 4:13; cf. Cranfield, *Romans*, 2:573). Paul does not want the Romans to be ignorant of this information that entails a particular **mystery** that serves a very practical purpose. Once known, this *mystery* will curtail Gentile pride and boasting against Jews. The term *mystery* in the New Testament means something previously unknown but presently revealed (BAGD, 530). Paul uses this term twenty-one times of which sixteen are used with this meaning (Rom 16:25; 1 Cor 2:1, 7; 4:1; 15:51; Eph 1:9; 3:3, 4, 9; 6:19; Col 1:26, 27; 2:2; 4:3; 1 Tim 3:9, 16). Here the content (hence the *hoti* clause) of the *mystery* revealed cannot refer to Israel's hardening for that was already revealed in 11:7-10, or that all Israel will be delivered because that was widely held by Jews in Paul's day (cf. Isa 27:9; 59:20, 21 quoted by Paul in vv 26*b*-27).

Therefore, this *mystery* entails the sequence of *how* Israel will be saved: **blindness** will temporarily come **to Israel until the fullness of the Gentiles has come in.** Then, salvation will come to the Jews, but not *until the fullness of the Gentiles* occurs. Various views exist to explain the meaning of this phrase.

(1) The *fullness of the Gentiles* may refer to the end of the seven years tribulation when God removes Gentiles from their place of blessing and when all Israel will be saved (cf. Rev 6:11). This view interprets the phrase "times of the Gentiles" (Luke 21:24) as the same event spoken here since similar terminology appears in both places. That is, Luke 21:24 refers to the "times of the Gentiles" that began in 586 B.C. and continuous to the end of the tribulation when Christ returns. In this view, Gentiles will continue to enjoy the primary place of blessing as God's people until the moment that Israel is saved.

(2) Yet, the *fullness of the Gentiles* may refer to the time when God completes His dealings with Gentiles and will again turn to Israel at the beginning of the tribulation. Numerous problems exist with view one that are absent in view two. First, Revelation 6:11 does not refer to Gentiles but to the full number of the Jewish servants that will be martyred for their faith. Second, the phrase *until the fullness of the Gentiles has come in* may also refer to a fixed number of Gentiles who will enter the spiritual body of Christ (Rom 6:4; 1 Cor 12:13; i.e., become believers) before the rapture occurs. Hence this view distinguishes the phrase in *fullness of the Gentiles* from the phrase "times of the Gentiles" (Luke 21:24) that will continue to the end of the tribulation (Rev 19:17-21). Thus, the "times of the Gentiles" refers to the cessation of Gentile domination when Christ returns to establish His millennial kingdom (19:17–20:6). Third, contextually since God's present dealings with Gentiles must leave time for Him to deal with Israel again

and fulfill Daniel's seventieth week prophecy (Dan 9:24-27), the *fullness of the Gentiles* must occur in a time period that leaves room for all of this to take place. Fourth, from Revelation 4–19 God focuses on Israel once more. Though Gentiles come to faith in that period, as they did in the Old Testament, they are not the main people of God in that period. Fifth, hence the term *Church* does not appear once from chapters 4–19. Moreover, the term *mystery* is used of the Church that presently form the people of God (Eph 3:3-6) that includes Jews (vv 4-6; Eph 2:11-22). Thus, if the Church (largely comprised of Gentiles) is removed at the rapture (1 Cor 15:50-55; 1 Thess 4:13–5:11), who is left for God to deal with but Israel? One thing is certain: After God accomplishes His mission with the Gentiles **all Israel will be saved**.

The phrase *all Israel will be saved* has been interpreted in numerous ways: (1) *All Israel* may refer to the Church made up of Jews and Gentiles. Romans 9:6 (*For they are not all Israel who are of Israel*) may support this view. However, Paul uses *Israel* ten times from chapters 9–11, and it always refers to ethnic Israel.

(2) *All Israel* may refer to the elect within Israel but not the nation as a whole. Because the phrase "fullness of the Gentiles" (v 25) cannot mean all Gentiles in history, most likely the phrase *all Israel* cannot mean *the whole nation* throughout history. Since a complete Israelite in the Romans 9:6 sense refers to regenerate Israelites, *all Israel will be saved* must mean only those elected from the nation who become believers, similar to 11:5. This is unlikely since contextually Paul refers to the entire race of Jews and Gentiles (11:13-25), not just a specific group. Therefore, a shift in meaning (without contextual evidence supplied) would be necessary to make *all Israel* mean *all of the elect within Israel.*

(3) *All Israel will be saved* throughout history. Israel's salvation cannot refer to all of Israel throughout history, because personal

faith in Christ is a prerequisite for justification that many Jews did not meet.

(4) This view takes a mediating position between the previous two. On the one hand, interpreting "the elect within Israel" may be too restrictive to fit the phrase *all Israel*. On the other hand, interpreting "all Israelites throughout history" *will be saved* is too inclusive to fit contextually the phrase *all Israel*, since the context refers to a future period when Christ returns. Thus, contextually, this view interprets *all Israel* to mean the bulk of the nation as a whole in contrast to the elect previously mentioned or Israel throughout history. Paul would then be making a general statement: the majority of the nation upon Christ's return *will be saved*. While this view is possible, it is unlikely for the reasons developed below.

(5) *All Israel* means the whole nation of Israelites who remain alive during the tribulation period (who are justified) will be delivered at the end of the tribulation wrath to enter the millennium and fulfill all of God's Old Testament promises. Isaiah declares how the nation will at once be regenerated (66:8). At Christ's coming at the end of the tribulation in Revelation 19 (cf. Zech 12–14) the nation will be delivered. If only the bulk of Israel or the elect within Israel (instead of all individual justified Jews that make up the whole) are in view, it allows for unjustified Jews to remain at Christ's return. Jesus in Matthew 23:37-39 speaks of not returning until the whole nation recognizes Him as Messiah. By inference this suggests all Jews will believe in Christ before or at His return.

Faith in Christ is exactly what Paul said has to occur before God turns to Israel (v 24). Revelation 13:18 and 14:9-10 leaves the impression that at this point of the tribulation (before Messiah arrives) a dividing line will be drawn to separate those who receive the mark of the beast (the unjustified) and those who do not (the justified).

Verses 28-32 also validates that Paul thinks of a nationally justified people that will be delivered since the focal point of these verses shows how *all Israel* will receive mercy upon believing in Christ.
This is part of *the gospel* Paul preaches (Fitzmyer, *Romans*, 625).
Other passages also teach that until Israel repents and believes in
Christ, the kingdom will not come (cf. Mark 1:14-15; Acts 2:37-40;
3:19-26) and deliverance from their enemies will not occur. Finally,
the meaning of the term *saved,* used by Paul throughout Romans,
refers to a deliverance from wrath to those who are already justified
(cf. 1:18; 5:9; 10:9-13). Though the term *wrath* does not appear
here, the concept does. Paul's quotation (from Isa 59:20-21) sits in
a context of great vengeance (cf. 59:16-21).

Thus contextually *all Israel will be saved* refers to the nation's
deliverance from Gentile rule (known as "the times of the Gentiles"
in Luke 21:24). However, theologically all Israelites left when
Christ returns to deliver them from their enemies at the end of the
tribulation wrath must be justified since unjustified individuals
cannot enter the millennium (cf. Matt 7:21-23; 25:31-46; John
3:3; Rom 9:26–10:1; 11:23-25

Paul quotes Isaiah 59:20-21 that God *will turn away ungod-*
liness from Jacob (cf. Ezek 20:34-38) to support that upon
Christ's return all Jews left will be regenerated at a moment in time
(Isa 66:7-8). Moreover, Paul's quotation of Isaiah 29:1, with allu-
sions of Jeremiah 31:33, validates God's fidelity to keep His
covenant with Israel (see chap 9 intro).

11.28-29. The lack of a connecting conjunction (called *asyn-*
deton) between v 27 and v 28 prompts commentators to see a break
in Paul's thought (cf. Cranfield, *Romans*, 2:579; Moo, *Romans*,
729). Thus, what follows from vv 28-32 summarizes not only vv 1-
27 but also the entire content of chapters 9–11 (Osborne, *Romans*,
309). Israel rejected **the gospel** (9:30–10:21; 11:7, 11; 1 Thess

2:14-16) and the nation became **enemies** causing God to reject them (9:6-29; 10:16-21; 11-24). In God's sovereign plan this occurred **for** the **sake** of Gentile salvation (11:11-15). Nevertheless, **concerning the election** (i.e., those chosen by God through grace; cf. 11:1-7) within the nation, *they are* **beloved for the sake of the fathers**. God's basis for setting aside anyone from a rebellious nation (or humankind as John 3:16) is His unconditional love outside of any merit found in the elect (cf. 9:11, 14-18; 11:4-7). God's special love for the elect is an outgrowth of His love (without merit contradicting rabbinical teaching; cf. Cranfield, *Romans*, 2:580) for the patriarchs (Abraham, Isaac and Jacob; cf. v 16) and the promises He made to them (Deut 7:7-8).

For (*gar*) further substantiates God's favor to the elect of v 28 by explaining how His free choice of *election* is based on His **gifts** ("that which is freely and graciously given," BDAG, 1081) and **callings** ("invitation to experience a special privilege," BDAG, 549; cf. 8:28-30). The bestowal of these *gifts* and *callings* are **irrevocable** (*ametameletos*, i.e., incapable of being recalled; or regretted and remorsed, BDAG, 53). Though the term *irrevocable* appears at the end of the English sentence, Paul emphasizes this act of God by placing it at the beginning of the Greek sentence. Paul emphatically believes that God will never renege on anything promised to Israel.

11:30-32. God evens the score at the end. **For** (*gar*) explains how God's electing love for Israel in vv 28-29 is further expressed in vv 30-32. As Gentiles (indicated by **you**; cf. v 12) were once **disobedient to God** (perhaps thinking of 1:18-32), they **have now obtained mercy** because of Jewish **disobedience** (perhaps thinking of 2:1–3:8). The idolatrous ways of Gentiles, not being privy to God's righteousness by faith in Christ (3:21–4:25), confirms their status of *disobedience*. Conversely, the legalistic ways of Jews, who had God's Law but did not understand His righteousness, also confirm their status of disobedience (3:9-20). Yet, because God showed **mercy** to undeserving Gentiles (i.e., understood contextually by the pronoun **you**) after the Jews rejected Christ, undeserving Israel (i.e., understood contextually by the pronoun **they**) will likewise receive mercy and believe in Christ at one point in the future (cf. vv 23, 26-27). Thus, Israel's disobedience is preparing them to be ready and willing to receive mercy when God again turns to them in the tribulation period that completes Daniel's 70th week prophecy (9:24-27; cf. Rom 9:26). Hence, at the end God levels the playing field, having **committed** (*sygkleiō*, i.e., to become imprisoned by giving people over to their compulsion, BDAG, 952; cf. 1:24, 26, 28) Jew and Gentiles (i.e., **them all**) **to disobedience** so that **mercy** can come equally to **all**.

c. God's wisdom vindicates Him (11:33-36)

11:33-36. The revelation of God's purposes and plans (possibly from 9–11 or more probable 1–11) cause the apostle to break out in an emotional doxology (hymn) praise to God. Paul's praise includes four elements, followed by two quotations, which elevate God to a level unimaginable to the feeble human mind. First, God's **riches** (recalls His mercy of 2:4; 9:23; 10:12; 11:12) encompass **wisdom and knowledge**. The term *wisdom* used by Paul elsewhere involves the infinite plan of God to save humanity through Christ (cf. 1 Cor 1:17–2:16; Col 1:27; 2:2-3). This *knowledge* **of God** and *wisdom* that modifies the term *riches* recall God's sovereign and gracious act to have an intimate relationship individually and corporately (cf. 8:29; 11:2-6) with people. Contextually the phrase *wisdom and knowledge of God* seems to be related to God's incredible plan delineated in Romans to save both Jews and Gentiles. Hence God's unique **judgments** and **ways** of dealing with humanity, as difficult passages (9:11, 14-18, 21-23; 11:2-6) come to mind, show that total comprehension is humanly impossible (cf. Job 42:3; Ps 147:5; Isa 40:28; 2 Baruch 14:8-9).

Thinking of God's unfathomable *ways* (v 33), causes Paul to employ quotations from Isaiah 40:13 and Job 41:11. This shows how no one has ever been able to know **the mind of the LORD..become His counselor** or place Him in a position of debt to humanity. God's actions toward humanity are by grace. Thus Paul concludes that no one has the right to demand anything from God, because He is the source (i.e., *ex autou*=lit. in Gk "out **of Him**"), sustainer (i.e., *di' autou*=**through Him**) and the goal (i.e., *eis auton*=**to Him**) of **all things**. Evidence suggests that first century Hellenistic Jews borrowed this three-fold formula from Greek Stoic philosophers and applied it to God in the synagogues, where Paul may have picked it up (cf. Dunn, *Romans 9–16*, 701; Philo, *Cherubim* 35§ 125-26 and *Special Laws I* 37§ 208). Perhaps Paul saw no other way to extol God than by using this three-fold formula that expresses God's sovereign hand in all (cf. 1 Cor 8:6; Col 1:16-17). Therefore, after asking the hard questions of life to no avail, the Christian's attitude should be Paul's attitude: to God **be** the **glory forever. Amen** (a strong affirmation that means *let it be so*, BDAG, 53).

In summary, chapter 9 expresses how God's sovereign choice in the *past* of electing Israel to proclaim His glory vindicates Him, because election is based on grace not justice. Thus, in chapter 10 one can see how Israel's rejection of Christ forms the basis that vindicates God for rejecting Israel in the *present*. Finally, chapter 11 shows that God, extending mercy to Gentiles in the present, does not preclude Israel from being saved permanently in the *future*. Thus, God's wisdom by extending mercy equally to Jews and Gentiles vindicates Him. Hence who can fathom the works of God?

12
BLUEPRINTS FOR CHRISTIAN LIVING

D. The Practical Outworking of the Gospel Serves in All Aspects: Only the Justified Can Serve and Express Gospel-Life to Others (12:1–15:13)

Romans 9–11 showed God's love and unfailing promises to Israel. This curbed Gentile arrogance since they likewise depend on God's mercy. However, chapters 9–11 also serve to vindicate God's faithful promises made to believers from 8:28-39 since the temporally unfulfilled Old Testament promises made to Israel may cause one to doubt God's promises made to the Church. Thus, after exhorting believers to suffer for God (8:17-30) in light of His sure love for them (8:31-39), one might expect Paul to immediately exhort these believers to continue their suffering for Christ with numerous applications. Yet, this does not occur until chapter 12–15:13. This section includes various themes that Paul taught elsewhere (12:1-2 and Eph 4:17-24; Rom 12:3-8 and 1 Cor 12; Eph 4:11-16; Rom 12:9-21 and 1 Thess 4:9-12; 1 Cor 13; Rom 13:8-10 and Gal 5:13-15; Rom 13:11-14 and 1 Thess 5:1-11; Rom 14:1–15:13 and 1 Cor 8–10; Moo, *Romans*, 745). Most of these books (including Colossians) also show the common Pauline practice of moving from indicatives (Rom 1–11; cf. intro to chap 6) to imperatives (12–15:13). Thus believers, after having believed the gospel, should know *how* to live the gospel (in all aspects of life) in light of God's mercies (12:1-2): Toward believers by exercising spiritual gifts to serve the Church (vv 3-8), toward the community and enemies by extending kindness to all (vv 9-21), toward the government (13:1-7) by living in light of the future (vv 8-14) and toward weaker believers by living in love (14:1–15:13).

1. Service of the Church (12:1-21)

Chapter 8 primarily addressed individual believers concerning overcoming sin (8:1-17*a*) and suffering by persevering (8:17*b*-30) in light of God's love for them (8:31-39). Paul reiterates this same love, called *mercies*, as the basis for obedience (12:1-2). Now, Paul explains how the life of a believer functions in light of the community, called the Church, which they belong: by exercising spiritual gifts to serve the Church (vv 3-8), by extending sincere love, by extending kindness toward the community and even to enemies (vv 9-21).

a. Expect to sacrifice in light of God's mercy (12:1-2)

12:1-2. Based on all of the doctrinal truth previously shared from chapters 1–11, *therefore* is Paul's way of concluding how instruction should lead to practice. Hence now he exhorts believers: **I beseech** is a typical Pauline term (Rom 15:30; 16:17; 1 Cor 4:16; 16:15; Phlm 10) used occasionally to introduce a practical section in a letter (cf. 1 Cor 1:10; 2 Cor 10:1; Eph 4:1; Phil 4:2; 1 Thess 4:1; 1 Tim 2:1). Paul's exhortation finds its basis in the phrase: **by** (*dia*) **the mercies of God.** Though the preposition *dia* may be interpreted as having an instrumental force (Dunn, *Romans 9–16*, 709) that can be translated *through* (YNG), contextually it seems best to view it as having a causal force understood as *because* (Schreiner, *Romans*, 643). Thus the grounds by which Paul motivates all believers to **present** (*parastēsai*, see below) their **bodies** (i.e., the Hebrew thought that viewed the *body* as the whole being as the vehicle representing the person; cf. Cranfield, *Romans*, 2:598-99; 6:6) as **a living** (*zōsan*, present active participle implies ongoing) **sacrifice** and **holy** (*hagios*, means set apart to serve God, BDAG, 10) is based on *the mercies of God* found in 9:11, 15-16, 18, 23; 11:30-32, or His love delineated through mercy (5:8; 8:35-39). Yet, one should not totally divorce the concept of God's prevenient grace that empowers a believer (cf. 12:3) to *present* himself to God (cf. 6:13, 16, 19). The infinitive *parastēsai* should be understood as a command (Schreiner, *Romans*, 643) as the two imperatives (*do not be conformed* and be *transformed*) of v 2 indicate.

Perhaps Paul has in mind the Old Testament sacrifice that served its purpose by dying and shedding its blood (Heb 9:22) for sins, which was **acceptable** (i.e., *pleasing*, NIV) to God. Now, this sacrifice is analogically applied to a believer's ongoing lifestyle (not just a one time act at the altar) of sacrificial obedience to God (6:13) by putting to death the corrupt deeds of the Adamic nature (8:13) as a **reasonable** (*logikos*, means "rational" implying a careful thinking through something; BDAG, 598) **service** (*latreia*) "in a dedicated spiritual sense" (BDAG, 598) of worship as the term *latreia* implies (BDAG, 587). Paul means that it is only rational that believers dedicate their entire life to God, by living in a spiritual way that worships Him (cf. John 4:24), based on all He has done for us.

God never places any value on animal sacrifices but on the spiritual principle and truth that they represent (BADG, 598; Heb 10:1-4, 6), since Christ's life and death is the only spiritual service acceptable to God (Heb 10:5-12). Now, the believer-priest identified with Christ as the ultimate High Priest (cf. Heb 7:23-28; 1 Pet 2:5, 9; Rev 1:6) ought to render the same spiritual service of a sacrificial lifestyle that requires dying daily for God (cf. 8:13).

While v 1 tells one *what* to do (*present you bodies*) to carry out spiritual service to God, v 2 explains *how* to do it. Paul mentions first the negative then the positive avenue to take. Christians are commanded **do not be conformed** (*syschēmatizesthe*, present passive imperative that means *to be molded after a pattern*; cf. BDAG, 979 and 1 Pet 1:14 as the only other occurrence of this term in the NT) **to this world** (*aiōni*, lit. means "age") **but** (*alla*, the strongest contrast in the Gk) **be transformed** (*metamorphousthe*, present passive imperative that means "to change inwardly in fundamental character or condition"; cf. BDAG, 639).

Believers are commanded to refrain from being molded after the cultural norms of this age. For if they do not participate in Church, prayer, and reading the Word, Christians will automatically become victims of the world which will mold them. Hence Paul used the passive tense of the verb *conformed* (*syschēmatizesthe*), which refers to the world's influence that will conform believers after its image. Consequently, a passive believer will be influenced to act and look like the people of this age unable to be distinguished as a child of God. These are carnal Christians. However, to be *transformed* inwardly, a **renewing of** the **mind** must take place. The Greek term *metamorphousthe* from which is derived our English word *metamorphosis* implies a transformation from the inside out. This same term is used in Matthew 17:2 for Jesus' transfiguration and in 2 Cor 3:18 for the believers' transformation via the Holy Spirit. The secret to accomplishing this change occurs through the believer's *mind* (*noos*). This is the control center where a believer's thoughts, feelings, attitudes and decisions take place (Eph 4:22-23). Paul uses the *noos* as a practical synonym of the "inward man" that can be "renewed" daily and "strengthened" by the Holy Spirit (cf. 7:23; 2 Cor 4:16; Eph 3:16). Hence Christians should actively seek to be influenced and changed by *the Spirit* through daily prayer, constant reading of God's Word and assembling with other believers for worship and instruction (cf. Rom 8:5-7).

Once believers begin to be *transformed* they **may prove** (*dokimazō*) that God's will is **good and acceptable and perfect** (i.e., complete). Two things must be noted here: (1) The Greek verb *dokimazō* means more than mere knowledge of God's will (2:18); it also implies *testing* (BDAG, 255) His will by doing it (cf. 1:28 and 14:22 where *dokimazō* is almost practically synonymous with "doing"). One can then become an expert of God's *good and acceptable and perfect* **will** (*thelēma*, neuter noun). (2) These three qualities are not attributes of God as the NIV translates it but are neuter adjectives describing the will of God man should practice.

b. Exercise spiritual gifts to serve the church (12:3-8)

12:3-5. For (*gar*) works to inform believers of *what* God's good, acceptable and perfect will looks like in detail. Before explaining *how* a believer's consecration to God should be lived out by exercising their spiritual gifts to serve the Church, the apostle Paul **through the grace given to** him (refering to his authority; cf. 15:15-16; 1 Cor 3:10; 15:9-10; Gal 2:9; Eph 3:2, 7-8; 1 Tim 1:12) warns believers: **not to think of** themselves **more highly** (*hyperphronein*, lit. "haughty"; cf. BDAG, 1034) than they should.

The renewed mind that Paul had just told them about (v 2) **ought** not **to** proudly **think** (*phroneō*, i.e., hold an opinion, BDAG, 1065) that some gifts are better than others, but should **think** (*phroneō*) **soberly** (*sōphronein*, i.e., careful consideration with a focus on self-control, BDAG, 1065, 986). Perhaps Paul (writing from Corinth) saw this attitude first-hand in believers there who suffered from this type of haughty attitude (cf. intro and 1 Cor 11–14). Having used the Greek verb *phroneō* in a word play four times in this verse, Paul emphasizes the thinking that leads him to conclude that human pride is wrong (cf. 3:27; 11:18, 20), since all special abilities or gifts come from **God**. These special abilities or gifts are correctly understood as a **measure** or "quantity" (1 Cor 7:17; 2 Cor 10:13; not "standard" *of faith* as if it were Jesus Christ or the gospel; cf., Moo, *Romans*, 761) **of faith** possessed by each believer (Schreiner, *Romans*, 652-53) to serve the Church a concept that is more fully developed in vv 6-8.

For (*gar*), Paul explains how this *measure of faith* works with an analogy to one's physical **body**, which has *many members* (arms, legs, feet, etc.) **but** with different **function**. This is similar to baseball players having different positions but playing together to achieve one goal: *to win games*. Similarly, the spiritual **body** (called the Church; cf. 1 Cor 12:6-31; Eph 4:11-16) **in Christ** (who is the head; Eph 5:23) has **individual members** to serve the church, each with different gifts. Therefore, one should not regard one gift above another (e.g., preaching vs. giving) since all are important and needed for the body/Church to work properly and achieve its goal: *to worship God*.

12:6-8. Paul now moves to identify the **differing** of those *gifts* (*charismata*, lit. grace-gifts) that should be exercised in spiritual service to the Church (vv 6-8; 1 Pet 4:10). The Greek term *charismata* refers to abilities that are God-given. Believers should serve with this in mind, knowing that each individual will exercise his gift **according to the grace that is given** to him.

Though a Christian may receive the same *kind* of gift as another (e.g. teaching, showing mercy, etc.), he does not possess the same *type* of gift. That is, Paul received the same kind of gift of apostleship (v 3) as others, but his type of apostleship set him apart from the other apostles (1 Cor 15:8-10). Hence two believers possessing the gift of teaching do not possess the same form of the gift, though both may possess the same kind of gift. Therefore one should cease in comparing gifts of the same kind among believers, since God gives different forms of the same gift to serve different people and purposes.

Paul then lists seven gifts: **prophecy** here refers to receiving spontaneous revelation and should not be equated with teaching or preaching since *teaching* appears in the list as a separate gift (v 7; cf. 1 Cor 14:6). Such a prophet ought to *prophesy* **in proportion to** his **faith**. There are two ways to interpret the latter statement: (1) Since the article *the* appears with the term *faith* in the Greek text, this could mean the prophet should *prophesy* according to the body of truth (i.e., Scripture) known as "the faith" (Rom 1:5; 14:1; 1 Cor 16:13; 1 Tim 1:19; 3:9, 13; 4:1; 5:8; 6:10, 21; 2 Tim 2:18; 3:8; 4:7; Titus 1:13). In this view the term *proportion* means "rule" or "standard" implying that those prophesying ought not to deviate from the apostolic doctrine found in Scripture (cf. Moo, *Romans*, 765-66; Fitzmyer, *Romans*, 647). This may be similar to the standards found in the Mosaic Law (cf. Deuteronomy 13 and 18).

(2) Though this view may be correct, another is preferable according to the phrase "measure of faith" that means *quantity of faith* in v 3 (Schreiner, *Romans*, 656). Hence, the prophet's faith (not **our** *faith* as the NKJV but "his faith" according to the NASB) in direct *proportion* to "his gift" is the referent here, which implies that everyone does not prophesy but only those elected by God. Contextually, Paul anticipates that believers can be tempted to go beyond the special abilities or gifts given to them by doing or saying something not of God. That is why in verses 3 and 6 he cautions believers to check their prideful attitudes by exercising their gifts in direct *proportion* to the quantity of *faith* granted to them by God. Thus a prophet should not *prophesy* more than God has revealed.

The same guiding principle mentioned in v 6 should be followed in regard to the use of the rest of the gifts. Those with the gift of **ministry** should devote themselves to serve. Paul seems to be using the term *ministry* in a general sense (cf. 1 Cor 12:5; 1 Pet 4:10-11) since this word is used in various ways: monetary assistance (Acts 11:29; Rom 15:25, 31), serving tables (Acts 6:1, 2; Luke 10:40), general ministry (Eph 4:12; 2 Tim 4:5, 11), the ministry of the Word (Acts 6:4), apostolic ministry (1:17, 25), the Spirit's ministry (2 Cor 3:8-9) and Paul's own ministry (Rom 11:13; 1 Tim 1:12). The gift of *teaching* is different from the gift of prophecy, as previously stated. The one who prophesies unfolds new information from God. He, **who teaches**, explains Scripture already recorded in light of Church traditions, cultural and historical-grammatical norms (Rom 6:17; 16:17; 2 Thess 2:15; 1 Tim 4:11; 6:1-2; 2 Tim 2:2; Titus 1:11). Though *exhortation* is sometimes used synonymously with teaching (1 Thess 2:3), in this passage **he who exhorts** refers to one who encourages another to take a bold course of action in regard to his faith (BDAG, 766). Thus, even if teaching and exhorting may overlap, here they are contextually distinguished (cf. 1 Tim 4:13). In regards to **he who gives**, it ought to be done with **liberality**, which means sincerely and sacrificially (cf. Bauernfeind, *TDNT*, 1:386-87). Giving of one's property, money, or possessions to help the needy, is what usually occupied Paul's thoughts (cf. Rom 15:25-26; 2 Cor 8:2; 9:11, 13). Believers ought to be generous in funding the kingdom of God: "For where your treasure is, there your heart will be also" (Matt 6:21).

Then, **he who leads** (*proistēmi*) must do it with **diligence** (*spoudē*, lit. commitment, eagerness, willingness and zeal; cf. BDAG, 939). Some scholars argue that *proistēmi* refers to one in charge of charity since the word is not placed at the beginning but between those giving and showing mercy (cf. Cranfield, *Romans*, 2:626; Dunn, *Romans 9–16*, 731). Yet, there are no instances where Paul uses words in a list to qualify a previous term, nor is there any criteria here or elsewhere indicating the priority of this term in a list (Schreiner, *Romans*, 660). Instead, *proistēmi* likely refers more to leaders of the church since it carries this same meaning elsewhere (1 Thess 5:12; 1 Tim 3:4-5, 12; 5:15). Perhaps, Paul exhorts to *lead* diligently since leaders have no one to oversee their task; thus they may give a halfhearted effort to ruling the flock. Finally, those who show **mercy** should do so **with cheerfulness**, not only out of duty but more out of loving devotion for the good of the person.

All believers possess at least one of these gifts and should be totally committed to developing that gift(s) to serve the church. Yet, this does not exempt one from practicing the others, because all believers at one point have to teach the Word (whether to a son or daughter), exhort (friends or family), give (to build God's kingdom), lead (others with lesser abilities) and show mercy (since God has shown it to us).

c. Extend sincere love, kindness and mercy to all (12:9-21)

12:9-13. Paul now moves from discussing the proper use of spiritual gifts (vv 6-8) to the motivation undergirding those gifts. Love is the foundation that should move believers to heed Paul's commands, from vv 9-21, to behave honorably among believers and unbelievers.

Beginning with vv 9-13, Paul develops the theme of **love** describing its characteristics or attributes. Mentioning love first conforms to Paul's use elsewhere (Rom 13:8-10; 1 Cor 12:31–14; Gal 5:14; Eph 5:2; Col 3:14; 1 Thess 4:9; 1 Tim 1:5). The text of vv 6-21 bear a striking resemblance to 1 Corinthians 12–13. First,

Paul discusses the proper use of spiritual gifts in vv 6-8 (=1 Cor 12), then these gifts propelled by *love* will cause one to abhor **evil** (cf. Ps 97:10; 119:104, 128, 163; Prov 8:13; 13:5; 28:16; Heb 1:9; Rev 2:6) and to act **good** (cf. 1 Pet 3:11) in vv 9-21 (=1 Cor 13:1-7). The terms *evil* and *good* appearing in v 9 and in v 21 form an *inclusio* (cf. 1:5 for definition) showing how the commands directed at Christians (to *abhor evil* and *cling to what is good*) in this section are propelled by love *without hypocrisy* (*anypokritos* means *genuine* and *sincere*, lit. "without play-acting", BDAG, 91). Elsewhere believers are commanded to express genuine love (2 Cor 6:6; 1 Pet 1:22), not just role-play as it were a job. Though numerous participles (*abhor, cling, preference, fervent, serving, rejoicing, patient, continuous, distributing, given*) describing the characteristics of *love* are not (technically speaking) imperatives, the context indicates Paul uses them as commands to obey specific mandates (cf. Schreiner, *Romans*, 663-64).

Christian love should manifest itself in concrete ways: *love* (*agapē*), **kindly affectionate** (*philostorgos*) and **brotherly love** (*philadelphia*) manifested towards **one another**. These are three (out of the four) different kinds of love in the New Testament that overlap but have different nuances. (1) The highest form of love is *agapē*, known as self-sacrificing for all. (2) The Greek word *philadelphia* refers to an affection one has for a fellow Christian friend (BDAG, 1055; Louw & Nida, *Lexical Semantics*, 25:34). (3) The other Greek word *philostorgos* refers to affection for the relatives of one's immediate family (Louw & Nida, *Lexical Semantics*, 25:41). (4) The final Greek word *eros* refers to a sensual type of love. This term does not appear in Scripture.

By using all three of these forms, Paul covers all angles of what type of love believers ought to manifest towards their spiritual brothers and sisters, and how they should practice it: *giving preference* to others by putting them first (cf. Phil 2:3; Büchsel, *TDNT*, 2:908-9), **not lagging** (lit. "lazy"; Matt 25:26) **in diligence** and be **fervent** which literally means "*to boil with heat*" (Thayer, *Greek-English Lexicon*, 271) **in** their **spirit** (cf. Acts 18:25; 1 Cor 5:3; 7:34; Col 2:5; 1 Tim 4:12) by the power of the Holy Spirit (cf. Schreiner, *Romans*, 665). Today, one expresses this way of **serving** (lit. means "slave" implying a total commitment; cf. 1:1) **the Lord** by the metaphorical phrase: *to be on fire*. Thus, Paul encourages believers to be excited and zealous in *serving* Jesus, not just go through the motions in a half-hearted way.

Then, if one is on fire for Jesus, he will be **rejoicing in hope**. Though *hope* in Romans primarily refers to the eternal destiny all believers will enjoy (Rom 4:18; 5:2; 8:17*a*, 30), there is also the potential *hope* of sharing in rulership with Christ as fellow-sufferers (5:3-5; 8:17*b*-25; cf. 1 Pet 1:3-9). However, to achieve this *hope*, one must be **patient** when **tribulation** comes. How does a Christian do this? By **continuing** (lit. "to persist" or "be devoted to," BDAG, 881) **steadfastly in prayer** (cf. 1 Thess 5:17). Constant communication with God is the lifeblood that gives a believer power to endure problems.

The final elements in Paul's list ought to be two of the major virtues that characterize Christians. First, believers should be **distributing** (*koinōneō*, lit. means "to share") **to the needs** of other **saints** (i.e., believers; cf. 1:7). Usually the word group associated with the verb *koinōneō* is often employed in the New Testament as helping those with financial or material needs (Acts 2:44; 4:32 Rom 15:26-27; 2 Cor 8:4; 9:13; Gal 6:6; Phil 1:5; 4:15; 1 Tim 6:18; Heb 13:16).

Second, one way to help was to be **given to hospitality** by sharing one's home with traveling Christians since in those days lodging was expensive and travelers lacked funds to acquire it (cf.

Heb 13:2; 1 Pet 4:9; 1 Clem 1:2; 10:7; 11:1; 12:1).

12:14-16. After expounding the attributes of love in vv 9-13, Paul addresses the proper attitudes that express love. Since love wishes no one wrong, Paul commands that believers love each other in the following ways: **Bless** (*eulogeō*, present imperative) **those who persecute you; bless and do not curse.** The Greek term *eulogeō* is where we get the English word "eulogy" that means "to speak well" or "praise" someone. Since both sentences are parallel, the second sentence indicates the specific meaning of the term *eulogeō* in context. Believers are to *bless* their persecutors. Hence, *eulogeō* cannot mean in this context "praise." For how could one praise a persecutor? Instead, "to speak well" with kind words rather than cursing them (cf. Acts 7:59-60; Luke 23:34) is Paul's meaning. Jesus' instruction (Luke 6:27-28; Matt 5:44) was probably in Paul's mind. In fact, such behavior promises a special reward (5:46; 1 Pet 3:9), since it is a supernatural response indicating a spiritual origin and maturity. Those who practice such behavior are rightly called: "sons of your Father in heaven" (Matt 5:45; cf. Rom 8:14-17).

A Christian that adopts this attitude will also be willing to share the joys and sorrows **with those who weep.** Love does not envy when others *rejoice* and will share in their sorrows (1 Cor 12:25-26) by being there for them (Phil 4:13). To be sure, one who curses persecutors will also envy and look away at another's suffering instead of offering help. Such a man will not have **the same mind** (*phroneō*, lit. "to develop an attitude based on careful thought," BDAG, 1066) **toward one another,** since he does not carefully consider the attributes of love (vv 9-13) that lead to proper attitudes about love (vv 14-16).

Paul continues to attack an arrogant (cf. 11:20; 12:3) attitude by commanding: **Do not set your mind** (*phroneō*, see above) **on**

high things (*hypsēlos*, means "arrogant, *exalted, proud, haughty,*" BDAG, 1044), **but associate with the humble** (cf. Jas 2:1-9; 1 Tim 6:17). Thus, Paul summarizes by commanding: **Do not be** (*ginesthe*, present middle imperative) **wise** (*phronimos*, lit. refers to "understanding," BDAG, 1066) **in your own opinion.** That is, believers should not depend on humanistic understanding that leads away from righteousness and revelatory truth (Prov 3:5-7; Rom 11:25). Having used the Greek verb *phroneō* word-group in a word play three times in this verse (cf. 12:3), Paul emphasizes how attitudes of disunity and pride (11:20, 25; 12:3; 15:5; 1 Cor 4:10; 2 Cor 13:11; Phil 2:2, 5; 4:2; cf. Schreiner, *Romans*, 668), which lead to wrong behavior, begin in one's thinking process (cf. Rom 8:5). Failing to subject one's thinking to God's thoughts and ways (cf. Phil 2:2-7) produces selfishness leading to human pride. Christians should never be arrogant since they owe everything to the grace of God.

12:17-21. Having dealt with the issue of how believers behave toward other believers (in vv 14-16) Paul shifts the focus to the behavior of the believer toward the unbeliever. Though the commands continue to relate primarily to believers, the secondary concern centers on how they will respond to unbelievers who mistreat them (v 20). Thus, 12:17–13:7 is mainly concerned in context with Christians not taking matters into their own hands. Paul's command proves this: **Repay no one evil for evil** (1 Thess 5:15; 1 Pet 3:9; cf. 1QS 10:17-21 where the term has similar use, and teaches man to rely on God to repay). Perhaps, Paul has Jesus' words in mind (Matt 5:38-39, 44-45; Luke 6:29, 35) as well as numerous Old Testament passages that censured retaliation against one's enemies (Exod 23:4-5; Prov 17:13; 20:22; cf. Sir 28:1). Believers should not repay verbal or physical abuse with verbal or physical abuse; instead, they should "feed" the "hungry" and give a "drink" to a "thirsty" "enemy" (v 20).

These are the **good things** (*kalos*, can mean "attractive" or "beautiful" but here it means *morally good*, i.e., of "moral quality," BDAG, 504) that will be witnessed **in the sight of all men**, because even the unsaved know that refraining from getting even is *good* (Schreiner, *Romans*, 672). However, Paul limits the command to *live peaceably with all men* by stating: **If it is possible, as much as depends on you.** Having peace with everyone in all situations will be impossible, for one cannot deny Christ to appease a king or compromise the truth of the gospel in order to win the majority consensus. Paul made many enemies by not caving in to the majority (cf. 3:8; 6:1).

After giving a brief qualifier (v 18), Paul resumes in v 19 the contextual theme of retaliation (begun in v 17) in a gentle—but firm—way by using the term: **Beloved**. He tells them **not to avenge** themselves and commands them to **give place** (*dote topon*, to turn over their revenge) **to** God's **wrath** (*tē orgē*, lit. "the wrath," see below). The two other places in the New Testament where the phrase *give place* appears has someone else as its executor (Luke 14:9; Eph 4:27). The idea here would then mean to "make room for, the wrath of God" (Cranfield, *Romans*, 2:646). Hence Paul makes this point with a quote from Deuteronomy 32:35, ***"Vengeance is Mine, I will repay."*** The context of Deuteronomy 32:35 refers to the repayment on Israel's enemies by God at a point in time. Thus, the phrase *the wrath* has the article of previous reference pointing to God's temporal wrath in 1:18 (cf. Lopez, *Wrath of God*, 65; Morris, *Romans*, 454, also views this as temporal wrath).

If believers take this humble route by refraining from getting even and doing "good" (cf. v 17) to their enemy, it will be like heaping ***coals of fire on his head*** (Prov 25:21-22). This metaphorical expression refers to an old Egyptian practice of carrying on one's head a tray of burning coals on a pan (Moo, *Romans*, 789). As one's coals were consumed and the fire went out, a person would then go to his neighbor to borrow coals. This neighbor would then carry the coals on his head, which involved much danger and discomfort. Yet, this was proof of the neighbor's love. Likewise, an antagonist will be shamed and could turn to God as a result of a believer's behavior. Thus, heaping *coals of fire* on one's *head* is a metaphorical expression that was used in a missionary sense to convict and win over one's enemy (cf. Lang, *TDNT*, 7:1095 n 5). By acting in kindness this will also show that good is a greater power than evil.

Therefore, to overcome evil with evil will only bring spiritual chaos and defeat. Hence Paul commands: **Do not be overcome** (*nikō*, present passive imperative) **by evil, but overcome evil with good**. To meet *evil* with *good* is to vanquish its effects, first in one's life by not retaliating and then perhaps in the lives of others by causing them to mull over their evil acts, bringing them guilt and shame. The use of *evil* (twice) and *good* (once) links this verse to v 17 in the immediate context and also to v 9 in the broader context and forms an *inclusio* (cf. 1:5 for definition).

Thus, love is the foundational force that moves one to act according to the principles and commands in vv 9-21 (cf. 1 Cor 13:1-7). The gracious character embedded in Paul's commands from vv 9-21 expresses how "the law of Christ" (Gal 6:2) is vastly different from the legalistic mandates of the Mosaic Law, where specific commands were tailored to fit specific situations. Explaining this difference Constable says: "The commands in verses 9-21, as well as in all of the New Testament, are much more general and are similar to principles. This is one reason we say the Israelites lived under 'law' and we live under 'grace'" (Constable's, *Notes on Romans*, 138).

13
RESPECTING AUTHORITIES

2. Service to the state (13:1-7)

Some scholars argue that 13:1-7 was added by an editor due to the absence of a syntactical connection to the previous verse (known as an asyndeton; cf. 11:28) and of the central theme love plays in vv 9-21 that relates to 13:8-10 (e.g. Käsemann, *Romans*, 352). Conversely, the lack of a grammatical connector in the Greek may prove the close connection that 13:1-7 has with 12:9-21. That is, submission to the Roman government (under Nero's reign— A.D. 54–68—who would soon persecute Christians) fits well with Paul's exhortation to "prove" God's will (12:2) and the "evil" they ought to overcome with "good" (v 21) that manifests love (vv 9-21). Hence, the same terminology and themes link both chapters (good/evil, 12:21; 13:3-4; wrath, 12:19; 13:4-5; avenge/avenger, 12:19; 13:4; all men/all, 12:17-18; 13:7).

Furthermore, since evildoers may appear to have their way, Christians may decide to take matters into their own hands (v 19). Hence Paul responds: God's wrath can come directly from Him or indirectly through the civil government as the executor of this wrath (cf. 13:4-5; Moo, *Romans*, 792).

The church is not a theocracy ruled religiously and politically, directly by God, like Israel was in the Old Testament. Therefore, clarifying the function of this new entity to earthly rulers in light of God's rule was necessary (cf. Matt 22:15-22; 1 Tim 2:1-3; Titus

3:1; 1 Pet 2:13-17). In 13:1-7, Paul addresses the single subject of the government's function and Christian response: Any believer honoring the state honors God, conversely, dishonoring the state dishonors God.

a. Honoring the state honors God (13:1-2)

13:1-2. The present context flows from 12:17, "Repay no one evil for evil." The Christian must depend on God's wrath to repay evil (v. 19). To curtail a spirit of vengeance Paul commands believers (with application to all) to obey the government rule of law: **Let every soul** (*psychē*, a Semitic expression meaning "person") **be subject** (*hypotassesthō*, the present imperative implies an on-going mandate) **to the governing authorities** (*exousia*). Though the term *exousia* refers to angelic authorities (e.g., 1 Cor 15:24; Eph 1:21; 1 Pet 3:22), contextually it clearly refers to earthly rulers (cf. v 3). Elsewhere Paul objects to a believer's submission to angelic authorities (Col 2:8-15). **For** (*gar*) Paul explains the reason believers should to submit: All **authorities that exist are appointed** (*tetagmenai*, perfect passive participle) **by God.** The perfect tense *tetagmenai* refers to a past action with continuous results meaning that all governments that exist (past, present and future) are ordained of God, whether good or bad. This does not mean He approves the actions of evil rulers that practice tyranny, corruption and brutality (e.g., the Assyrians, Stalin, Hitler and the beast). Nevertheless, it remains a fact that in God's sovereign plan all regimes are divinely ordained (2 Sam 12:8; Prov 8:15-16; Isa 45:1; Jer 27:5-6; Dan 2:21, 37; 4:17, 25, 32, 34-35; 5:21; Wis 6:1; Sir 17:17; Rev 13:5, 7).

Therefore to resist governmental **authority** equates to opposing **God**, and believers **will bring** divine and civil **judgment on themselves** as the context dictates. The only exception to this rule is when the government orders a believer to disobey God by violating a scriptural mandate or renouncing Christ (cf. Acts 4:19; 5:29). Hence there are times when Christians will have to incur the wrath of men for the sake of God (cf. Acts 4:1-4; 5:17-21, 40). Many did in Nero's persecution as believers were dipped in tar and lit as torches for parties and covered in animal skins and thrown to wild dogs. Apart from this exception, the rule stands: Honoring the state honors God.

b. Dishonoring the state dishonors God (13:3-7)

13:3-5. The common rule follows that **rulers are not a terror to good works, but to evil**. No matter how terrible the government, it normally opposes lawlessness: killing, stealing, abuse and different forms of corruption. Hence believers who do not retaliate but resolve to do **what is good** (i.e., obey the rule of law) will even receive **praise from the** government. By Christians obeying the government, referred to as **God's minister** (which equates to obeying Him; cf. v 6), they need not **be afraid**. As Proverbs 16:7 says, "When a man's ways please the LORD, He makes even his enemies to be at peace with him."

However, dishonoring the state by committing a terrible crime could incur a capital offense: **for he** (i.e., *God's minister*) **does not bear the sword in vain**. Though the word *sword* itself is not a technical term for capital punishment, it was an instrument of death in Paul's day (cf. Acts 12:2). Ever since sin entered humanity, the world took a turn for the worse (Gen 6:5). Thus, after the flood, God established an earthly government with power to execute capital punishment (Gen 9:5-6) and this power remains today. Some object to this rule citing Exodus 20:13, "You shall not kill" (NET), but the Hebrew word *rāṣaḥ* means "murder" (BDB, 953). Capital punishment is not murder but justice that was prescribed by the Law for serious offenses (Exod 21:12, 15-17, 29; 22:19; 31:14, etc…).

All governments are as good as the men who comprise them. Thus no earthly government is perfect, except for the future reign of Jesus Christ (cf. Dan 2:44-45; Rev 20:1-6). Yet, any government is better than no government, for that leads to anarchy. Hence Paul states the government has the right as **God's minister** to *execute wrath* on one that commits crimes. Both occurrences of *wrath* in 13:4-5 refer to the temporal punishment inflicted by *God's ministers* (i.e., the government through whom God works). Christians should not avenge themselves by repaying evil with evil, thus incurring punishment from governing authorities (cf. Jas 5:20; 1 John 5:15-16, both of which refer conceptually to Christians experiencing wrath). On the contrary, believers must repay evil with good (v 21; 13:3-4).

Therefore (*dio*, cf. 2:1) Paul's summarizes in v 5, Christians should submit to the state for two reasons: To avoid civil punishment called **wrath** (cf. 12:19; 13:4) and **for conscience' sake**. Believers should heed their *conscience* to obey the government, not only to avoid potential punishment, but also because it is the right thing to do since governments are God ordained.

13:6-7. Therefore, believers should not feel burdened to **pay taxes**; because the state acts as **God's ministers** (cf. v 4), appointed by Him to keep order. Cheating the government equates to cheating God. Around this time (A.D. 57-58) taxes were enormously high (cf. Suetonius, *Lives* [Nero] 6.10 §1, p 101) and complaints emerged about tax collectors' extortions (cf. Tacitus, *Annals* 13.50-51, pp 89-91; Schreiner, *Romans*, 678). Hence believers, weary of such practices, may have resorted to cheating the government. Paul quickly curtails such a thought by commanding (like Jesus in Luke 20:25) Christians to: **Render therefore to all their due: taxes to whom taxes *are due*.** No matter how unethical the government may be, believers are always encouraged to support

God ordained institutions. Even the widow, who gave two cents to a religious system operated by the corrupt Jewish rulers, was praised for it instead of being persuaded against it (cf. Mark 12:38-44). Entities that aid the functions of society like firefighters, police, court officials and others, carry out God's will and are entitled to support. Though some officials may be corrupt and misuse funds, this should never be used as an excuse to cheat the state. Proper channels exist to address and correct such abuses, while continuing to **fear** and give **honor to whom honor** is *due* (cf. v 8).

3. Serve by loving others in light of the future (13:8-14)

Paul transitions by linking owing the government to a believer's unending debt to serve by loving others. He then encourages them to behave this way in light of the future.

a. Serve by loving others (13:8-10)

13:8-10. Still thinking of the Christian's obligation to fear and honor the state (v 7), Paul transitions with a command: **Owe no one anything**. This command does not prohibit borrowing (cf. Ps 37:21; Matt 5:42) though it may seem contradictory. Instead the translation "Let no debt remain outstanding" in the NIV captures the correct meaning. That is, one must repay all debts, not that one should never borrow. The word **except** is the logical connection to the debt believers will always have: **to love one another** (John 13:34-35; 1 Cor 16:14; Eph 5:2; Col 3:14; 1 John 3:14, 23; 4:7, 11). By using **for** (*gar*) Paul explains how this command summarizes how one **fulfilled the law** (cf. Matt 22:39; Rom 8:4). The Mosaic Law required this as well (Lev 19:18) but did not provide the permanent ability to love that believers now possess through the power (cf. chap 8) of the Spirit (Gal 5:14, 22-23). Thus since a believer is obligated to keep the law of love till death, one can never cease to *owe* love to his neighbor on this side of heaven.

Since the essence of love expresses itself in concrete ways, Paul cites five of the Decalogue **commandments** that address horizontal relationships among men: *"You shall not commit adultery ... murder ... steal ... bear false witness ... covet"* (Exod 20:13-17). Any **other commandment** not mentioned in this list Paul summarizes in one pithy statement (as Jesus did in Matt 22:39): *"You shall love your neighbor as yourself."* In other words, Paul says: **Love does no harm to a neighbor**; because one is too busy seeking his neighbor's good (as in 12:9-21). Hence Paul reiterate (v 7): **love *is* the fulfillment of the law** (cf. Rom 8:4; John 13:34-35; 1 John 3:23; 4:21). Only by walking in the Spirit's power can one fulfill the Law through love. Attempting to live by the Law leads to breaking it (cf. 7:5, 13-25). Concentrating on God's mandate to love by the Spirit's power will result in fulfilling it (8:1-13).

b. Serve in light of the future day (13:11-14)

13:11-14. To further encourage believers to persevere in love Paul points to the imminent return of Christ. As children are urged to behave based on their parents' imminent arrival, so Christians are likewise motivated. Paul opens v 11 by saying: **And *do* this**. This phrase may hark back to the ethical norms that form God's perfect will (12:3) mentioned from 12:1–13:10 (Moo, *Romans*, 820). Yet, elsewhere the construction *do this* refers back to what precedes by summarizing the content of previous thoughts (cf. 1 Cor 6:6, 8; Eph 2:8; Phil 1:28; 13:8-10), which may be the least strained and most natural way to understand it here.

Being aware of **the time** will cause believers **to awake** from their spiritual **sleep**. The term *sleep* is a metaphor used to convey moral laxity as in 1 Thessalonians 5:6-7. Hence all lethargy must be put away in light of the believer's **salvation** that *is* **nearer than when we *first***

believed. At the moment of faith this *salvation* was in view looking ahead to delivering one from any kind of wrath. Unlike the conditions laid to escape God's wrath (1:18–3:20), by believing in Christ (3:21–4:25) and by living the resurrection life in union with Christ (5:9–6:23), there are no conditions for this *salvation* (known as glorification; cf. 8:30). Yet, like the rest of Romans, this *salvation* also refers to deliverance from wrath. That is, the future tribulation wrath that Paul mentions in 2:5. This *salvation* parallels the "salvation" in 1 Thessalonians 5:9. Both contexts are similar. Other words, including *sleep* and *salvation*, found in 13:11-14 are also found in 1 Thessalonians 5:1-10: "time" (v 1), "night," (vv 2, 5, 7, 10), "darkness" (v 5) and "day" (see below). Since both contexts use almost identical terminology, this *salvation* (like 1 Thess 5:9) refers to a future deliverance from the tribulation wrath guaranteed by Christ's imminent return. Therefore, in light of the believer's deliverance from impending wrath Paul commands them to live in a holy manner.

The **night is far spent** may refer to the present evil age where Satan and his followers are still at work (cf. John 3:19-21; 2 Cor 4:4; Eph 2:2; 1 Thess 5:7). Very soon however, this work will cease as **the day** approaches (2 Pet 1:19; i.e., **at hand** refers to the final stage of time; cf. BDAG, 871). The term *day* expresses a key concept in defining when this future *salvation* will arrive. In 1 Thessalonians 5:2, 4, 5, 8, this *day* refers to the tribulation wrath that believers will not experience, because Christ will deliver them (1 Thess 1:10; 5:9). This *day*, also known as "the day of the Lord," is a common theme in many Old Testament (Isa 13:6, 9; Joel 1:15; 2:1, 11, 31; 3:14; Zeph 1:7, 14; Zech 14:1; Mal 4:5) and New Testament (Matt 24:42-44; Acts 2:20; 1 Cor 5:5; 2 Cor 1:14; 1 Thess 5:2ff; 2 Thess 2:2; 2 Pet 3:10) passages.

Because this *day* of wrath approaches and this evil age is almost over, Paul commands believers to live morally upright lives with the

following two contrasting phrases: **cast off works of darkness** and
put on the armor of light. This *armor of light* is a common
metaphor that describes the equipment a Christian soldier must
wear to win the war against evil (Eph 6:10-17; 1 Thess 5:8).
Wearing this *armor* allows believers to **walk** (i.e., "behave") **properly, as in the day,** by not caving in to the Adamic desires of the
flesh (cf. v 14) described by the list of vices that follow: **revelry,
drunkenness, lewdness, lust, strife and envy** (cf. Gal 5:16-21).
These vices are usually associated with *night/darkness* (John 1:5;
3:19-20; 8:12; 12:35, 46; Eph 5:8, 11; 6:12; 1 Thess 5:7; 1 Pet 2:9;
1 John 2:9, 11) but behaving *properly* is associated with *the
day/light* since that is usually when good deeds are carried out (cf.
John 3:19-21; 1 John 1:5-7).

Christians can accomplish this when they **put on the Lord
Jesus Christ.** To be clothed with Christ means to have Christ-like
behavior or practices (cf. *put on,* Gal 3:27; Eph 4:24; 6:11, 14; Col
3:10, 12). Though believers *put on* Christ when they believe in
Him (Gal 3:27), in another sense they *put on* Christ when they
behave like Him (Matt 10:24-25). Since believers will be like Him
in that future day (Rom 8:29; 1 John 3:2), they are to behave like
Him now so that "we may have confidence and not be ashamed
before Him at His coming" (1 John 2:28).

When the world sees believers they should see Christ, but this will
not occur unless believers **make no provision for the flesh, *to fulfill
its* lusts.** There are ways to curtail the desires of the flesh: (1) Believers
must restructure their way of thinking by learning the Word. A new
believer's mind is like a computer's hard drive running on old soft-
ware. By reading the Word, praying and attending Church, one's
thoughts will begin to change (cf. Rom 8:5). (2) Yet, there must be a
deliberate act to turn away from the flesh's desires (Rom 6:11-14; 8:1-
13; 2 Tim 2:22; 1 Pet 2:11) and toward the things of God.

14

THE SENSITIVE SERVANT

4. Serve by being sensitive to others (14:1–15:13)

In chapter 13, Paul dealt with a Christian's responsibility to honor and serve the government, and to love others, while waiting for Christ's return. However, special problems existed among believers, probably Jews and Gentiles (cf. Acts 15:1-23; Gal 2:11-15). Thus a detailed discussion of these problems with their solutions must be addressed for believers to comply with God's mandate to love others (12:9-21; 13:8-10) who are less mature in the faith. This is also what God's will entails (cf. 12:2) in detail since the Mosaic Law, with all of its 613 specific mandates, no longer applies.

In order to serve correctly, Paul addresses the theme of being sensitive to others in four major sections: (1) 14:1-12, (2) 14:13-23, (3) 15:1-6 and (4) 15:7-13.

a. Practice love by not judging on nonessential issues (14:1-12)

14:1-4. Paul does not suggest but commands: **Receive** (*proslambanesthe*, the present imperative implies an ongoing command to keep receiving) those who are less mature in **the faith** (i.e., apostolic teaching; cf. 1:5). Perhaps these spiritual babes have not had enough training in grace and other matters to release them from a legalistic conscience. Thus immature believers should not be engaged in **disputes over** their "opinions" (as the NASB translates it, not **doubtful things**; cf. *diakrisis* and *dialogismos* in BDAG, 231-32). Believers should not break fellowship over secondary or nonessential issues.

According to other sections of the letter (e.g., 1:16; 2:1–4:25; 9–11:36) and details of what correct foods and certain days to keep, the Jew and Gentile were at the center of such disputes. After commanding the mature not to engage the immature believers in their opinions over nonessential issues, Paul gives a concrete example. The mature Christian knows it is acceptable to **eat all** kinds of food (shrimp, oysters, lobster, beef or ham), but the immature believer **eats *only* vegetables**. Perhaps these mature believers knew of Christ's words (Mark 7:15), Peter's story (Acts 10:10-15) or what Paul would later write in his first letter to Timothy (4:4-5; cf. Rom 14:14, 20) that all foods are clean. The text does not state why some chose to eat *only vegetables*. Yet, in Paul's day when disputes involving Jews and Gentiles arose (similar to that of 1 Cor 8–10) over eating certain foods it was almost always a faith issue. Thus one can conclude the issue at stake is eating meats offered to idols or non-kosher foods.

A believer's scruples are not the main issue, but the mutual acceptance of each other as they are. Hence Paul commands again: the one who **eats** *all things* (the strong) is not to **despise** (*exoutheneitō*, present imperative) the one **who does not eat** (the weak) all things; and the one *who does not eat* is **not** to **judge** (*krinetō*, pres imper) **him who eats**. The reason (**for**) Paul gives to the "weak" to receive the "strong" is direct: **God has received him** (*auton*, third person singular). Though later Paul states that God accepts both groups (cf. vv 7, 10), understanding *him* to refer to both groups here does not do justice to the text (Cranfield, *Romans*, 2:702; Schreiner, *Romans*, 717). At this point of the argument Paul shifts to the "weak," since in vv 1-2 (and later vv 13*b*-23) his command was directed to the "strong" to receive the "weak." From vv 3*b*-9, Paul dealt with the temptations of the weaker brother. While this is relevant to both groups, what follows especially applies to the weaker brothers.

Paul continues to confront the "weak" in typical fashion by using a rhetorical question (cf. 2:1): **Who are you** (*sy*, second person singular) **to judge** (*krinō*) **another's servant?** Two reasons point to the weak being in view: (1) The singular *sy* is used. (2) The same verb *krinō* is used above for the non-eaters that continues to be a factor in describing and distinguishing both in v 10, the weak with the noun *krinō* and the strong with the verb *exoutheneō* (cf. vv 3, 10). For the weak believer to condemn another is like becoming his master. He reverses the role since all believers are *servants* (lit. Gk meaning, "slave," cf. 1:1) not masters. The strong brother has **his own master** whom he will answer to for his beliefs and actions. Whether the strong **stands** or **falls** is anticipated by the weak to end up in failure, but Paul anticipates God's power working in the strong for his success to **stand** at Christ's Judgment Seat (cf. v 10 where *stand* refers to appearing before Christ). To *stand* does not refer to the judgment of one's eternal-salvation; God has already guaranteed this victory (since these are already believers; contra Schreiner, *Romans*, 718-19); instead, to *stand* refers to the strong *servant's* success that God guarantees at Christ's Tribunal, since the issue of eating becomes irrelevant for believers at the Judgment Seat of Christ since there is no sin in eating any kind of food. Rather, whether one obeys Paul's command not to condemn *another's servant* concerns both groups (cf. vv 12-13) because that is not guaranteed by God and will be judged at Christ's Tribunal.

14:5-6. Another area of dispute centered around the observance of *one* **day above another.** Some of the Jewish believers probably held to keeping Old Testament holy days of the Mosaic

Law, while others thought **every day** was the same. Paul did not see anything wrong with keeping any Old Testament ritual, but not for justification or sanctification as Galatians shows; for even he, for the sake of not offending Jews after becoming a Christian, on numerous occasions participated in such practices (Acts 21:18-26; 24:11-12; 1 Cor 9:20). Though Paul taught the abolishment of Old Testament holy days elsewhere (cf. Col 2:14-17), this was irrelevant to his main point here. He was simply concerned whether the believer acted of his own conviction (cf. v 23). All days are of God and should be lived with that emphasis. One should not be a Sunday morning Christian and act like a pagan Monday through Saturday.

Perhaps some believers pointed to days and diets to validate their spirituality above someone else's. On the other hand, other believers having more training in grace became arrogant and criticized their weaker brothers (cf. 1 Cor 8:1-13). Whether one **observes the day** or **eats** is not the point. The issue is a Christian's conviction and commitment **to the Lord**. That is, do believers' actions show their relationship to *the Lord* (not superiority over others), and do they manifest a spirit of thankfulness? This is the key.

14:7-9. For (*gar*) is an explanatory conjunction showing in vv 7-9 the logical reason why v 6 makes sense (cf. Cranfield, *Romans*, 2:707). That both types of Christians follow their own path in these matters is not the point, but since they belong to Christ they ought not gratify themselves (in life or death) but the Lord.

Believers are indicated by the phrase **none of us lives** or **dies to himself.** Paul reiterates in v 8 what he just said in v 7. That is, a Christian's total existence and experience should be to serve Christ in life or death. Even when believers die, their souls will be in Christ's presence (cf. 2 Cor 5:8), perhaps serving in some way (cf. Rev 6:9-10).

Then Paul supports vv 7-8 in v 9 by explaining why the Lord has the right to be sovereign over all believers: **For to this end Christ died and rose and lived again, that He might be Lord of both the dead and the living.** Since Christ's death reconciled the world (cf. 5:10) everyone is accountable to Him (cf. 2:16). If this principle applies universally because Christ is the author of all things (Col 1:16-17), how much more does it apply to Christians who Paul addresses here? Because Christ paid for the right to be our Lord by dying for our sins and rising from the dead, Christians owe their full allegiance to Him (2 Cor 5:15; Acts 10:36).

14:10-12. The implication of Christ's lordship (indicated by the word "Lord" appearing seven times in vv 6-9) should cause both groups to stop condemning each other over certain days and diets, because it is not their right. Only the Lord has the right, and He does not condemn anyone on these issues.

As in v 3, Paul addresses both groups, but this time he commands the weak not to **judge** and the strong not to **show contempt** (cf. vv 3-4). **For** (*gar*) is a conjunction explaining why this should not happen: **all** believers are accountable to their "master" and must **stand** (v 4) **before the judgment seat** (cf. 1 Cor 3:12-15; 2 Cor 5:10;) **of Christ**. Some ancient manuscripts support the reading "of God" (Aleph and B from the fifth century A.D) instead of "of Christ" supported by the majority of manuscripts. The latter seems best for three reasons: (1) The majority of all Greek manuscripts attests to it, not just a few earlier texts. (2) Early church writers like Marcion, Polycarp, Tertullian and Origen also supported the reading "of Christ." (3) Since John 5:22 and 2 Corinthians 5:10 attests that Christ will also be judging believers along with Philippians 2:10-11 that refers to bowing and confessing Christ as Lord, it is highly likely that *Christ* not God (the Father) is the referent here.

To confirm the event of all believers appearing before Christ, Paul quotes from the LXX by conflating two passages found in Isaiah 49:18 (i.e., *As I live, says the LORD*) and 45:23 (i.e., *Every knee shall bow ... And every tongue shall confess to God*). Although this passage in the prophets applies universally, it contextually applies to believers. One day all believers will have to *bow* and **give** an **account of himself to God**, which contextually refers to Jesus Christ (cf. vv 6-9).

b. Practice Christian-liberty but not above Christian-love (14:13-23)

Paul began dealing with the temptation of the strong (vv 1-2) but turned to address the weak in the previous section (cf. vv 3*b*-9). In the rest of chapter 14 he deals with the temptation the stronger believer faces to flaunt his freedom in grace against the weaker believer. From vv 13*b*-21, Paul tailored his exhortation in a chiastic structure directed to the stronger brother (Moo, *Romans*, 850):

> A. Warning about stumbling blocks (13*b*)
>   B. Nothing is "unclean" in itself (v 14*a*)
>   C. Do not "destroy" one for whom Christ died (v 15*b*)
>   C.' Do not tear down "the work of God" (v 20*a*)
>   B.' All things are "clean" (v 20*b*)
> A.' Do not do anything to cause the fellow believer to stumble (v 21)

14:13. Therefore is Paul's way of summarizing his argument from vv 1-12 while preparing to address what is ahead from vv 13-23. Do **not judge** each other **anymore** about days and diets. By this point Paul has covered this extensively. If believers spend more time checking themselves, instead of criticizing others, there would be no time to **put a stumbling block** (cf. vv 20-22; 1 Cor 8:9) that **cause** (*skandalon*, lit. "trap") a brother **to fall**. The term *skandalon* literally refers "to a device for catching something alive" in a *trap* (BDAG, 926; cf. Matt 16:23; 1 Cor 8:13). Therefore, whether a believer wants to or not, to condemn a brother over these issues will trap him. Consequently this will stunt a person's spiritual growth (cf. 1 Tim 6:3-4; Titus 3:9), since arguing about such issues may cause one to become more stubborn and ingrained in his belief.

14:14-18. Returning to the issue of one's diet, Paul believed, perhaps **by** what **the Lord Jesus** said in Mark 7:15, that **nothing is unclean** (*koinos*, lit. "common/profane"; cf. 1 Macc 1:47, 62; Rom 14:2, 20). The term *koinos* refers to *unclean* foods, like pork prohibited by the Mosaic Law (cf. Lev 11:4, 42; Deut 14:8, 10), but now permissible to eat (cf. v 2), although some Christians still consider sinful to eat these types of foods. Thus, if the weaker brother **considers** (i.e., "believes/thinks") **anything to be unclean**, then **to him** *it is* **unclean**. This does not mean that certain foods are unclean but that the strong brother should not offend the weak brother because he believes otherwise. Clearly Paul agrees with the stronger brother, but his point is to use this liberty with caution. "For" (*gar*) translated by the NASB better expresses the meaning than the NKJV translation of **Yet**, because this conjunction explains (not contrasts) v 14 in v 15. Thus, Paul explains that to persist in one's conviction to eat **food** disapproved by the weaker brother, considering his pain, violates the greatest principle of grace, *love*. If one sits down with an immature believer (who thinks the laws of kosher foods are still in effect) and insists on his right to eat pork, oyster, shrimp or lobster, he is **no longer walking in love**. To such Paul commands: **Do not destroy** (*apollye*, present imperative) **with your food** this brother.

The words *grieved* and *destroy* describe two stages that a weaker brother experiences. If a person sees another doing what his conscience condemns, this causes grief (1 Cor 8:7-12). When this person proceeds to practice it himself, he violates his conscience and sins leading to "moral destruction" (Constable's, *Notes on Romans*, 149). How terrible to temporally *destroy* someone for whom **Christ died,** by paying the ultimate penalty, for him to live eternally. Thus to persist on one's liberty could result in being **spoken of as evil** and ruining the stronger Christian's reputation. Why? Because, to persist on issues that others are not prepared to accept, by their lack of maturity, will be misunderstood.

The explanatory conjunction **for** (*gar*) connects to vv 15-16 by way of describing why the strong believer should not insist on his right and ruin the weaker brother: Paul appeals to the essential issues that lay at the core of **the kingdom of God**. This *kingdom* may refer to the sphere where only the regenerate exists and where God rules in the lives of His own. Yet, out of the eight times the expression *the kingdom of God* occurs in Paul's epistles (14:17; 1 Cor 4:20; 6:9-10; 15:50; Gal 5:21; Col 4:11; 2 Thess 1:5), it is more consistent to interpret it as a literal future *kingdom*, with operative principles now to be fully realized in the future. Hence Alva J. McClain says: "For surely in the present life no one can deny the importance of meat and drink; but so far as the Church is concerned in the future Kingdom, these things will be of no consequence. Therefore, since the Church is to reign in that Kingdom, its members should not grieve one another in such matters here and now" (*The Greatness of the Kingdom*, 434).

Thus, God's rule in the lives of Christians does not pertain to physical practices like **eating and drinking** but to spiritual principles belonging to a future kingdom that are operative now: Practiced by living **righteous** (Rom 6:13, 16, 18-20), being at **peace** with your brother (Rom 12:16, 18; 14:19) and with God (Phil 4:7) **and** having **joy** (Gal 5:22-23) that comes from **the Holy Spirit**. These principles, on which this *kingdom* is founded, exist now but still lie in the future.

A Christian who practices these principles **serves** (*douleuōn*, the present participle means "one who continuously serves as a slave") **Christ,** proves to be mature and becomes **acceptable to God**. Consequently, instead of building a bad reputation, everyone will think highly of him (cf. v 16).

14:19-21. Therefore (*ara oun*, lit. "so then"; cf. 5:18) is Paul's way of summarizing his basic argument: The strong brother should **pursue** being sensitive, by practicing restraint in Christian liberties that offend the weaker brother; this leads to **peace** and "mutual edification" (NIV; cf. 15:2; 1 Thess 5:11). By giving up one's right to enjoy temporary pleasures, like eating lobster and drinking wine, while in the presence of one who thinks it is wrong, a strong brother will keep the peace and allow God time to work in the weaker person's heart. Hence Paul commands: **Do not destroy the work of God**. Unlike v 15, this refers to God's dealing in the life of the weak believer. God works in everyone uniquely and at a different pace. To dispute over nonessential matters **of foods** with an immature believer disrupts his spiritual growth. This is like giving an infant a piece of meat that his body is not yet able to tolerate since the physical organs are not fully developed. It could cause choking and lead to death. Thus, mature Christians should be cautious in exercising their liberty because using such freedom liberally could trap immature believers by hurting their conscience which will stunt their growth (cf. v 13).

The phrase **the man who eats with offense** may refer to the weaker brother who, under pressure from a mature believer, violates his conscience (cf. vv 14, 23). However, it seems best to understand it as a reference to the mature believer who, by insisting on his right, will cause the immature believer to be offended and be stunted spiritually (cf. vv 13, 21). In light of the context, this seems to be addressing the "strong." Furthermore, this understanding makes more sense in light of the following verse: It is *evil* and not **good** to **eat** and **drink wine** if it damages the immature believer who is not ready to understand that these things are not wrong. To be a glutton and a drunkard is wrong, but to indulge in moderation is not (cf. Luke 7:33-34). However, a weaker brother's welfare should take precedence over a Christian's liberty (1 Cor 8:13).

14:22-23. By such restrictions Paul does not require mature believers to abandon their convictions on issues that are not wrong. Instead, Paul encourages one to **have faith** in these matters, but discourages such practices when sharing a meal with immature believers. Such restrictions are not limited to the immature, for in principle to drink wine in front of mature believer who is a recovering alcoholic may also cause stumbling. Mature believers are free to practice these things privately **before God**, but if one chooses to do it publicly before others he should exercise caution at all cost.

Thus mature Christians who have a clear conscience on these matters and practice them in private may consider themselves, **Happy** (lit. "blessed"), because such Christians know they are not violating Scripture or harming the immature believer. However, if an immature believer **doubts** whether eating certain foods and drinking wine is right and does it anyway, he stands **condemned** by his conscience before God. Such actions are not derived **from faith**. That is, the meaning of *faith* here does not refer to apostolic doctrine (cf. v 1), but to what a person believes God wants for him. The moment one acts contrary to personal conviction, whether right or wrong, that person sins. He is not trusting God but has shifted his trust on what someone else believes. Opting to follow someone else's spiritual beliefs contrary to personal conviction falls into the category of behavior not stemming **from faith** and **is sin**. For the weak brother to act in a way he believes to be sinful (or at best doubtful) before God is wrong, because this action of rebellion is contrary to what he thinks God wants for him. Hence, even if the weak Christian's faith is deficient, God expects him to live up to his conviction (cf. Osborne, *Romans*, 374). To do otherwise *is* to *sin*.

The Majority Text places 16:25-27 here. This disrupts the flow of the argument making it the harder reading. Hence, since textual criticism usually prefers the harder to a smoother reading (perhaps done by a scribe), placing it here may be correct. Furthermore, placing these verses here eliminates having what seems to be a double ending since 16:24 concludes quite nicely. Nevertheless, even if placing this ending after 14:23 makes for a nice benediction and bookend, by correlating the phrase "obedience to the faith" with 1:5, some may call into question the authenticity of chapters 15–16, which would seem superfluous if the book ended previously. Perhaps Paul wrote two copies of the letter (one with and without chaps 15–16) to be sent to different places (cf. Metzger, *A Textual Commentary*, 470-73).

A better solution indicates that placing 16:25-27 after 14:23 works best (without calling into question chaps 15–16) as a doxology praising God's ability to establish Christians, despite their shortcomings. Then those who are established "ought to bear with the scruples of the weak" (15:1ff.). Regardless of one's view no major doctrines are called into question here. Thus one should not be dogmatic.

15

CHRISTIAN UNITY

c. Put others before ourselves: imitate Christ (15:1-6)

Having commanded the mature believer to resist despising and judging the weak on nonessential issues (14:1-12) and to practice Christian-liberty but not above Christian-love (14:13-23), Paul continuous to address the most important Christian principle: putting others before ourselves by imitating Christ, and create unity. Logically, Christians should behave in a Christ-like manner.

15:1-4. Summarizing the topic of 14:14-23, Paul includes himself in vv 1-4 (**We**) as one who practices the principle he preaches: The **strong ought to bear** (*opheilomen*, lit. "obligated," BDAG, 743) **with the scruples of the weak** by being unselfish. By placing the verb *opheilomen* (with its plural pronoun prefixed) at the beginning of the Greek sentence and further adding an unnecessary Greek plural pronoun, Paul emphasizes the basis for Christian conduct: do not live **to please ourselves**. Instead mature believers are commanded to seek the **good** (done in love; cf. 12:9-21) that leads to **edification** (cf. 14:19). Paul exemplified this behavior through Christ who **did not please Himself** as the quote from the messianic Psalm 69:9 supports. Christ had the right to stay in heaven but that would not have remedy the sin problem. Having renounced His heavenly pleasures and rights as God, Christ incurred earthly problems for the sake of humanity. Christians have rights, but acting on one's right is not always a guide for good conduct. Laying aside all rights Christ took on infirmities for humanity's sake. That is love (cf. Phil 2:1-8). That is how mature Christians ought to act towards immature Christians on the nonessential issues.

By this Paul does not mean mature Christians must be people-pleasers by acting on the whims of others (cf. Gal 1:10; Eph 6:6; Col 3:22; 1 Thess 2:4). Rather building others up should be the basis that motivates godly behavior (1 Cor 9:19-23).

After quoting from the Psalms, Paul explains the purpose of using Old Testament Scripture. It serves to teach one how to behave. As a result of **learning**, the Scriptures will give the believer **patience** to overcome adversities **and comfort** in times of distress. These results cultivate **hope** (cf. 5:2-5; 8:20, 22-25; 15:12-13) but not that the weaker brother will change, although he may. Instead the Scriptures give believers *hope* in various ways: (1) Others have gone before us who were able to accomplish this. (2) Hence one can have confidence to endure. (3) Obedient believers can expect to be rewarded (14:10-11; 8:20, 22-25; 1 Cor 9:17, 24-27). (4) Most importantly, *hope* in this context (accomplished through Jesus' vicarious suffering for others mentioned in Ps 69:9) guarantees a future unity of Jews and Gentiles (cf. vv 9-12) that ought to be exemplified in one's present behavior. This *hope* gives believers confidence to live in unity now since this is only a foretaste of what will come in full at a later date.

15:5-6. Thinking of this "hope" causes Paul to break into prayer asking **the God of patience and comfort** (since He is the source of Scripture that serves one this way; cf. v 4; cf. 11:33-36) to aid believers in becoming imitators of Christ's unselfish love **toward one another**. As a result this will unify believers (cf. Eph 4:3, 13), instead of dividing them. If believers resist becoming judgmental on nonessential issues, they will be of **one mind** (cf.

12:16) and achieve the goal of the Church and ultimately of human existence: To **glorify the God and Father of our Lord Jesus Christ** (cf. 2 Cor 1:3; Eph 1:3; 1 Pet 1:3 for similar terminology). Although this glorification occurs verbally (i.e., through the *mouth*), one cannot exclude a believer's course of action that leads to unity making God's glorification possible. That is, praising God verbally on Sundays always depends on how one practices God's mandates on Mondays.

d. Praise God together: Jews and Gentiles (15:7-13)

15:7-12. Therefore (*dio*, cf. 1:24; 2:1) serves to summarize the conclusion of the section discussed, from 14:1, where Paul commanded the mature to "receive" the immature believer. Yet here the command is directed at both groups to **receive one another.** Again Paul used **Jesus Christ** as the model for believers to follow (cf. v 3) since "Christ also received us" when we were still "without strength," "ungodly," "sinners," and "enemies" of God (cf. 5:6-10). Thus, if Christ did for *us* something so great, clearly one can do the lesser act to accept those who differ on secondary issues. Hence Paul explains how Christ **has become** (*gegenēsthai*, perfect tense, signifies He became in the past and continuous in the present) **a servant to the** Jews (cf. Mark 10:45; Matt 15:24; Gal 3:16) to validate God's two-fold **truth:** (1) **to confirm** (*bebaioō* is a legal term used to guarantee something as true, MM 108) **the promises** *made* **to the fathers** (Abraham, Isaac and Jacob) and (2) **that the Gentiles might glorify God** since they are also recipients of *His* **mercy** and are included as part of those *promises* in Scripture (Gen 12:3; 18:18; 22:18; 26:4; cf. John 4:22; Rom 4:9-17; commentary in 9:7; 11:13-24). By default one can see how these *promises made to the fathers* (that were fulfilled because of Christ's service; cf. 14:9; 15:8) would cause Gentiles to praise God. Contextually, reminding the Roman Christians of this truth serves to exhort Christians to "receive one another" (v 7; cf. Moo, *Romans*, 875).

To support how God intended for Jews and Gentiles to praise God together in unity, Paul cites four passages taken from the three-fold division of the Old Testament (the Law, the Prophets and the Writings) written by three of the greatest Israelite leaders (Moses, David and Isaiah). (1) The first quote (v 9) pictures David rejoicing in song for God's victory over Gentile enemies who will serve Him (cf. 2 Sam 22:50; Ps 18:49). (2) The second quote (v 10) describes Moses' farewell song that expresses how Gentiles will praise God with Israel when God vindicates "His servants" (Deut 32:43). (3) The third quote (v 11), coming from the middle of the Bible and shortest chapter in Scripture, shows how Gentiles will praise God in a context where "mercy" and "truth" are mentioned (Ps 117:1). (4) The last quote (v 12) describes Gentile praise through the hope found in the Messiah (Isa 11:10).

Perhaps Paul had two reasons for citing these passages: (1) To encourage the weaker Jewish Christians to accept their Gentile brothers, since they were to form part of God's family (cf. 10:20; 11:11-12; see above). (2) To exhort the stronger Gentile believers to accept their Jewish brothers. Thus, since the promises come through the Jews that Gentile Christians partake, they should be sensitive and not despise their weaker Jewish brothers.

15:13. Thus, Paul concludes (the nonessential issues section begun in 14:1) with a benedictory prayer (v 6). He asks **God** as the source **of all hope** to **fill** believers with **joy and peace** (14:17) by **believing** in the *hope* mentioned in context, which guarantees a future day of unity that Jews and Gentiles (cf. vv 9-12) will share. Consequently, one's behavior should exemplify this unity now in light of that future day. This **hope** like that mentioned in 14:17 comes **by the power of the Holy Spirit**. A believer filled with this kind of *hope* has little time to engage in nonessential issues since this *hope*, which is based on that future day when Jews and Gentiles will live in peace, instills confidence to unify now.

This verse also concludes the section dealing with the practical aspect of the gospel that reveals specifically God's perfect will that exhorts believers to serve in all aspects. Only the justified can experience gospel-life by serving others in love (12:1–15:13; cf. intro to section).

This section also concludes the body of the epistle that unfolds the Gospel (1:18–15:13). *Problem*: Paul shows that humanity suffers God's wrath because they are unrighteous (1:18–3:20). *Solution*: By grace through faith alone in Christ anyone can attain God's righteousness (3:21–4:25). *Maintenance*: As a result, those who are justified can now experience the resurrection-life of Christ by the Spirit and escape God's wrath that falls on those who persist on sinning (6:1–8:39). *Misunderstandings*: Turning to Gentiles due to Israelite disobedience does not place God's gospel promises to Jews in danger, since He has fulfilled some and will ultimately fulfill them all one day (9:1–11:36). *Manual for Ministry*: Paul ends by giving believers specific exhortations on how to behave in key relationships within the church and the world (12:1–15:13).

A. Paul's Present Ministry and Future Plans (15:14-33)

The epistle's conclusion and introduction are framed like bookends by repeating similar contents in 1:1-16 that correspond to 15:14-33 and 16:25 (See chart on 280).

Unlike other closing remarks of Paul's epistles, by far this letter contains the longest conclusion. Similar to the introduction, in the conclusion Paul shares personal matters, with the exception of a few places in the body (7:7-25; 9:1-3; 10:1-2; 11:1). Perhaps, since

Gospel	1:1, 9, 15-16 = 15:16, 19-20, 16:25
Commendation of the recipients	1:8 = 15:14; 16:19
Obstacle in coming to Rome	1:3, 13 = 15:15b-21
Indebtedness to help	1:14 = 15:27
Ministering for reciprocal blessings	1:11-12 = 15:29
Praying for others	1:9-10 = 15:30-33

he had not visited Rome yet, he wanted to establish personal warmth. Thus, Paul wanted to lay the groundwork before arriving at Rome. He informs the Romans of his previous work (vv 14-21), present (vv 22-29) and future plans (vv 30-33).

15:14-16. Having discussed debatable issues (14:1–15:13) that perhaps plagued the Roman congregation, Paul emphatically (**I myself am confident**) assures them of not being prompted to write due to any overwhelming deficiency found in them. Instead he commends them: **you also are full of goodness, filled with all knowledge, able also to admonish one another.** Commending a Church (1:8) that one has never visited may cause the readers to think Paul evokes empty rhetoric, unless he was informed of the Romans' situation by someone (perhaps, Priscilla and Aquila; cf. 16:3). Obviously Paul does not mean they were flawless or had no absolute need of apostolic guidance and authority (v 20). Words like *full, filled* and *all* are hyperboles (i.e., exaggerated language) used to give the Roman Christians credit on *some* **points** (*apo merous*) they already knew but needed **reminding**. In fact, the Greek phrase *apo merous* is best translated "in part" or "partly." This establishes one of Paul's reason for writing: *partly to remind his readers by virtue* **of the grace given to me by God** (cf. Fitzmyer, *Romans*, 711). Hence Paul's intent beyond *reminding* was to impart new information. Since the phrase *the grace given to me* refers to Paul's apostolic authority (cf. 12:3), one may think the other purpose for writing was to establish his apostolic authority. Yet, if he had nothing new to say what difference would that make? This phrase was not an apologetic defense of Paul's apostleship but refers to his authority to impart information his readers knew (thereby strengthening them) and did not know (thereby informing them). This congregation obviously knew many basic truths shared by Paul since they were already believers (1:7-8) but could not have know all, unless "they were a collection of the most insightful theologians who ever lived!" (Moo, *Romans*, 889).

Paul's apostolic authority as a **minister** (*leitourgos* refers to the formal office of priesthood used metaphorically here, BDAG, 592; cf. Heb 8:2) **of Jesus**, specifically over the Gentile mission field, forms part of his purpose for writing. By preaching **the gospel** (cf. vv 1, 15-16) to **Gentiles** he will present them as an *offering* (metaphorically speaking as it were an Old Testament animal sacrifice; cf. 12:1) **acceptable** to God (cf. 1 Pet 2:5), since they have been **sanctified** (*hēgiasmenē*, perfect passive participle, lit. "set apart") **by the Holy Spirit** (cf. 1:7). Jews regarded Gentiles as unclean; hence this becomes highly important (Morris, *Romans,* 511) because now God has cleansed them (cf. Acts 15:15). Though this refers to positional sanctification (by being set-apart at regeneration the perfect passive tense *hēgiasmenē* refers to an action completed in the past by the *Spirit*) it cannot exclude progressive sanctification for the following reasons (since the perfect passive tense also carries an ongoing effect also performed by the *Spirit* upon the believers obedience): The gospel developed in Romans (and specifically in this context, cf. "gospel" in vv 20-21) will only achieve its goal when Gentiles are not only justified but sanctified and experience deliverance from wrath (cf. 1:1, 15-16; 5:9). This means more than imputed righteousness by faith alone. Hence

Paul uses the perfect passive tense *sanctified* to capture the entire thrust in Romans. Thus only when believers live resurrection-life by the Spirit's power (cf. 6:1-23; 8:1-17) can this offering be *acceptable* to God in the fullest sense by making "Gentiles obedient" (v 18; cf. 12:1).

15:17. Therefore (*oun*) points to Paul's special ministry due to God's grace in vv 15-16 that furnish the ground **to glory** (*kauchēsis*, lit. "boasting," BDAG, 537) **in Christ Jesus.** Since the success among the Gentiles is attributed to God, his boasting is valid since God is the source of success (cf. 4:2; 5:3).

15:18-19. Thus Paul knows that all of his success belongs to what **Christ** has done **through** him. His goal is **to make the Gentiles obedient.** Obedience is an adequate term used to encapsulate both concepts of believing in and obeying Christ that Paul unfolds in Romans: To obey the command to believe in Christ and to obey the command to follow Christ (cf. 1:5; 10:16 for discussion). Obviously Paul not only brought God's message through doctrine and actions expressed by the frequent combination of the phrase *word and deed* (i.e., a person who practices what he preaches; cf., Luke 24:19; Acts 7:22; 2 Cor 10:11; Col 3:17; 2 Thess 2:17; BDAG, 390, contrast to a person devoid of actions mentioned in Jas 1:25; 2:14-26) but **in mighty signs** (*sēmeion*) **and wonders** (a phrase used that authenticates apostolic authority; cf. 1:1; Acts 2:22, 43; 4:30; 5:12; 2 Cor 12:12; Heb 2:4) through **the power of the Spirit** (cf. Rom 15:13). Many Gentiles through Paul's *sēmeion* came to faith in Christ. The term *sēmeion* occurs exclusively out of the four Gospels in John with the purpose of bringing people to faith in Christ (cf. John 20:30-31). As a result of the Spirit's power Paul had great success, **from Jerusalem** to **Illyricum** (i.e., modern-day Yugoslavia and northern Albania), in preaching **the gospel** (cf. 1:1, 15-16) **of Christ.** Obviously Paul did not preach to every individual. Rather he covered these areas by planting the seed where Christ was never preached (see below).

15:20-21. After naming the region of ministry Paul states his outreach strategy: **I have made it my aim to preach the gospel** (cf. 1:1, 15-16)**, not where Christ was named.** Paul was a true pioneer in fulfilling the Great Commission (Matt 28:19-20) by going to uncharted territory as his main focus in ministry: to plant churches. The reluctance **to build on another man's foundation** reflects part of Paul's purpose to visit Rome. This is probably why the Spirit limited his ministry in Phrygia, Galatia, Asia, Mysia and Bythinia (cf. Acts 16:6-7) since Peter went to those areas (cf. 1 Pet 1:1). Thus, since the Roman Church was not initially founded or visited by an apostle (cf. "Purpose" in Intro.), perhaps they were in need of apostolic doctrine to strengthen them and establish further truths of *the gospel.*

Nevertheless, Paul does not disparage the necessary work *to build on another man's foundation* vital for growth that was done by others (e.g., 1 Cor 3:5-8). Though this is the rule, there are exceptions. For example, Paul had ministries in places where others had also visited (e.g., Antioch; cf. Gal 2:11; cf. Moo, *Romans*, 897).

In Romans, Paul validates typically his doctrine and action by citing the Old Testament (cf. 1:2; 4:1). Perhaps he had three reasons for quoting Isaiah 52:15*b:* (1) It justifies why his primary ministry goal was to evangelize those who have not heard, since this passage supports his action. (2) By targeting unbelieving Gentiles, understood contextually by terms "nations" and "kings" (Isa 52:15*a*), Paul validates his Gentile ministry. (3) Finally, Isaiah's prophecy (52:13-–53:12) fulfilled in Christ serves as a perfect picture that forms the basis for taking the gospel to Gentiles who have not heard of Jesus Christ (cf. Moo, *Romans*, 897-98).

15:22-24. For this reason expresses (by linking the previous verses) why Paul's zeal to preach Christ to unbelievers **hindered** him **from coming** to Rome sooner (cf. 1:10, 13). **But now** is a phrase that contrasts the past to present accomplishment having preached the gospel from Jerusalem and its surrounding regions to Illyricum (v 19; i.e., **in these parts**). Thus Paul can now material- ize his visit to Rome and other parts like **Spain** (cf. 15:28). Spain was on the outer limits of the empire and was occupied by Rome since 200 B.C. but was now completely organized by Rome (cf. Moo, *Romans*, 900). Then, after enjoying a short stay at Rome, Paul expects to be **helped** (perhaps financially; cf. 1:12; 15:25-27) **on** his **journey** *to Spain*. Paul treats his trip to Rome as a layover on his way to Spain.

15:25-27. But now indicates something else takes precedence before Paul fulfills his desired visit to Rome on his way to Spain: **I am going** (*poreuomai*, pres tense implies he is preparing to leave as he writes; cf. Moo, *Romans*, 902) **to Jerusalem to minister to the saints** (i.e., Jewish Christians; cf. 1:7). Evidence from that time shows a famine struck Judea around A.D. 46–48 (cf. Acts 11:27- 30; Josephus, *Ant.* 20.5.2 §101, p 531) that affected the mother church. Hence the main focus of Paul's third missionary journey was to gather financial means to help the poor in *Jerusalem* (Acts 11:27-30; Gal 2:10) to which he devoted considerable attention (cf. Acts 24:17; 1 Cor 16:1-4; 2 Cor 8–9; Gal 2:10).

For explains in vv 26-27 why **it pleased those from Macedonia and Achaia to** help financially the Christian **saints who are in Jerusalem**. Perhaps Paul's intent to mention *Macedonia* (=modern northern Greece composed of the Philippians, Berean and Thessalonian churches) and *Achaia* (=modern southern Greece composed of the Corinthian church and perhaps converts of Athens; cf. Acts 17:33-34) was three-fold: (1) To mention the con- tributing regions closest to Rome (since churches in Asia probably contributed), (2) hence showing Gentile inclusion into God's family and (3) perhaps to provoke Jews to jealousy so that they would come to faith in Christ (cf. Schreiner, *Romans*, 776-77). Though their *contribution* was completely voluntary, **it pleased them** and was appropriate because they had gained all of their **spiritual wealth** (cf. Rom 9:7 [see commentary there]; 11:11-12, 17-18; 15:12; Gal 3:14; Eph 3:6) from the Jerusalem church, which is where it all began since "salvation is of the Jews" (John 4:22). Therefore, it is not too much to expect Gentiles to help their Jewish brothers **in material things** since these brothers are the source of their spiritual blessings. Though no one compelled Gentiles to give legally, it did not preclude them from giving out of moral obligation (Moo, *Romans*, 904). This principle not only applies here, but Paul uses it elsewhere to argue for the obligation that all Christians have to support their ministries and ministers (1 Cor 9:9-14; Gal 6:6; 1 Tim 5:18).

15:28-29. Therefore indicates a transition from what has just been said to mark Paul's original plan. Until Paul had **performed this** mission **and** brought **sealed to them this fruit** (i.e., the monetary collection), he will not visit Rome via **Spain**. The sense of the expression *sealed to them this fruit* means: "*when I have placed the sum that was collected safely (sealed) in their hands*" (BDAG, 980). Only after Paul delivers this collection safely to Jerusalem does he feel confident about getting to Rome in order to share **the fullness of the blessing** found only in **the gospel of Christ** (cf. 1:11). Though Paul finally arrived in Rome, it did not occur like he expected (Acts 27–28), and whether he ever visited Spain no one knows absolutely. Paul testified of Christ in Rome as a prisoner, in front of the emperor's representative, where he was ultimately beheaded for his faith at another time (Bruce, "Paul the Apostle," *ISBE*, 3:718-19; cf. 2 Tim 4:6-18). Hence one should plan ahead but not be dogmatic in how or when things are accomplished, because the fulfillment of all plans depends on God (Jas 4:13-15). Paul knew this, which is why he prayed: "that I may come to you with joy by the will of God" (v 32; 1:10).

15:30-33. Paul ends the section by exhorting (cf. 12:1) the Christian **brethren** to **strive** (implying a "struggle" [Thayer, *Greek-English Lexicon*, 600] or "wrestling" on the basis of their relationship with **the Lord Jesus Christ** and **the love** inspired by **the Spirit**) with him in prayer for the success (cf. Eph 6:19-20; Col 4:3-4; 1 Thess 5:25; 2 Thess 3:1-2; Phlm 22) of his future plans. These plans entail four specific prayer requests: (1) Paul wanted to be **delivered** (i.e., rescued) from the unbelieving Jews **in Judea** who wanted to kill him (cf. Acts 20:3).

(2) He desired that his **service** (i.e., monetary collection) would be acceptable to **the** Jewish **saints** (cf. vv 25-26). Since Paul mingled with Gentiles some immature Jewish Christians may be offended (Acts 15; 21:17-22). Perhaps some would also view this gift as a degrading charity. Thus, "It often takes more grace to be on the receiving end than on the giving end" (MacDonald, "Romans," in *BBC*, 1740).

(3) Not only does Paul understand that his arrival at Rome depends on God's *will* (v 29; 1:10) but also desires that the trip be full of **joy**. He emphasizes the kind of trip he wishes to have by placing the word *joy* at the beginning of the Greek sentence (lit. "that with joy I come").

(4) Finally, after having a turbulent time at Jerusalem, Paul wishes to be **refreshed together** (i.e. *rest* and *relaxation*; BDAG, 965) **with** the Roman Christians. Having entrusted all of his plans to God's will, ironically God does not answer Paul exactly how he expects: (1) Paul was rescued by the unbelieving Jews but only by being imprisoned for two years. (2) His collections appear to have

been accepted by most (if not all) of the Jewish Christians (cf. Acts 21:17), but his arrest may have cast a shadow on his entire work. (3) He did not arrive at Rome in a joyful manner but as a prisoner (cf. commentary on 15:29), and (4) he had ample time to relax with the Roman Christians but not in the manner desired (cf. Moo, *Romans*, 911). That is, he was probably in house arrest around A.D. 60-62 (Acts 28).

Finally Paul closes by giving his third benediction (vv 5, 13): **God** who is the source **of peace** (cf. 16:20; cf. "God of patience and comfort," in v 5, "God of hope" in v 13) **be with you all.** By having the *God of peace* (cf. Lev 26:6; Judg 6:24; Ps 29:11; Isa 26:12; 2 Cor 12:11; Phil 4:9; 1 Thess 5:23) one can rest assured He is the source of *peace* needed to unite the Roman church (cf. 14:17, 19). Paul concludes formally by affirming the prayer: **Amen** (cf. 1:25; 9:5; 11:36).

16

FINAL WARNINGS AND CONCLUSIONS

B. Personal Greetings to Paul's Friends (16:1-16)

Friends are a blessing. Scripture highlights numerous close friendships (e.g., Moses and Joshua, David and Jonathan, Ruth and Naomi and Paul and Luke). Hence Romans 16:1-16 becomes highly important since Paul mentions by name 27 people (and others in general terms) that he had some type of relationship.

Furthermore, having traveled for a number of years, Paul had time on numerous occasions to meet these brothers, and perhaps stay in their homes and build close relationships. Since Rome was the capital of the empire it drew people from everywhere, including people Paul stayed with while traveling. This helps explain how Paul knew so many people in Rome, besides knowing others by reputation (1:8-9). Since Paul had not visited Rome yet, perhaps he wanted to begin establishing personal warmth.

16:1-2. Desiring that the Roman Church accept the one who perhaps delivered the letter from Corinth, Paul said: **I commend** (see below) **to you Phoebe** (means "bright" or "radiant," Robertson, *Word Pictures*, 4:425) **our sister**. Obviously Paul means she was a spiritual *sister*, **who is** also **a servant** (lit. "deacon") **of the church in Cenchrea** (the port city of Corinth; cf. Acts 18:18). The term *servant* may be used generically as performing various functions of the church (cf. Rom 15:8; 1 Cor 3:5), or technically for the office of deacon (Phil 1:1; 1 Tim 3:8, 10, 12). No one knows for sure, but she probably held the office of deacon for three reasons: (1) The term *servant* appears connected to the phrase *of the church* suggesting she served in a special capacity since this is the only place where both concepts are linked. (2) Right in the midst of addressing deacons in 1 Timothy 3:8-12 Paul discusses, in v 11, either wives of deacons or women as deacons. The latter is more likely since it is odd that Paul would address the behavior of a deacon's wife and not the more important role of an elder's wife. (3) In an environment where strict separation of sexes was the norm, women deaconesses were probably necessary, perhaps to perform baptisms on women, to disciple and visit them (cf. Robertson, *Word Pictures*, 4:425).

By commending *Phoebe,* not only as a fellow believer and letter bearer, Paul desires that the believers **assist** her in lodging and perhaps in financial support to carry out the **business** of the ministry. Paul commends her even more by giving a pithy résumé: **she has been a helper of many and of myself also.** Typical of the ancient world commendations served to acquire aid for unknown emissaries (cf. Acts 18:27; 2 Cor 3:1; 4:2; 5:12; 10:12; 12:11; 3 John 9-10; 1 Macc 12:43; 2 Macc 9:25).

16:3-4. Having the longest list of greetings of any epistle, by mentioning 27 people by name and many others including nine women, Paul begins: **Greet Priscilla and Aquila.** Paul met this outstanding couple (who are never mentioned separately, perhaps because they served so well together) in Corinth on his second missionary journey when Claudius commanded all Jews to leave Rome (Acts 18:2).

Since Paul was a tentmaker like them this helped solidify even more the relationship (Acts 18:3). When Paul left Corinth they left with him (Acts 18:18) and stayed at Ephesus (Acts 18:19) where they ministered to Apollos (Acts 18:26). Later they again ministered to Paul while staying in Ephesus on his third missionary journey (1 Cor 16:19). Later *Priscilla and Aquila* went back to Rome to continue as **fellow workers in Christ Jesus** with Paul. Perhaps because Nero blamed the Christians for burning Rome in A.D. 64, the couple fled under persecution and ended in Ephesus (2 Tim 4:19).

Not only were they close associates of Paul in the ministry, but he also reveals (having probably occurred at Ephesus) how they even **risked their own** life for him. This emulates Christ's love that believers should have for each other (John 15:13). Since *Priscilla and Aquila* ministered to numerous people and in numerous places; hence, along with Paul, **all the churches of the Gentile** are thankful to them.

16:5-7. With the same warmth for the hosts of the church (hence **Likewise**), Paul greets **the church** that meets **in their house**. Roman Christians probably met in many house churches. Unlike today, mega-churches were unknown. Hence, Paul speaks of the "saints" (16:2) who he later greets individually by name (Rom 16:3-16; cf. Intro.).

Many of the people on this list require no extensive comments except for noticing various key elements. Like an open book at the Judgment Seat of Christ showing the believer's works that either condemn or commend (2 Cor 5:10-11), out of the 27 names in this list only 10 are commended (cf. vv 3-7, 9-10, 12). In the same way, the day believers appear before Christ not all will be "approved" (cf. v 10).

Paul sends greetings to **Epaenetus** the first convert in the area of **Achaia** (instead of the NU text reading of Asia that contradicts the majority of mss). This location is found in southern Greece from Corinth where Paul wrote the letter (cf. 15:26). **Mary** (perhaps *Mariam* a Jewish name as the best and majority of Greek mss record instead of *Marian*) receives greetings and praises as one who

labored much for Paul and his associates. Since the majority and best Greek manuscripts (*Aleph* and p^{46}) read *Mariam*, the Hebrew form identifies her as a Jew. Another prominent couple **Andronicus and Junia** are greeted by Paul. He not only acknowledges their ethnicity as Israelites (i.e., **countrymen** with reference to racial kinship; cf. 9:3; 16:11, 21) and bondage with him (cf. 2 Cor 11:23), but as being recognized **among the apostles**. The phrase *among the apostles* can mean *distinguished as apostles*. Since the term *apostles* is used in a general sense as those commissioned directly by the apostles of Christ (e.g., Barnabas, Silas and others called apostles who had not seen the risen Lord; cf. 1:1; Acts 14:4, 14; 2 Cor 8:23; 11:13; Phil 2:25; 1 Thess 2:6 [v 7 in Gk]), this could be the meaning. Yet, here it probably means the couple was well known to the apostles, because no record of them appear anywhere else. Apparently the couple came to faith before Paul, which may place them as those who formed part of the original group at Pentecost who returned to establish the church in Rome (Acts 2:10; cf. intro.). Hence they were well known to the apostles.

16:8-11. Paul also greets the *beloved* **Amplias**, *fellow worker* in the ministry **Urbanus** and *beloved* **Stachys**. Impressively, since 2 Corinthians 10:18 says that one who commends himself is *not* approved, but *only* whom the Lord commends, Paul writes that **Apelles** is **approved** (*dokimos*), a representative *approved* **in Christ**. The term *dokimos* is used to indicate one's faithfulness after being tested that usually results in being eternally rewarded (cf. 1 Cor 9:24-27; 2 Cor 13:7; 2 Tim 2:15 [cf. context vv 12-13]; Jas 1:12). Since Paul does not apply this term to anyone else (not that he was the only one worthy in this list), he wanted this to be a distinguishing factor for this person for reasons unknown. Perhaps Paul does not greet **Aristobulus** (possibly the grandson of Herod the Great) and *Narcissus* directly, but only those **of the**

household, because they may not be believers, or perhaps because they were deceased (Moo, *Romans*, 925). Paul also greets **Herodion** as a fellow **countryman** (i.e., Jew; cf. v 7).

16:12-15. Paul notices three women who worked hard for the Lord, besides Mary in v 6. Notice the gradation of the first two to the last one: First, **Tryphena and Tryphosa** (perhaps sisters or even twins) had **labored** compared to **Persis, who labored much** in Christ. Perhaps this **Rufus** who Paul greets is the same one mentioned in Mark 15:21. If so, he was the son of Simon the Cyrene who carried the cross of Christ (Matt 27:32). Paul also greets **his mother**, who the apostle attributes as his own by saying **mine**. Obviously Paul did not mean she was his physical mother, for he would not refer to her in such a casual way. Instead, he only meant she acted toward him in motherly love.

Paul concludes the list of names without extra information, because he only knew of them as Christians who hosted church meetings in their homes. Hence he greets them in general terms **all the saints who are with them**; the plural pronoun *them* refers to those that met either in one or various churches, perhaps hosted by those named above.

16:16. What might sound rash in Western culture by commanding one to: **Greet one another with a holy kiss**, is the norm in the ancient Near Eastern culture (Stählin, *TDNT* 9:121-22). Such request was a common way for Paul to end letters (cf. 1 Cor 16:20; 2 Cor 13:12; 1 Thess 5:26; cf. also 1 Pet 5:14). An equivalent custom in Western culture would be a handshake. Paul's intention is not to command believers to duplicate Eastern customs in Western culture. Instead, his principle idea refers to receiving believers with warmth and caring, not a mere casual greeting. The principle not the Eastern custom is what Paul wants believers to duplicate. Thus, he ends with a general greeting from all the

churches of Christ he represents throughout the region.

C. Final Exhortation (16:17-20)

16:17-20. With a stern warning Paul gives a final exhortation to **note** (*skopeō*, lit. "pay close attention") **those** causing **divisions** by arguing over nonessential issues or false teachings by placing traps (i.e., a better rendering of the Gk *skandalon* than **offenses** cf. 14:13) before believers by inducing them to sin, either by heated debates or following false doctrine. Since the Romans knew (from Paul and others) apostolic doctrine, they are now to apply what they have **learned**. Thus, after identifying such a man Paul commands to **avoid** (*ekklinete*, present imperative, "continue to turn away") him.

There is no way to identify what specific group Paul had in mind: either unbelievers or believers. On the one hand, Paul describes unbelievers as "savage wolves" that will try to devour "the flock" (Acts 20:29; cf. Phil 3:2; 2 Tim 3:1-9). On the other hand, believers can teach false doctrine (cf. Acts 20:30; 2 Tim 2:15-18). Paul teaches to *avoid* such believers (cf. 1 Cor 5:5-13; 2 Thess 3:6; 2 Tim 2:16; Titus 3:10).

For (*gar*) explains further v 17 by giving two reasons to avoid these false teachers: first, they **do not serve our Lord Jesus Christ, but their own belly** (cf. 14:18). The phrase *their own belly* has been interpreted in various ways: (1) gluttony (i.e., intemperance lifestyle), (2) those emphasizing Mosaic food laws (cf. 14:1–15:13) or (3) the "flesh" understood as a synecdoche (i.e., emphasizing a part of the person for the whole man) of one who follows a self-seeking lifestyle (Phil 3:19). Though all three may be in view since all are related, the last option fits best because it parallels the previous phrase by contrast: they *do not serve our Lord* but instead they *serve themselves.*

One might term such a man: a smooth operator with **flattering**

speech. That is, their arguments are persuasive and seem logical but when scrutinized by Scripture and sound interpretation methods, prove false. Second, one must "avoid" them because they **deceive** believers untrained in Scripture (that Paul calls infants in Eph 4:14).

However, Paul does not hesitate to affirm the Romans as those not untrained in Scripture, because many have confirmed their **obedience** (cf. 1:5, 8; 15:18; 16:26). Instead, Paul is **glad** that they are not deceived but says: **I want you to be wise in what is good, and simple** (*akeraios*) **concerning evil** (cf. 1 Cor 14:20). The only way to have good judgment is to continually study the Bible. The term *akeraios* means *pure, innocent* or *unmixed* (BDAG, 35). In the Greek period it was used to specify undiluted wine and of unmixed gold (i.e., to remain pure; Kittel, *TDNT*, 1:209-10). Thus Paul desires that believers not contaminate themselves with any form of evil that surrounds them (cf. Matt 10:16; Phil 2:15), but to be transformed from worldly practices (cf. 12:2). To comply with both of Paul's desires one must diligently study to know and practice the truth of Scripture. To assure the Romans further, Paul confirms that the **God** who is the source of all **peace** (cf. 15:33) guarantees future *peace* by crushing **Satan under** their **feet shortly** (cf. Gen 3:15). Soon God will establish an earthly kingdom that will be peaceful (cf. Dan 2:34-35; 7:27; Rev 20:1-6). Then, as in other places, Paul concludes with another benediction of the **grace of our Lord Jesus Christ** (cf. v 24; 1 Cor 16:23; Gal 6:18; Phil 4:23; 1 Thess 5:28; 2 Thess 3:18; 1 Tim 1:14; Phlm 25; cf. Rev 22:21). This *grace* takes one back to the same grace Paul desired for his readers to have (1:7).

D. Personal Greeting from Paul's Friends (16:21-24)

16:20-24. Before ending Paul allows his associates, who helped him on his third missionary journey, to send greetings. Others were leaders of the Corinthian church. Perhaps Paul wants to establish a personal bond between his helpers and readers so that later they may be sent to Rome on his behalf.

Timothy, very young in the faith, joined Paul on his second missionary journey at Lystra (Acts 16:1). He was like a son to Paul (2 Tim 2:1) and became Paul's greatest pupil and associate in ministry. Paul sent him everywhere (cf. Acts 19:22 [Macedonia]; 20:1-3 [where Paul wrote to Rome]; 1 Cor 4:17; 16:10-11; 2 Cor 1:1; Phil 2:19-24; 1–2 Tim [Ephesus]). **Lucius, Jason, and Sosipater** were Paul's Jewish **countrymen** (cf. 9:3; 16:7). Since Luke who wrote the Gospel and Acts was a Gentile, *Lucius* could not be referring to him since this man is Jewish. Perhaps *Jason* hosted Paul in Thessalonica (cf. Acts 17:5-9) and *Sosipater* was probably Sopater of Berea who accompanied Paul to Asia when he left Greece (Acts 20:4). These names appear in other accounts (cf. Acts 13:1; 17:5-9; 20:4; perhaps they are alluded in 2 Cor 9:4).

Tertius was Paul's secretary who **wrote** the letter while Paul dictated it. Perhaps because of bad eyesight Paul usually used amanuenses to write letters (cf. Gal 6:11; 1 Cor 16:21; 2 Thess 3:17). *Tertius* sends greetings along with **Gaius** who not only hosted Paul but **the whole church** at Corinth. Gaius Tititus Justus may be the same man where Paul stayed, which house was next to the synagogue (Acts 18:7). *Gaius* was a common name; therefore, this was probably not the Gaius who traveled with Paul (Acts 19:29). Instead he was probably the one who Paul baptized at Corinth (cf. 1 Cor 1:14). **Erastus**, an important high official who was the **treasurer** at Corinth, along with **Quartus, a** spiritual **brother**, also greet the Romans. Perhaps *Erastus* was the same man who Paul sent to Macedonia (cf. Acts 19:22; 2 Tim 4:20). Again Paul concludes by expressing his desire that the **grace of** the **Lord Jesus Christ be with** the Romans (cf. v 20). **Amen**, let it be (cf. 11:36).

E. Praise Concluding Doxology (16:25-27)

16:25-27. If this section belongs after 14:23, then this doxology was designed to praise God's ability to **establish** Christians, despite their shortcomings on nonessential issues (cf. 14:23). The word *establish* appears in Romans only in one other place (cf. 1:11). At the beginning of the letter Paul began expressing his intent of going to Rome: To *strengthen* the faith of the Roman believers (to live and overcome problems in life), Paul imparts the *spiritual benefits* developed in the book. The power of God that strengthens believers comes by means of the **gospel** (cf. 1:1, 15-16) that concerns the person and work of Jesus Christ (3:21–8:39; 12:1–15:13) and the impact it had on *salvation history* (i.e., God's plan to redeem man unfolding in history seen through revelation, known in theology by the German word *Heilsgeschichte* [history of salvation]; cf. 9:1–11:36).

Because this *gospel* involves much more than justification, Paul can speak of it as a **mystery** that was **kept secret since the world began**. This *mystery* refers to the good news plan of salvation that Jews and Gentiles now form part of God's family called the church (cf. 11:25; Eph 2:11-22; 3:1-13; Col 1:26). Though this is true, there are two ways to understand this *mystery* that is now revealed: (1) This truth is *now* revealed *by the prophetic Scriptures* of the New Testament, not those of the Old Testament, since the church is not in the Old Testament. Since *mystery* means completely covered or hidden, it would be wrong to understand this as being *partially* uncovered in the Old Testament that is now fully revealed. These *Scriptures* are *now made known to all nations* through inspired apostles and prophets whose writings are also called Scripture (2 Tim 3:16; 2 Pet 1:20; 3:16). (2) While this is true, Paul uses the term *Scriptures* in Romans as Old Testament prophecies of Christ's coming to validate New Testament doctrine (cf. 1:2-3; 3:20). Hence the close connection of *mystery* with Christ's coming, that validates New Testament doctrine here, refers to the part that was hidden in the Old Testament of how Jews and Gentiles would become united in one body. Though the Old Testament Scriptures do not reveal the New Testament church, it shows that Gentiles would receive blessings through Christ's coming (Gen 12:3; cf. Isa 11:1; 42:1, 6; 49:6; 60:3; 65:1; 66:12; Amos 9:11-12; Mal 1:11; Rom 10:18-21).

Yet until **now** it was not fully **made manifest** *how* that would happen. Thus *how* Gentiles would receive blessings, mentioned in germ form through Old Testament **prophetic Scriptures**, is part of the *mystery* revealed at Christ's coming that was completely hidden. Having shown in the Abrahamic covenant that Gentiles would receive blessings, now God **made known to all nations** their equal status with Jews in this plan after Christ's coming (Matt 16:18; Acts 20:28; Eph 1:19-22). This mystery forms part of the "gospel" that **the everlasting God** ordained (cf. Eph 1:4) and commands *all nations* to know in order that they obey **the faith**. This means *obedience to believe consists of faith and obedience to follow is produced by faith* "so that all nations believe and obey him" (NIV; cf. 1:5 [see commentary]; 15:18) and be delivered from wrath (cf. 1:18).

After revealing such magnificent truths throughout Romans, Paul identifies through this doxology (cf. 11:33-36) the source and object of his wisdom: **to God, alone** who is **wise**. In the Greek text, the latter phrase is immediately followed by the other phrase: **through Jesus Christ**. By this Paul indicates that God's wisdom manifests itself *through Jesus Christ* (cf. Col 2:3; Eph 3:20-21). Then, in the Greek, text Paul places last the following doxology to end Romans: *to whom be the glory* **forever**. **Amen** (cf. 11:36).

BIBLIOGRAPHY

Abbott-Smith, G. *A Manual Greek Lexicon of the New Testament.* Edinburgh: T. & T. Clarck, 1937.

Barrett, C. K. *The Epistle to the Romans,* Revised ed. Black's New Testament Commentary, ed. Henry Chadwick, vol. 6. London: A & C Black Limited; [Peabody]: Hendrickson Publishers, 1957.

Bauer, W., W. F. Arndt, F. W. Gingrich and F. W. Danker. *A Greek English Lexicon of the New Testament and Other Early Christian Literature.* Revised and Edited by Frederick William Danker, 2d ed. Chicago: University of Chicago Press, 1979.

Bauer, W., F. W. Danker, W. F. Arndt, and F. W. Gingrich. *A Greek English Lexicon of the New Testament and Other Early Christian Literature.* Revised and Edited by Frederick William Danker, 3d ed. Chicago: University of Chicago Press, 2000.

Blass, F., A. Debrunner, and R. W. Funk. *A Greek Grammar of the New Testament and Other Early Christian Literature.* Chicago: University of Chicago, 1961.

Boice, J. M. *Romans 9–11.* 3 vols. Grand Rapids: Baker Book House, 1993.

Brown, Francis, S. R. Driver and Charles A. Briggs. *A Hebrew and English Lexicon of the Old Testament with an Appendix Containing the Biblical Aramaic.* Oxford: Clarendon Press, 1906. Reprint, *A Hebrew and English Lexicon with an Appendix Containing the Biblical Aramaic.* Peabody, MA: Hendrickson, 1979.

Bruce, F. F. "Paul the Apostle." In *The International Standard Bible Encyclopedia,* ed. Geoffrey W. Bromiley, vol. 3. 4 vols., 696-720. Chicago: Howard-Severence, 1915. Reprint, Grand Rapids: Wm. B. Eerdmans Publishing, 1986.

Bruce, F. F. *The Letter of Paul to the Romans,* revised ed. Tyndale New Testament Commentary, ed. Leon Morris. Grand Rapids: William B. Eerdmans, 1985.

Bullinger, E. W. *Figures of Speech Used in the Bible: Explained and Illustrated.* London: Eyre and Spottiswoode, 1898. Reprint, Grand Rapids: Baker Book House, 1968.

Buswell, James Oliver, Jr. *A Systematic Theology of the Christian Religion.* 3 vols. Grand Rapids: Zondervan Publishing House, 1962.

Byrne, Brendan. *Romans.* Sacra Pagina, ed. Daniel J. Harrington, vol. 6. Collegeville, MN: Liturgical Press, 1996.

Calvin, John. *Epistle of Paul the Apostle to the Romans.* Translated by John Owen. Calvin's Commentaries, ed. John Owen. Edinburgh: The Calvin Translation Society, no date. Reprint, Grand Rapids: Baker Books House, 2003.

_____. *Genesis.* Translated by John King. Calvin's Commentaries, vol. 1. 22 vols. Edinburgh: Calvin Translation Society, no date. Reprint, Grand Rapids: Baker Books, 2003.

Carballosa, Evis L. *Romanos: Una Orientación Expositiva y Práctica.* Grand Rapids: Editorial Portavoz, 1994.

Carson, D. A., Peter T. O'Brien, and Mark A. Seifrid, eds. *Justification and Veriegated Nomism: Volume I, The Complexities of Second Temple Judaism.* Tübingen: Mohr Siebeck, 2001: Reprint, Grand Rapids: Baker Academic, 2004.

Carson, D. A., Peter T. O'Brien, and Mark A. Seifrid, eds. *Justification and Veriegated Nomism: Volume 2, The Paradoxes of Paul.* Grand Rapids: Baker Academic, 2004.

Congdon, James R. "The New Realm and Rules of the Christian Life: Romans 6:1-14." In *Abiding to Be Bold: Essays in Honor of Zane C. Hodges,* ed. Stephen R. Lewis. Eugene, OR: Wipf & Stock, 2004.

Constable, Thomas L. *Notes on Romans.* Online: http://sonic light.com, 2000. Accessed April 14, 2001.

Cranfield, C. E. B. *A Critical and Exegetical Commentary on the Epistle to the Romans.* International Critical Commentary. 2 vols. Edinburgh: T. & T. Clark, 1975, 1979.

Delitzsch, F. *Isaiah.* Translated by James Martin. Commentary on the Old Testament in Ten Volumes, vol. 7. 10 vols. n.p.: n.p., n.d. Reprint, Grand Rapids: William B. Eerdmans Publishing, 1980.

Dillow, Joseph C. *The Reign of the Servant Kings: A Study of Eternal Security and the Final Significance of Man.* Miami Springs, FL: Schoettle Publishing, 1992.

Dodd, C. H. *The Epistle of Paul to the Romans.* Moffatt New Testament Commentary. London: Hodder & Stoughton, 1932.

Dunn, James D. G. *Romans 1-8.* Word Biblical Commentary. Waco, TX: Word Book Publisher, 1988.

Edwards, James R. *Romans.* New International Biblical Commentary. Peabody, MA: Hendrickson Publishers, 1992.

Evangelical Dictionary of Theology. ed. Walter A. Elwell. Grand Rapids: Baker Book House, 1984.

Fitzmyer, Joseph A. *Romans: A New Translation with Introduction and Commentary.* Anchor Bible, ed. William Foxwell Albright and David Noel Freedman, vol. 33. New York: Doubleday, 1993.

Fung, Ronald Y. K. "The Impotence of the Law: Toward a Fresh Understanding of Romans 7:14-25." In *Scripture, Tradition and Interpretation: Essays Presented to Everett F. Harrison by his Students and Colleagues in Honor of his Seventy-fifth Birthday /,* ed. W. Ward Gasque and William Sanford LaSor, 34-48. Grand Rapids: W. B. Eerdmans Publishing, 1978.

Glasscock, Ed. *Moody Gospel Matthew Commentary.* Chicago: Moody Press, 1997.

Godet, Frederick L. *Commentary on the First Epistle of St. Paul to the Corinthians.* Translated by A. Cusin. Classic Commentary Library, vol. 1. No city: T. & T. Clark, 1886. Reprint, Grand Rapids: Zondervan Publishing House, 1957.

Gromacki, Robert G. *New Testament Survey.* Grand Rapids: Baker Book House, 1974.

Gundry, Robert H.. *A Survey of the New Testament,* 3 ed. Grand Rapids: Zondervan, 1994.

Graves, Robert. *I, Claudius.* Special ed. New York: Time, 1965.

Harrison, Everrett F. "Romans." In *The Expositor's Bible Commentary: with The New International Version of the Holy Bible,* ed. F. E. Gaebelein, J. M. Boice, and M. C. Tenney, vol. 10. 12 vols., 2-171. Grand Rapids: Zondervan Publishing House, 1976.

Hart, John. "Why Confess Christ? The Use and Abuse of Romans 10:9–10." *Journal of the Grace Evangelical Society* 12 (Autumn 1999): 3-35.

Hodge, Charles. *Commentary on the Epistle to the Romans.* Grand Rapids: William B. Eerdmans Publishing, 1947.

Hodges, Zane C. *Absolutely Free: A Biblical Reply to Lordship Salvation.* Grand Rapids: Zondervan Publishing House, 1989.

Holy Bible. Young's Literal Translation.

The Holy Bible. New International Version. Nashville: Holman Bible Publishers, 1978.

Holy Bible. New King James Version. Nashville: Thomas Nelson Publishers, 1982.

Josephus, Flavius. *The Works of Josephus: Complete and Unabridged.* Translated by William Whiston, New Updated ed. Peabody, MA: Hendrickson Publishers, 1987.

Judaeus, Philo. *The Works of Philo: Complete and Unabridged.* Translated by C. D.

Yonge, New Updated ed. Peabody, MA: Hendrickson Publishers, 1993.

Kaiser, Walter C., Jr. "Leviticus 18:5 and Paul: Do This and You Shall Live (Eternally?)." *Journal of the Evangelical Theological Society* 14 (1971): 19-28.

_____. *Toward Rediscovering The Old Testament.* Grand Rapids: Zondervan Publishing House, 1987.

Käsemann, Ernst. *Commentary on Romans.* Translated by Geoffrey W. Bromiley, 4th German Edition. Grand Rapids: William B. Eerdmans Publishing Company, 1980.

Kittel, Gerhard, Gerhard Friedrich, and Geoffrey W. Bromiley, eds. *Theological Dictionary of the New Testament.* Translated by Geoffrey W. Bromiley, index compiled by Ronald E. Pitkin ed. 10 vols. Grand Rapids: William B. Eerdmans Publishing, 1964-76. Reprint, 1999.

Leupold, H. C. *Exposition of Genesis,* vol. 1. Grand Rapids: Baker Book House, 1942.

Liddell, Henry George, R. Scott, H. S. Jones, and R. McKenzie, eds. *A Greek-English Lexicon,* Redvised and Augmented by Henry Stuart Jones, and Roderick McKenzie, 9th ed. With revised supplement 1996, ed. P. G. W. Glare and A. A. Thompson ed. Oxford: Oxford University Press, 1940.

Lopez, René A. "Do Believers Experience the Wrath of God?" *Journal of the Grace Evangelical Society* 15 (Autumn 2002): 45-66.

Lopez, René A. "Old Testament Salvation–From What?" *Journal of the Grace Evangelical Society* 16 (Autumn 2003): 49-64.

Louw, J. P., and E. A. Nida. *Lexical Semantics of the Greek New Testament: A Supplement to the Greek-English Lexicon of the New Testament Based on Semantic Domains.* Atlanta: Scholars Press, 1992.

Lowe, Chuck. "'There Is No Condemnation' (Romans 8:1): But Why Not?'" *Journal of the Evangelical Theological Society* 42 (June 1999): 231-50.

MacArthur, John F., Jr. *The MacArthur Student Bible: The New King James Version,* ed. John F. MacArthur Jr. Nashville, TN: Word Publishing, 2000.

MacDonald, William. *Believer's Bible Commentary,* ed. Arthur L. Farstad. Nashville: Thomas Nelson Publishers, 1995.

Metzger, Bruce M. *A Textual Commentary on the Greek New Testament,* 2d ed. Stuttgart: Biblia-Druck, 1994.

Minirth, Frank, Paul Meier, and Stephen Arterburn, eds. *The Complete Life Encyclopedia: A Minirth Meier New Life Family Resource.* Nashville, TN: Thomas Nelson Publishers, 1995.

Moo, Douglas J. "'Law,' 'Works of the Law,' and Legalism in Paul." *Westminster Theological Journal* 45 (Spring 1983): 73-100.

Moo, Douglass. *The Epistle to the Romans.* The New International Commentary on the New Testament, ed. Gordon D. Fee. Grand Rapids: William B. Eerdmans Publishing, 1994.

Morris, Leon. *The Epistle to the Romans.* The Pillar New Testament Commentary. Grand Rapids: William B. Eerdmans Publishing, 1988.

Moulton, James Hope, and George Milligan. *The Vocabulary of the Greek Testament.* London: Hodder & Stoughton, 1930. Reprint, Grand Rapids: William B. Eerdmans Publishing, 1997.

Murray, John. *The Epistle to the Romans: The English Text with Introduction Exposition and Notes.* The New International Commentary of the New Testament. 2 vols. Grand Rapids: William B. Eerdmans Publishing, 1959–65.

Needham, David C. review of *Birthright: Christian, Do You Know Who You Are?*, by Frederic R. Howe, *Bibliotheca Sacra* 141 (January–March 1984): 69-78.

Nygren, Anders. *Commentary on Romans.* Translated by Carl C. Rasmussen. Philadelphia, PA: Muhlenberg Press, 1949.

Osborne, Grant R. *Romans.* The IVP New Testament Commentary Series, ed. Grant R. Osborne. Downers Grove, IL: InterVarsity Press, 2004.

Pentecost, J. Dwight *Designed to Be Like Him: Understanding God's Plan for Fellowship, Conduct, Conflict, and Maturity.* Chicago: Moody Press, 1966. Reprint, Grand Rapids: Kregel Publications, 1994.

Robertson, A. T. *A Grammar of the Greek New Testament in the Light of Historical Research.* Nashville: Broadman, 1934.

Robertson, A. T. *Word Pictures in the New Testament.* 6 vols. Grand Rapids: Baker Book House, 1931.

Robinson, John A. T. *The Body: A Study in Pauline Theology.* Studies in Biblical Theology, ed. C. F. Moule, J. Barr, P. Ackroyd, F. V. Filson, and G. E. Wright. London: SCM Press, 1952. Reprint, 1963.

Ryrie, Charles C. *So Great Salvation.* Wheaton: Victor Books, 1989.

_____. "The End of the Law." *Bibliotheca Sacra* 124 (July-September 1967): 239-47.

Sanday, W., and A. C. Headlam. *A Critical Commentary on the Epistle to the Romans.* International Critical Commentary. Edinburgh: T. & T. Clark, 1902.

Sanders, E. P. *Paul and Palestinian Judaism: A Comparison of Patterns of Religion.*

Philadelphia: Fortress Press, 1977.

Schreiner, Thomas R. *Romans*. Baker Exegetical Commentary New Testament. Grand Rapids: Baker Book House, 1998.

————. "Does Romans 9 Teach Individual Election Unto Salvation? Some Exegetical and Theological Reflections." *Journal of the Evangelical Theological Society* 36 (March 1993): 25-40.

Shank, Robert L. *Life in the Son: A Study of the Doctrine of Perseverance*. Minneapolis, MN: Bethany House Publishers, 1960.

Showers, Renald E. "The New Nature." Th.D. diss., Grace Theological Seminary, 1975.

Strack, Hermann L., and Paul Billerback. *Kommentar zum Neuen Testament aus Talmud und Midrash*. 6 vols. München: C. H. Beck, 1961.

Suetonius. *The Lives of the Caesars*. Translated by J. C. Rolfe. Vol. 2. 2 vols. The Loeb Classical Library, ed. G. P. Goold. Cambridge, MA: Hardvard University Press, 1914. Reprint, 1992.

Tacitus. *The Annals of Tacitus*. Translated by Clifford H. More. Vol. 4. 5 vols. The Loeb Classical Library, ed. T. E. Page, E. Capps, and W. H. D. Rouse. Cambridge, MA: Hardvard University Press, 1937.

Thayer, J. H., ed. *Thayer's Greek-English Lexicon of the New Testament*. Edinburg: T. & T. Clark, 1986. Reprint, Peabody: Hendrickson Publishers, 2000.

Vine, W. E. *An Expository Dictionary of New Testament Words: with their Precise Meanings for English Readers*. Old Tappan, NJ: Fleming H. Revell Company, 1940.

Wallace, Daniel B. *Greek Grammar Beyond the Basics: An Exegetical Syntax of the New Testament*. Grand Rapids: Zondervan Publishing House, 1996.

Witmer, John A. "Romans." In *The Bible Knowledge Commentary: An Exposition of the Scriptures by Dallas Theological Seminary Faculty*, ed. John F. Walvoord and Roy B. Zuck, 435-503. Colorado Springs, CO: Chariot Victor Publishing, 1983.

Ziesler, J. A. *Paul's Letter to the Romans*. TPI New Testament Commentaries. Philadelphia: Trinity Press International, 1989.

Scripture Index

Author Index

SUBJECT INDEX

317